◌ human rights *first*

2008 Hate Crime Survey

Table of Contents

About Human Rights First

Human Rights First believes that building respect for human rights and the rule of law will help ensure the dignity to which every individual is entitled and will stem tyranny, extremism, intolerance, and violence.

Human Rights First protects people at risk: refugees who flee persecution, victims of crimes against humanity or other mass human rights violations, victims of discrimination, those whose rights are eroded in the name of national security, and human rights advocates who are targeted for defending the rights of others. These groups are often the first victims of societal instability and breakdown; their treatment is a harbinger of wider-scale repression. Human Rights First works to prevent violations against these groups and to seek justice and accountability for violations against them.

Human Rights First is practical and effective. We advocate for change at the highest levels of national and international policymaking. We seek justice through the courts. We raise awareness and understanding through the media. We build coalitions among those with divergent views. And we mobilize people to act.

Human Rights First is a nonprofit, nonpartisan international human rights organization based in New York and Washington D.C. To maintain our independence, we accept no government funding.

This report is available for free online at www.humanrightsfirst.org

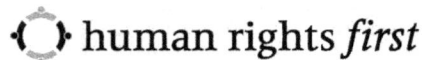

HRF's Fighting Discrimination Program

The Fighting Discrimination Program has been working since 2002 to reverse the rising tide of antisemitic, racist, anti-Muslim, anti-immigrant, and homophobic violence and other bias crime in Europe, the Russian Federation, and North America. We report on the reality of violence driven by discrimination, and work to strengthen the response of governments to combat this violence. We advance concrete, practical recommendations to improve hate crimes legislation and its implementation, monitoring and public reporting, the training of police and prosecutors, the work of official anti-discrimination bodies, and the capacity of civil society organizations and international institutions to combat violent hate crimes. For more information on the program, visit www.humanrightsfirst.org/discrimination or email FD@humanrightsfirst.org.

Acknowledgements

Human Rights First gratefully acknowledges the generous support of the Ford Foundation, the Righteous Persons Foundation, the David Berg Foundation, and the Richard and Rhoda Goldman Fund.

This report was prepared by Tad Stahnke, Paul LeGendre, Innokenty Grekov, Michael McClintock, Alexis Aronowitz, and Vanessa Petti.

{ } human rights *first*

Headquarters

333 Seventh Avenue
13th Floor
New York, NY 10001-5108

Tel.: 212.845.5200
Fax: 212.845.5299

Washington D.C. Office

100 Maryland Avenue, NE
Suite 500
Washington, DC 20002-5625

Tel: 202.547.5692
Fax: 202.543.5999

www.humanrightsfirst.org

Preface

Human Rights First's *2008 Hate Crime Survey*—our second annual study—is a review of the rising tide of hate crime covering the region from the Far East of the Russian Federation and the Central Asian states across Europe to North America: the 56 participating states of the Organization for Security and Cooperation in Europe (OSCE).

Human Rights First continues to document and analyze the reality of violent hate crime. We have reviewed available reports on violence motivated by prejudice and hatred, including the findings of the few official monitoring systems that provide meaningful statistical information. This data—combined with the findings of nongovernmental monitoring organizations as well as media reporting—provides important insights into the nature and incidence of violent hate crimes.

Our aim is to raise the profile of these insidious crimes and the challenges they pose to societies that are becoming increasingly diverse. Hate crimes are everyday occurrences that result in broken windows and burnt out homes, mental distress and bodily harm—sometimes fatal. Hate crimes threaten whole communities who identify with the victim based on race, religion, or other attributes, leaving many to live in fear and alienated from the larger society. This report seeks to overcome official indifference and indecision in the fight against such crime.

In the first part of this report, we examine six facets of hate crime in sections on **Violence Based on Racism and Xenophobia, Antisemitic Violence, Violence Against Muslims, Violence Based on Religious Intolerance, Violence Against Roma,** and **Violence Based on Sexual Orientation and Gender Identity Bias**. In the second part, we assess government responses to violent hate crimes in sections on **Systems of Monitoring and Reporting** and **The Framework of Criminal Law**.

Although not included in this compilation, the *2008 Hate Crime Survey* also includes separate sections on the **Russian Federation** and **Ukraine**, where hate crime has been on the rise and where governments have not responded adequately. No state is immune from the prejudice and bigotry that stand behind bias-motivated violence. A **Country Panorama** section profiles hate crime cases from 30 countries and includes in-depth descriptions of hate crime in France, Germany, and the United Kingdom—three countries where considerable efforts have been undertaken to combat hate crimes. Similarly, there has generally been a vigorous government response to hate crime in the **United States**, even though the problem continues. In a separate substantive section on the U.S., we outline recommendations to enhance the government's response. These sections are available at the Fighting Discrimination website: www.humanrightsfirst.org/discrimination.

Human Rights First is concerned that governments are not doing enough to combat violent hate crimes. In this survey, we offer a **Ten-Point Plan** for governments to strengthen their response. In particular, we are calling on governments to establish systems of official monitoring and data collection to fill the hate crime information gap. We are likewise urging them to improve criminal law and law enforcement procedures required to combat hate crimes. Stronger laws that expressly address violent hate crimes are necessary to more effectively deter, detect, and hold perpetrators accountable. International organizations also have an important role to play, and this Survey provides **Recommendations for Strengthening the OSCE**, in particular by advancing the organization's tolerance and nondiscrimination agenda—of which combating hate crime is an important component

Overview

European and North American governments are failing to keep pace with a wave of violent hate crime that continues to rise across the region. Racism, xenophobia, antisemitism, anti-Muslim and anti-Roma hatred, religious intolerance, homophobia: the list of biases that fuel these crimes is a long one. Attacks range from lethal assaults to threats and harassment to vandalism and desecration of religious and community property. The perpetrators are individuals acting alone, or in concert with neighbors, coworkers, and fellow students, as well as loosely-knit or more organized groups that share ideologies of hatred and act on them. The violence can ruin lives, or end them. It can terrorize whole communities, driving away vulnerable minorities or forcing them to stay out of sight. Violent hate crime, especially when the official response to it is weak or nonexistent, also attacks the society at large, undermining the very notions of equality and the equal protection of the law.

This *2008 Hate Crime Survey* examines six facets of violent hate crime in the 56 European and North American countries that comprise the Organization for Security and Cooperation in Europe (OSCE): **Violence Based on Racism and Xenophobia**, **Antisemitic Violence**, **Violence Against Muslims**, **Violence Based on Religious Intolerance**, **Violence Against Roma**, and **Violence Based on Sexual Orientation and Gender Identity Bias.**

Based on a review of available information, violent hate crime—individuals or property targeted with violence on account of race, religion, ethnicity, sexual orientation, disability or similar status—is occurring at historically high levels in many OSCE countries. Indeed, the violence increased in 2007 in many areas for several types of hate crime. Among the findings:

- There were moderate to high rises in the overall recorded numbers of violent hate crimes motivated by racism and xenophobia in 2006 and 2007 in **Finland**, **Ireland**, the **Slovak Republic, Sweden,** the **United Kingdom**, and the **United States.** In the absence of official data, information from nongovernmental monitors show rising levels of racist violence in **Greece**, **Italy**, the **Russian Federation**, **Switzerland**, and **Ukraine**. Individuals of African origin and Roma were particularly targeted in acts of racist and xenophobic violence in 2007 and in the first half of 2008.

- In 2007, overall levels of violent antisemitic attacks against persons increased in **Canada**, **Germany**, the **Russian Federation**, **Ukraine**, and the **United Kingdom** according to official statistics and reports of nongovernmental monitors.

- Available data indicates that violence based on sexual orientation and gender identity bias is a significant portion of violent hate crimes overall and is characterized by levels of physical violence that in some cases exceed those present in other hate crimes.

- Although there is ample evidence of violence targeting Muslims and those perceived to be Muslims across Europe and North America, only five governments—**Austria**, **Canada**, **Sweden**, the **United Kingdom**, and the **United States**—publicly report on violent incidents motivated by this form of bias.

Victim surveys and other data suggest that only a small portion of violent hate incidents are even reported to the police. Thus, the information that is available—and that paints such a sobering picture—is certainly only the tip of the iceberg.

The Survey also assesses government responses to violent hate crime. These vary considerably across the 56 OSCE countries. While several governments have responded in significant ways to hate crime, just as many downplay the problem, despite media and other reports that suggest that violence is taking place. Every government can do more to combat violent hate crime; many of the region's governments need to do much more.

To make this claim with specificity, the Survey examines two critical elements of an effective government strategy: official monitoring, data collection and public reporting; and legislation and its implementation. A systematic survey of each of the 56 OSCE countries on the basis of these two benchmarks can be found on our Web-based **Hate Crime Report Card**, available at: www.humanrightsfirst.org/discrimination.

Assessing **Systems of Monitoring and Reporting**, we conclude that most European governments are failing to live up to their commitments to the OSCE to monitor and collect data on violent hate crime, a prerequisite to an effective official response. Only 13 of the 56 participating states of the OSCE have adequate reporting systems, while over 40 states collect and publish either limited or no information specifically on the incidence of violent hate crimes. This gap in data collection can distort the full picture, as the countries that take the steps necessary to collect and publish the data can appear to be the ones with the highest number of incidents.

In the absence of government data, civil society groups have demonstrated the existence of the problem, pointing out failures in the government's response. Yet there are larger gaps in the information than such groups currently have the capacity to fill. Indeed, increased support and training is sorely needed for civil society groups in many countries to enhance their capacity to monitor and advocate.

Reviewing **The Framework of Criminal Law**, we report that over 30 OSCE countries have laws criminalizing or establishing enhanced penalties for a range of violent crimes motivated by racial or religious bias, but 23 countries do not, despite reports that violent hate crimes are taking place in many of those countries. Moreover, only 12 countries have laws that extend to sexual orientation bias; only seven extend to disability bias. Even when these laws are in place, it is nearly impossible to know the extent to which they are being implemented. Even the best official data collection systems do not generally assess how well police are responding to incidents and the disposition of cases in courts. There is virtually no systematic data on this from nongovernmental sources as well.

The Survey includes a **Ten-Point Plan** for all governments to strengthen their response to violent hate crime, and among those points are the following:

- condemn attacks when they occur and make clear that there is zero tolerance for violent hate crimes;

- instruct and adequately train police and prosecutors to investigate and prosecute cases, working in partnership with victims, their communities and civil society groups;

- improve monitoring, data collection, and public reporting in order to ensure the accountability of law enforcement and sound public policy;

- strengthen criminal laws to cover all forms of bias-motivated violence.

This Survey also provides **Recommendations for Strengthening the OSCE**, in particular by advancing that organization's tolerance and nondiscrimination agenda—of which combating hate crime is an important component.

The Survey also looks in more detail at two countries where violent hate crimes have been on the rise and makes specific recommendations for government action. Of particular concern is the **Russian Federation**, where the number of bias-motivated attacks on individuals continues to grow steadily, with 2008 on track to be the fourth record-setting year in a row and with an annual number of bias-motivated murders approaching 100. Though government officials have begun to recognize the problem posed by neo-Nazi violence, the official response has been sorely inadequate.

In **Ukraine**, too, racial, antisemitic and other bias motivated violent crimes are on the rise. The government there has undertaken a number of steps to combat hate crimes, although its overall response to this problem has been inconsistent and insufficient.

But though the level of violent hate crime and the adequacy of government responses may vary from one country to another, no state is immune from the prejudice and bigotry that stand behind such violence. A **Country Panorama** section profiles hate crime cases from 30 countries. We draw particular attention in that section to the rising levels of hate crimes in **Germany** and the **United Kingdom**, and continued high proportions of violent hate crime against individuals in **France** —countries where governments have mounted significant efforts to combat the problem in recent years.

Similarly, in the **United States**, the government has generally responded vigorously to violent hate crimes, in both rhetoric and action. Yet hate crime there constitutes a serious and continuing problem, and several specific recommendations are made to further strengthen the government's response.

The sections on **Russia**, **Ukraine**, the **United States**, and **Country Panorama** are not included in this compilation, but available at the Fighting Discrimination website: www.humanrightsfirst.org/discrimination.

The Survey finally provides **Foreign Policy Recommendations for Government of the United States**, which has played a leading role in international forums in addressing the problem of racist, antisemitic and some other forms of violent hate crimes. We outline a number of concrete steps that could be taken by the United States to demonstrate continued international leadership at the OSCE, to advocate combating hate crimes in bilateral relationships, and to support civil society groups that are working to address this region-wide problem.

Recommendations for Governments

Recommendations for all Governments of the 56 Participating States of the OSCE

We call on all governments of the 56 participating states of the Organization for Security and Cooperation in Europe (OSCE) to implement the following **Ten-Point Plan** for combating violent hate crimes within their own countries as well as the recommendations for strengthening the capacity of the OSCE in this area:

Ten-Point Plan for Combating Hate Crimes

1. ***Acknowledge and condemn violent hate crimes whenever they occur.*** Senior government leaders should send immediate, strong, public, and consistent messages that violent crimes which appear to be motivated by prejudice and intolerance will be investigated thoroughly and prosecuted to the full extent of the law.

2. ***Enact laws that expressly address hate crimes.*** Recognizing the particular harm caused by violent hate crimes, governments should enact laws that establish specific offenses or provide enhanced penalties for violent crimes committed because of the victim's race, religion, ethnicity, sexual orientation, gender, gender identity, mental and physical disabilities, or other similar status.

3. ***Strengthen enforcement and prosecute offenders***. Governments should ensure that those responsible for hate crimes are held accountable under the law, that the enforcement of hate crime laws is a priority for the criminal justice system, and that the record of their enforcement is well documented and publicized.

4. ***Provide adequate instructions and resources to law enforcement bodies***. Governments should ensure that police and investigators—as the first responders in cases of violent crime—are specifically instructed and have the necessary procedures, resources and training to identify, investigate and register bias motives before the courts, and that prosecutors have been trained to bring evidence of bias motivations and apply the legal measures required to prosecute hate crimes.

5. ***Undertake parliamentary, interagency or other special inquiries into the problem of hate crimes***. Such public, official inquiries should encourage public debate, investigate ways to better respond to hate crimes, and seek creative ways to address the roots of intolerance and discrimination through education and other means.

6. ***Monitor and report on hate crimes***. Governments should maintain official systems of monitoring and public reporting to provide accurate data for informed policy decisions to combat violent hate crimes. Such systems should include anonymous and disaggregated information on bias motivations and/or victim groups, and should monitor incidents and offenses, as well as prosecutions. Governments should consider establishing third party complaint procedures to encourage greater reporting of hate crimes and conducting periodic hate crime victimization surveys to monitor underreporting by victims and underrecording by police.

7. ***Create and strengthen antidiscrimination bodies***. Official antidiscrimination and human rights bodies should have the authority to address hate crimes through monitoring, reporting, and assistance to victims.

8. ***Reach out to community groups***. Governments should conduct outreach and education efforts to communities and civil society groups to reduce fear and assist victims, advance police-community relations, encourage improved reporting of hate crimes to the police and improve the quality of data collection by law enforcement bodies.

9. ***Speak out against official intolerance and bigotry***. Freedom of speech allows considerable latitude for offensive and hateful speech, but public figures should be held to a higher standard. Members of parliament and local government leaders should be held politically accountable for bigoted words that encourage discrimination and violence and create a climate of fear for minorities.

10. ***Encourage international cooperation on hate crimes***. Governments should support and strengthen the mandates of intergovernmental organizations that are addressing discrimination—like the Organization for Security and Cooperation in Europe, the European Commission against Racism and Intolerance, and the Fundamental Rights Agency—including by encouraging such organizations to raise the capacity of and train police, prosecutors, and judges, as well as other official bodies and civil society groups to combat violent hate crimes. Governments should also provide a detailed accounting on the incidence and nature of hate crimes to these bodies in accordance with relevant commitments.

Strengthening the OSCE

Advance the OSCE's tolerance and nondiscrimination agenda by raising hate crime issues at OSCE forums and advocating the following:

■ The fulfillment by participating states of their OSCE obligations to combat racism, xenophobia, antisemitism, and other forms of intolerance and discrimination, in particular the obligations to collect hate crime data and to report that data to the Office for Democratic Institutions and Human Rights (OSCE/ODIHR).

■ The reappointment by the Greek Chairmanship in 2009 of the OSCE Chairman-in-Office's three personal representatives on tolerance with their distinct mandates.

■ Expanded administrative resources, either from the Chairmanship or elsewhere within the OSCE, to support the three Personal Representatives in carrying out their mandates.

■ Continued support for the ODIHR's Tolerance and Nondiscrimination Unit (TnD), in particular to encourage:

▪ Efforts to ensure that the Law Enforcement Officer Program on Combating Hate Crime (LEOP) has the support it needs and that participating states are taking part in this program.

▪ The ODIHR to convene regular meetings of the National Points of Contact on Combating Hate Crimes, with the full participation of civil society groups and representatives of specialized antidiscrimination bodies, and consider as a topic in 2009 the building of trust and cooperation between law enforcement agencies and victims, their communities and civil society groups.

▪ Wide dissemination of the ODIHR's forthcoming legislative guidelines on hate crimes.

▪ Agreements between the ODIHR and participating states on programs of technical assistance to combat hate crime.

▪ Sufficient funding for the TnD unit and its programs and activities on hate crime through the regular OSCE budget and through extrabudgetary contributions.

- Immediate preparations for a high-level conference on combating hate crimes in 2009 in order to generate political support for the implementation of tolerance and nondiscrimination commitments as well as to reinforce the activities of the personal representatives on tolerance and the ODIHR. Action must be taken immediately to identify a host country, develop an agenda and proposed outcomes, and take steps to ensure high-level participation. Because hate crime is a problem that poses serious threats across the region and an issue that combines multiple forms of discrimination and intolerance, this conference could bring together governments and a wide range of civil society actors with a view to developing a common program of action to respond to hate crime while recognizing the unique factors that characterize different types of bias motivation.

- Implementation by participating states of the recommendations from the June 2004 Paris meeting on the internet and hate crimes, as set forth in Decision 633 of the OSCE Permanent Council on Promoting Tolerance and Media Freedom on the Internet.

Recommendations for the Government of the United States

We call on the government of the United States to demonstrate international leadership at the OSCE, advocate measures to combat hate crime in bilateral relationships, and expand efforts to support civil society organizations throughout the OSCE area, by taking the following steps:

Demonstrate International Leadership at the OSCE

Advance the OSCE's tolerance and nondiscrimination agenda by taking a leading role in furthering the above-mentioned recommendations related to "Strenghtneing the OSCE."

Provide for extrabudgetary contributions, secondment of personnel, and other in-kind support for OSCE programs to combat violent hate crimes, including by making available its law enforcement expertise. In this connection, undertake a process to assess and reform the current mechanism of budget allocation by the State Department to ensure that the United States meets its funding obligations to the OSCE in a timely manner.

Advocate in Bilateral Relationships and Offer Technical Assistance

Promote stronger government responses to violent hate crime among OSCE participating states through U.S. reporting as well as the bilateral relationships of the United States with those countries, by:

- Maintaining strong and inclusive State Department monitoring and public reporting on racist, xenophobic, antisemitic, anti-Muslim, homophobic, anti-Roma, and other bias-motivated violence—including by consulting with civil society groups as well as providing appropriate training for human rights officers and other relevant mission staff abroad.

- Raising violent hate crime issues with representatives of foreign governments and encouraging, where appropriate, legal and other policy responses, including those contained in Human Rights First's **Ten-Point Plan** for governments to combat violent hate crime and its specific recommendations on the Russian Federation and Ukraine.

■ Offer appropriate technical assistance and other forms of cooperation, including training of police and prosecutors in investigating, recording, reporting and prosecuting violent hate crimes as well as translation of Department of Justice and Federal Bureau of Investigation (FBI) materials on hate crimes. Moreover, the FBI's International Law Enforcement Academy should include a hate crime component in its training of law enforcement personnel in emerging democracies of Eastern Europe and the former Soviet Union.

■ Organize International Visitors Programs on combating bias-motivated violence for representatives of law enforcement, victim communities, human rights groups and legal advocates.

Support Civil Society Organizations

Expand funding and other support to build the capacity of civil society groups in the OSCE region to combat violent hate crimes, by:

■ Providing extra-budgetary support to expand ODIHR's civil society training program on combating hate crimes.

■ Focusing on combating hate crimes in the next phase of USAID's democracy and governance assistance in Russia in order to expand the capacity of civil society groups in Russia to monitor and report on hate crimes, engage in national and international advocacy and to respond to cases and support victims at the local level.

■ Providing funding to expand the network of monitors on violent hate crime by civil society groups in Ukraine.

■ Ensuring that groups working to combat all forms of violent hate crime have access to support under existing U.S. funding programs, including the Human Rights and Democracy Fund and programs for human rights defenders.

Congressional establishment of a long-term funding program at the State Department, USAID or an outside agency to provide financial support for civil society groups in the OSCE region to monitor and report on violent hate crime, to advocate more effective laws and policies and stronger official responses to hate crime incidents, to provide services to victims, and to develop and implement programs to prevent and respond to hate crime.

The Reality
of Hate Crime

Violence Based on Racism and Xenophobia

Table of Contents

Executive Summary

Racist and xenophobic violence rose in several of the 56 countries of the Organization for Security and Cooperation in Europe (OSCE) in 2007, according to official statistics and reports by expert bodies and nongovernmental monitors. Although comprehensive and systematic data collection systems are unavailable in most OSCE states, government monitoring systems in a number of countries showed moderate to high rises in the overall numbers of hate crimes in 2006 and 2007—the latest figures available. These include **Finland**, **Ireland**, the **Slovak Republic**, **Sweden**, the **United Kingdom**, and the **United States.** Over a longer period of time—between 2000 and 2006—eight European countries experienced an upward trend in recorded racist crime: **Denmark**, **Finland**, **France**, **Germany**, **Ireland**, **Slovakia**, and the **United Kingdom**.

Information from nongovernmental monitors provided evidence of rising levels of racist violence in 2007 in **Greece**, **Italy**, the **Russian Federation**, **Switzerland**, and **Ukraine**. Available figures may only be the tip of the iceberg, however. Media and NGO surveys suggest that in many cases violence was not being reported to or recorded by police. This assertion is bolstered by the *2007 European Crime and Safety Survey*, which revealed high levels of hate crimes reported in 2007 by respondents of immigrant background in **Greece**, **Italy**, **Portugal**, and **Spain**, while there was no relevant official criminal justice data on racist violence and crime from these countries.

Cutting across religious and cultural divides, racism and xenophobia threaten communities distinguished by ethnic or national origin, including both national minorities and people of immigrant origin, citizens and noncitizens, longtime residents and newcomers.

People of African origin, regardless of their citizenship status, were subjected to some of the most persistent and serious attacks, and were among the principal victims of racist and xenophobic violence in Europe and North America. A series of incidents involving hangman's nooses and burning crosses served as a reminder that racist intimidation and other hate crimes against African-Americans remain a serious problem—and that African Americans continue to be the largest group targeted for hate crime violence in the United States.

In Eastern Europe and the former Soviet Union, people of African origin faced particularly virulent racism and violence. People of Asian origin also faced high levels of racist violence, with racism confronting South Asians often overlapping with and exacerbated by religious hatred and prejudice toward those of a Muslim background, or those perceived to be Muslim. Anti-Muslim violence is addressed in a separate section of the *2008 Hate Crime Survey*: ***Violence Against Muslims***.

In Western Europe, discrimination and violence targeted in particular the Afro-European descendants of people from the former European colonies in the Caribbean, North Africa, and Sub-Saharan Africa. Roma and Sinti, who are often described as Europe's largest minority, continued to be particular targets of discrimination and hate crime violence in their countries of citizenship and as immigrants. Immigrant Roma within the expanded European Union faced extraordinary violence in 2007 and 2008. Anti-Roma violence is addressed in a separate section of the *2008 Hate Crime Survey*: ***Violence Against Roma***.

Immigrants and citizens of recent immigrant origin face particular problems of racism and xenophobia throughout Europe and North America. Anti-immigrant bias is a form of prejudice and hatred founded on multiple forms of discrimination that can attack the physical appearance, religious affiliation, and cultural characteristics of the victims. Immigrants are often highly visible even in multicultural societies. Refugees and asylum seekers, especially those concentrated in small areas amidst largely homogenous populations, are particularly vulnerable to violent attacks.

In Western Europe, new trends of internal immigration in the expanded European Union have led to an increase in anti-immigrant discourse and violence directed at people from new member states of the E.U. Those targeted for vilification and violence included immigrant workers of Roma background and other immigrants of a wide range of ethnicities and national origins from the new E.U. member states.

In the most extreme examples of the new anti-immigrant discourse in Europe, immigrant groups were made scapegoats in 2007–2008 for social ills ranging from crime to unemployment. In **Germany**, **Greece**, and **Switzerland**, new strands of anti-immigrant scapegoating combined with manifestations of racist violence targeting immigrants. In **Italy**, anti-Roma rhetoric in concert with aggressive anti-immigration policies provided the backdrop for incidents of racist violence that occurred at a level unprecedented in recent history.

In the **United States**, recent debates on immigration have polarized society and provided the backdrop for a surge in reported violent assaults against people of Hispanic origin, both citizens and immigrants, in the last several years.

I. Racist Violence: What Available Data Reveals

Government statistics, NGO monitoring, and other surveys paint a picture of racist violence that is either rising or holding steady at historically high levels. Although comprehensive and systematic data collection systems are unavailable in most OSCE states, government monitoring in **Finland**, **Ireland**, the **Slovak Republic**, **Sweden**, the **United Kingdom**, and the **United States** showed moderate to high rises in the overall numbers of hate crimes in 2006 and 2007– the latest figures available. In **France**, official figures showed an overall decline in racist and xenophobic hate crimes, even as the proportion of these crimes involving violence and direct threats against persons rose. In **Germany**, official figures released through the third quarter of 2007 showed a significant rise in violent hate crimes, although year end figures showed a slight decline.

Information from nongovernmental monitors provided evidence of rising levels of racist violence in **Greece**, **Italy**, the **Russian Federation**, **Switzerland**, and **Ukraine**.

A. Data Reported to the Fundamental Rights Agency

Intergovernmental bodies that have focused on hate crime data collection—particularly the European Union's Fundamental Rights Agency (FRA)—have been useful sources of comparative information. FRA has most recently concluded that of the 27 E.U. Member States, only 11 collect sufficiently robust criminal justice data on racist violence and crime to allow for a trend analysis of the problem over time.[1]

Based on the data collected by these eleven E.U. governments, FRA noted that between 2005 and 2006, seven of the eleven states had experienced an upward trend in recorded racist crime: **Austria**, **Finland**, **Germany**, **Ireland**, **Slovakia**, **Sweden**, and the **United Kingdom**. Over a longer period of time—between 2000 and 2006—eight countries experienced an upward trend in recorded racist crime: **Denmark**, **Finland**, **France**, **Germany**, **Ireland**, **Slovakia**, and the **United Kingdom**.[2]

In the absence of reliable official data in the majority of E.U. states, the FRA has noted the utility of crime surveys. For example, the 2007 report draws upon the *2007 European Crime and Safety Survey*, which asked respondents of immigrant background whether they or members of their household were victims of a hate crime during the previous year.

The survey revealed high levels of hate crimes reported by respondents of immigrant background in **Greece**, **Italy**, **Portugal**, and **Spain**, while there was no relevant official criminal justice data on racist violence and crime from these countries. The study found that in a 12-month period, hate crimes were experienced by 14.5 percent of respondents in Spain and by 16.4 percent in Greece. On the basis of this study, FRA observed that in the original fifteen member states of the European Union, "on average 9.9 percent of respondents with an immigrant background indicated that they or a member of their immediate family were the victim of hate crime."[3]

B. Countries with Good Monitoring Systems

In **France**, the National Consultative Commission on Human Rights (CNCDH), the official body that reports annually on racist, xenophobic, and antisemitic hate crimes, reported a continuing trend in 2007 toward violent attacks and threats against individuals, even as overall numbers of incidents declined. The proportion of violent acts directed at individuals increased from 45 percent of total hate crimes in 2006 to 51 percent in 2007; the total number of racist and xenophobic crimes declined by 9 percent.[4]

In **Germany**, between 2003 and 2006, official figures on violent crimes with a "right-wing extremist" motivation increased steadily from 759 in 2003 to 1,047 in 2006. In 2007, for the first time since 2003, the incidence of right-wing violent crimes decreased to 980, although remaining at historically high levels. Similarly, official figures showed a slight decline in violent xenophobic crime—a subset of right-wing violent crime—from 484 in 2006 to 414 in 2007.[5]

Other German sources reported a rise in these crimes in 2007. Uwe-Karsten Heye, the head of the German antixenophobia group *Gesicht Zeigen!* (Show Your Faces!), said in March 2008 that a record number of attacks were reported in 2007—consistent with official reports through the first three quarters of the year. These included incidents in which some six hundred people were attacked by neo-Nazis, as well as systematic attacks on immigrant-run businesses.[6]

In **Sweden**, in 2007, the Swedish National Council for Crime Prevention (Brå), reported 3,536 hate crimes—an 8 percent increase over the 3,259 hate crimes reported in 2006. "Xenophobic" crimes—the majority subset of hate crimes overall—also registered a year-on-year increase, up 13 percent to 2,489 such crimes in 2007 from 2,189 in 2006.[7]

In the **United Kingdom**—the only country to report on incidents (acts which may fall short of criminal offenses) as well as offenses—61,262 racist incidents were reported to the police in 2006/2007, an increase of 3.7 percent over the previous year. Among these, there were 42,551 racially or religiously aggravated offences, representing a 2.6 percent increase in the number of offenses over the previous year. Just over half of all police forces recorded an increase in the number of offences motivated by a religious or racial bias.[8]

In Scotland, there were 1,022 incidents of racist violence in Lothian and the Borders regions in 2006/2007, twice the 2002/2003 number.[9] In Strathclyde, police reported 1,853 hate crimes during the 2006/2007 year, a 7.5 percent rise over the previous year, and an almost 20 percent rise over 2002/2003 levels.[10]

C. Good Monitoring Systems with a Data Lag

In some countries where data for 2007 is not yet publicly available, available statistics for earlier periods show a rise in racist violence over 2005 levels.

In **Finland**, there was a steady rise in the incidence of racist crimes and violence between 2004 and 2006.[11] In 2006, police filed reports on 748 suspected racist crimes. The most common offence was assault (assaults and attempted assaults accounted for 40 percent of all cases).[12] The police registered 669 and 558 incidents of racial violence in 2005 and 2004, respectively.[13]

In **Ireland**, according to annual police reports, police registered 174 racist incidents in 2006 as compared with 94 in 2005 and 84 in 2004.[14] Early reports from Ireland's antiracism body—the National Consultative Committee on Racism and Interculturalism (NCCRI)—suggest a further rise in 2007. In March 2008, the NCCRI said that, according to incident reports it had received, the number of reported assaults, cases of harassment, and other types of abuse in 2007 had risen to 99, compared to the 2006 figure of 65.

Incidents monitored by the NCCRI included both crimes of violence—such as an attack by Cork teenagers on a Burundian man—and cases of racist speech, including racism on the internet.[15] The report said that "the most significant victims of racist incidents were black African males," with others targeted including people of Asian origin and members of the Traveller community. Half of the incidents were reported in the Dublin area.[16]

In the **Slovak Republic**, the police in 2006 reported on 188 registered criminal offenses motivated by racial, ethnic, or other intolerance, up from 121 reported offenses in 2005.[17]

In the **United States**, the Federal Bureau of Investigation's (FBI) hate crime statistics are disaggregated to include data on crimes motivated by race (including "antiblack" bias) and ethnicity (including "anti-Hispanic" bias). In 2006, there was a rise in both categories over figures from 2005. In 2006, the FBI reported 4,737 race-based offenses (up from 4,691 in 2005) and 1,233 ethnicity-based offenses (up from 1,144 in 2005).[18]

The highest levels of violent hate crime continue to be directed toward members of the African American community and others of African origin, in what the FBI's annual hate crime reports refer to as antiblack bias attacks. In the latest report, covering 2006, the FBI found that over a third of hate crime victims were targeted because of antiblack bias. Local monitors confirmed the statistics. The Los Angeles County Commission on Human Relations, in its annual hate crime report for 2007, found that antiblack hate crimes were not only by far the most numerous—310 of the total of 510—but also increased 21 percent compared to 2006. This represented 58 percent of all hate crimes, although African Americans constitute just 9 percent of Los Angeles County's population.[19]

NGO reporting and analysis in the United States added to the picture provided by the FBI statistics. *The Year in Hate*, the Southern Poverty Law Center's annual report for 2007, revealed a 35 percent rise in hate crimes against people of Hispanic origin between 2003 and 2006—based on an analysis of Federal Bureau of Investigation crime reports. An FBI spokesman interviewed by National Public Radio confirmed the 35 percent rise.[20]

D. Nongovernmental Organizations and the Data Gap

As in some of the aforementioned countries, NGO monitoring can often be a useful supplement to available government statistics. In countries where governments do not record or publicly report specifically on racist violence, NGOs may be the only source of data on hate crimes.

In **Greece**, where no official statistics on hate crimes are available, racist incidents reported by the Hellenic League for Human Rights in 2006 included the stabbing to death of a Georgian and an Albanian immigrant in Crete. There were sixteen other "major" incidents of racist violence against immigrants and refugees, two attacks on Roma, and two on religious minorities. In the annual report for 2007, the Hellenic League for Human Rights reported a steady increase in racist attacks on immigrants and other minorities, while condemning the indifference of Greek law enforcement bodies toward the attacks.[21]

In **Italy**, where no statistics on violent hate crimes are regularly made available by official sources, news media and nongovernmental monitors highlighted a spike of anti-Roma and anti-immigrant violence in 2007 and 2008.

In the **Russian Federation**, the number of violent hate crimes against individuals continues to grow steadily, with 2008 on track to be another record-setting year. According to the SOVA Center for Information and Analysis, the leading nongovernmental monitor of hate crimes, in 2007 there were at least 667 victims of racially motivated violence, including 86 murders.[22] In comparison, there were 568 victims of violent hate crimes, including 63 murders, registered in 2006. The beginning of 2008 has shown a dramatic growth of hate violence. Already in the first eight months of 2008, 65 people were killed and 318 injured as a result of racial and other bias-motivated assaults.[23]

In **Spain**, the Spanish Commission to Aid Refugees (CEAR) reported three hundred racist attacks in 2006, mostly on people of immigrant origin, and spoke out on continuing racist attacks during 2007 and 2008.[24]

In **Switzerland**, in June 2008, the Swiss Foundation against Racism and Antisemitism issued the annual review on racism, finding a rise of some 30 percent in racist incidents in 2007 from 2006 levels: from 87 to 118. Incidents recorded included personal assaults, arson or use of gunfire, harassment, and vandalism.[25]

In **Ukraine**, nongovernmental monitors documented eighty-six bias-motivated attacks on persons in 2007, including five murders, as compared with fourteen attacks, including two murders, in 2006. This constituted a sharp rise over 2005 figures.[26] In the first 6 months of 2008, there were at least four murders of foreigners and numerous serious attacks in which there was a suspected racist or other bias motivation.

II. Patterns of Violence Based on Racism and Xenophobia

Particularly pernicious patterns of violence and intimidation in many parts of Europe and North America are driven by racism and xenophobia. Members of minority groups may be victimized because of the color of their skin or other physical attributes, while such prejudice is sometimes exacerbated by religious intolerance or cultural stereotypes.

The principal victims of racist and xenophobic violence are often described as members of "visible minorities," although this term may be misleading. Even a minority that is not easily distinguished by physical features may stand out as "different" because of language, religion, and a variety of other cultural indicators.

In the 2008 annual report, the European Union's Fundamental Rights Agency noted that its national contact points "continue to indicate that visible minorities in Europe, such as Black Africans, Roma, or Muslim women wearing headscarves, are disproportion-ately vulnerable to racist victimization," taking into account their relatively low numbers in the population.[27]

In many cases, discrimination against particular groups combines racism and xenophobia with hatred and prejudice founded on religious intolerance. Distinguish-ing the forms of discrimination faced by some communities as predominantly driven by either racism or religious bias is sometimes neither possible nor particularly helpful in countering these forms of discrimination.

An overlay of multiple forms of discrimination is present in prejudice and hatred toward immigrants, where fear of the foreign or unknown—a standard definition of xenophobia—blurs together prejudice against differences in appearance, culture, religion, and other factors. But

the same combination of biases is also present with regard to national minorities and other communities that may stand out in their own countries.

Gender bias, too, often combines with racism and xenophobia. Women may be attacked because their customs and dress do not fit gender stereotypes. At times, racist assaults take particularly vicious and gender-specific forms. Women are frequently attacked because their particular gender-specific forms of dress—such as the Islamic hijāb or the long dresses worn by many Roma—are taken as a symbol of difference, or of defiance. In numerous reported cases of racist and religiously motivated attacks in Europe, assailants have shouted obscenities at Muslim women and attempted to tear off their headscarves.

In many countries, and notably in countries of the former Yugoslavia, members of national minorities are similar in appearance and share a common ancestry. But distinct communities within a country or region, defined by custom, language, and religion rather than ethnicity, may be no less "visible" and susceptible to become targets for racist violence.

Attacks motivated because an individual was *perceived* to be a member of a hated group were also frequently based on misconceptions that underscored the broad reach of racism. Non-Muslim people of South Asian origin, including Sikhs and Hindus, have been targeted—particularly in the United States—by attackers shouting anti-Arab and anti-Muslim epithets. Others suffered antisemitic or other bias attacks because they were mistaken for Jews, immigrants, or other "visible minorities." In one case, a Russian prosecutor ac-counted for a hate attack on a Russian citizen who *appeared* to be dark-skinned by explaining "in the nighttime, due to lack of natural and artificial lighting," the victim was simply "mistaken for a non-Slav."[28]

The rise in racist and xenophobic violence in the region has been reported in the context of widespread harassment and intimidation of minority populations through both physical and symbolic means. A range of symbols and slogans have emerged within the specific national contexts of particular countries or regions, from "Russia for the Russians" and "Germany for the Germans" to the more adaptable slogan "Foreigners Out"—a variation on the emblematic antisemitic slogan of German Nazism, "Juden Raus/Jews Out."

The symbols of German Nazism were used to send a message of hatred and exclusion to members of a broad range of religious and ethnic minorities, even as they retained their particular antisemitic significance when targeting Jewish families and communities. Modern-day adherents of racial supremacy theories painted swastikas on refugee hostels, the offices of human rights organizations, and foreign students' housing, as well as on Jewish, Christian, and Muslim graves. Combined with the swastikas daubed on homes, memorials, community institutions, and schools, these manifestations of hatred sent a chilling message to all who stand outside the chauvinist ideal of extreme nationalists.

Across the OSCE region, anti-immigrant and antiminority aggression led to incidents of extreme violence and everyday harassment and intimidation. Racist violence often took the form of persistent abuse that held families and whole communities in a pervasive state of fear, even if most abuse fell short of serious threats to life. This was the kind of "low level and mundane racism," that regularly went unreported, and when reported, often went without response.[29] But even low-level violence that persisted day after day—egg throwing, broken windows, threatening graffiti, and verbal abuse—brought with it an implicit threat of more serious violence and crime.

In many cases, police remained unaware of hate crime incidents. A serious shortcoming lies in the failure, sometimes due to unwillingness, of law enforcement agencies to establish relations with particular minority communities, resulting in many crimes not being reported to the authorities. Similarly, some police agencies also fail to appropriately record the evidence of bias attacks when victims do in fact come forward.

III. Victims of Violence Based on Racism and Xenophobia

Racism and xenophobia victimize a wide range of communities across Europe and North America by reason of their origins, and the color of their skin. These communities under threat, often distinguished by their ethnic or national origin, include both national minorities and people of immigrant origin, citizens and noncitizens, longtime residents and newcomers. Among them are Roma and Sinti, often described as Europe's largest minority—a people whose situation is touched upon here but whose unique circumstances are addressed in a separate section in this survey on *Violence Against Roma*. Racism is also a factor in antisemitism and anti-Muslim bias that combines with religious hatred and prejudice. These issues, too, are discussed in separate sections on *Antisemitic Violence* and *Violence Against Muslims.*

A. People of African Origin

Whether citizens or noncitizens, people of African origin stand out as among the principal subjects of racism and xenophobia in many parts of Europe and North America. In the United States, African American citizens continued to represent the largest group of victims of hate crime violence—a legacy of systemic state sanctioned discrimination that began to be remedied only in the 1960's. In Western Europe, citizens of African origin, many of them descended from the people of former colonies, faced ongoing discrimination and violence.

In parts of Eastern Europe and the former Soviet Union, small populations of citizens and immigrants of African origin were highly visible and often vulnerable targets of racism and xenophobia. In the **Russian Federation** and **Ukraine**, where relatively few people of African origin

reside, the rate of violence was extraordinary: African refugees, students, visitors, and the handful of citizens and permanent residents of African origin lived under constant threat of violence.

Numerous incidents of hate crime violence against people of African origin were reported throughout the region.

In September 2007, attackers in Tartu, **Estonia**, threw stones at a dark-skinned French student. Although the head of an association of foreign students there said the incident was part of a larger problem of neo-Nazi violence, a local police officer downplayed the incident, claiming foreign students in the past two years had been caught up in only a few cases of "robbery, fights, or insults."[30]

In **Germany**, numerous serious attacks on people of African origin were reported throughout 2007 and 2008.

- On May 24, 2008 in Viersen, North Rhine-Westphalia, four men with shaved heads and wearing bomber jackets approached a man of African origin, threatened him with knives and an iron rod, and then beat him.[31]

- On March 2, 2008, in Berlin, a 20-year-old woman yelling racial slurs pushed a dark-skinned man into the path of an oncoming train. The 19-year-old victim, assisted by two people, was able to jump up from the tracks in time.[32]

- On October 20, 2007, in the Spandau borough of Berlin, a group of young men harassed and beat an African-American; four men were arrested and an investigation was reportedly opened.[33]

- In June 2007, in Berlin, three attackers assaulted a man of African origin at a subway station and knocked him off the platform; the victim suffered head injuries and was in a coma for several days.[34]

An acquittal was reported in June 2008, in Potsdam, for an April 2006 attack on a man of Ethiopian origin. This was one of the most widely reported incidents in the lead-up to Germany's hosting of the World Cup that year and had precipitated a national and international debate on racist violence in the country.[35]

In the **Russian Federation**, despite the small number of people of African origin, foreign students have been particularly vulnerable to attacks.

- In October 2007, in Moscow, an assailant stabbed and seriously injured Cameroonian Vansi Jeanu. Police said a young man had been detained in relation to the attack, which was similarly being investigated as act of hooliganism.[36]

- On February 4, 2007, in Saint Petersburg, attackers described as skinheads assaulted a postgraduate student from Cameroon at a metro station, causing serious injuries requiring hospitalization. Prosecutors said the attack was under investigation as hooliganism.[37]

In Bratislava, **Slovakia**, in March 2007, attackers knocked a Nigerian man to the ground reportedly shouting obscenities. The nongovernmental organization People Against Racism (PAR) reported that when police arrived and the man pointed out his attackers, the police officers told him to "shut up."[38]

The Swiss Foundation Against Racism and Antisemitism, in the annual review on racism in **Switzerland**, reported that the principal victims of racist violence were Muslims, people of African origin, and Jews. Incidents included 15 personal assaults, 5 cases of arson or use of gunfire, 6 of harassment or threats, and 12 of vandalism.[39] The foundation's 2006 report said that

one-third of hate crime cases recorded concerned people of African origin.[40]

- On May 1, 2007, in a Zurich suburb, unknown men shouting obscenities about Africans attacked Antonio da Costa, a 43-year-old refugee from Angola. The attackers used chainsaws to rake da Costa's face, neck, and chest, nearly severing his left thumb, and severely slashing one arm; he required six hours of emergency surgery. There were reportedly no arrests, although a prosecutor said video surveillance footage was being used in the investigation.[41]

- In Thun, on January 28, 2007, six skinheads assaulted and injured three young people, including a 22-year-old Swiss citizen of African origin, who was told that he had no business being in Switzerland. Police arrived but made no arrests; in April, 2008, a 23-year-old with a record of political extremism was fined for involvement in the attack.[42]

The African community in Kyiv, **Ukraine** had already held four funerals for victims of racially motivated violence in the first half of 2008, following the murders of a Nigerian, a Sierra Leonean, and two Congolese immigrants in the course of the year. One victim's funeral turned into a march against racism. In an act of protest over the worsening conditions for foreigners in Ukraine, friends and family of the brutally murdered Gbenda-Charles Victor Tator of Sierra Leone walked in a procession through the streets of Kyiv from the morgue to the cemetery.

In the **United Kingdom**, people of African origin continued to be targeted for extreme violence. On May 13, 2007, in Garston, England, four men shouting racial epithets attacked 21-year-old Marlon Moran, who was of mixed race, with a metal bar, a cleaver, sticks, and knives. Moran was killed by a knife wound to the stomach. Four suspects were tried for murder aggravated by racism in November 2007; one was sentenced to three-and-a-half years in prison on the lesser charge of manslaughter and the three others were released.[43] In the course of the trial, Moran's family protested that in the aftermath of the murder they suffered constant racial harassment and threats.[44]

In the **United States**, people of African descent are most likely to become victims of hate crimes, in line with longstanding patterns of violent hate crimes. The annual hate crime survey produced by the Federal Bureau of Investigation (FBI), covering 2006, reported 3,332 victims of antiblack bias crimes, in 2,640 incidents. This represented 66.4 percent of the victims of racial bias crimes, and some 34.5 percent of the 9,652 victims of hate crimes overall.[45] Antiblack bias crimes were also predominantly violent crimes against persons, in contrast to crimes against property.

B. Immigrants and Citizens of Immigrant Origin

Immigrants and citizens of immigrant origin face particular problems of racism and xenophobia. Singled out because of race or ethnicity, language, culture, and often religion, immigrants and those perceived to be immigrants are often highly visible even in multicultural societies.

Official classifications and data collection agencies often describe members of many minority populations in Europe as "of immigrant origin," although many of them are descendants of people that came to Europe generations ago. Racist and xenophobic prejudices indiscriminately victimize people regardless of their official citizenship or residency status.

Discrimination and racist violence against immigrant foreign nationals is generally both underreported and underrecorded. Many immigrants, both legal and illegal, have fears of encounters with police and public authorities. People without or with uncertain legal residence status may fear that reporting will not only result in retaliation on behalf of the attackers, but will

also draw the attention of immigration services, set in motion by the very authorities from which they seek protection. Accordingly, people with no legal residence status are far more likely to suffer discrimination and violence in silence.

In **Germany**, members of the large Turkish minority—both German citizens and nonnationals—faced harassment and violence in many parts of the country. People of African and South Asian origin were also among the targets of persistent and sometimes extreme violence there. Foreign-owned shops were targeted for vandalism and arson; members of minorities were attacked in the street, at public events, and on public transport. In the state of Brandenburg alone, according to the NGO *Gesicht Zeigen* (Show Your Faces!), there were eleven recorded attacks on immigrant-run businesses, as part of what a representative of the organization called "a strategy to destroy livelihoods and drive out immigrants."[46] Members of minorities in Germany are routinely referred to as *Ausländer* ("foreigners") regardless of their actual citizenship status.

In **Ireland**, official hate crime monitors and the media reported increased hate crime attacks on immigrants, including immigrant workers from Eastern European countries newly admitted to the European Union. The National Consultative Committee on Racism and Interculturalism (NCCRI) said that "the most significant victims of racist incidents were black African males," with others targeted including people of Asian origin and members of the Traveller community. Half of the incidents were reported in the Dublin area.[47]

In one case in Dublin, on March 14, 2008, a group of youths attacked Cida Jeangros, a 30-year-old Brazilian woman, subjecting her to racist verbal abuse and beating and kicking her. There was no effort to rob the woman—the intent appeared simply to do harm. Jeangros said she had previously been subjected to verbal abuse, and that many migrant workers live in fear of attacks in Dublin.[48]

In **Latvia**, anti-immigrant discourse was accompanied by racist attacks on immigrants belonging to visible minorities. Although Latvia has adopted legal provisions imposing more serious sentences for bias-motivated crimes, there is little evidence that these amendments are being applied with vigor. In June 2007, a Riga City Court gave suspended sentences to two convicted men, characterized as neo-Nazis, for attacking a Brazilian woman with a bottle while shouting xenophobic expletives.[49]

A major concern in Latvia, identified by the European Commission against Racism and Intolerance (ECRI) in a 2007 report, is "the widespread denial of the problem of racist violence both on the part of the public and the authorities." Latvian authorities "tend to remain indifferent and/or undermine the problem by speaking of "isolated cases" without recognizing or being aware of the real number of violent manifestations of intolerance in the country."[50]

In the **United States**, although the largest number of reported hate crimes continues to be committed against African-Americans, a dramatic rise in anti-immigrant violence accompanied a new mainstreaming of anti-immigrant rhetoric and fears.[51] The rising violence was reflected both in the media reporting and in the statistical data available from annual national hate crime statistics.

The Southern Poverty Law Center revealed a 35 percent rise in hate crimes against people of Hispanic origin between 2003 and 2006, based on an analysis of FBI crime reports. The incidents reported ranged from violent assaults to vandalism and arson.[52] For example, on October 8, 2007, in Omaha, Nebraska, arsonists set fire to vehicles owned by a family of Hispanic origin, while spray-painting two cars with white power slogans and a swastika.[53]

In San Diego, California, Deputy District Attorney Oscar Garcia, who specializes in hate crime prosecutions, confirmed that Hispanic Americans were being expressly targeted, with illegal immigrants and U.S. citizens alike victimized in his district. Places at which migrant workers gather to meet employers were particular targets of racist abuse: "day labor sites seem to attract hate mongers who use that as an excuse and hide behind the flag and claim they're merely trying to express political views."[54] According to official statistics from the state of California, anti-Hispanic offenses increased over 7 percent, from 218 in 2006 to 234 in 2007.[55]

There were also important cases in the **United States** in which serious hate crimes led to prosecutions and heavy sentences. Two young men were sentenced in December 2007 for the April 22, 2006 attack near Houston, Texas, on Mexican-American teenager David Ritcheson, who was tortured and verbally abused. The attackers broke his jaw, burned him with cigarettes, attempted to carve a swastika in his chest, and poured bleach on him. The most severe injuries were caused when they violently sodomized Ritcheson with a patio umbrella pole. Ritcheson was hospitalized and required thirty surgeries for his injuries, but never fully recovered from the physical and psychological trauma of the attack. He subsequently collaborated with the Anti-Defamation League in creating an antihate program at his high school, and one year after the attack testified before the U.S. House of Representative's Judiciary Committee in hearings concerning the strengthening of federal hate crime laws. Three months later David Ritcheson committed suicide.[56] The accused were sentenced to life imprisonment and ninety years, respectively, for aggravated sexual assault; an appeal by one of the defendants was dismissed in March 2008.[57]

Anti-Immigrant Violence in the Expanded European Union

The expansion of the European Union coincided with racist violence that reflected new patterns of immigration from new member states to other parts of the E.U. At the same time, the new members of the European Union should be held to the E.U. standards in their response to longstanding patterns of racist violence.

On November 24, 2007, in Zlin, in the **Czech Republic**, three young men described as skinheads shouted racist insults and attacked Sri Lankan student Pradeep Manohara Mahadura as he waited with friends at a bus stop. He was beaten and knocked to the ground and then kicked in the stomach and head before a passerby intervened to help.[58]

In **Ireland**, violence against immigrants from Eastern European E.U. states was on the rise, while the criminal justice system has yet to include provisions for penalty enhancement even for the most serious bias crimes.

■ On February 22, 2008, in the Dublin suburb of Drimnagh, Polish migrant workers Marius Szwajkos and Pawel Kalite were murdered by a group of youths, suffering lethal stab wounds in the head and throat.[59] Irish Prime Minister Bertie Ahern, who was on a state visit to Poland at the time of the killings, called the killings a result of "hooliganism," while the families of the victims said it would probably "never be known" if they were motivated by xenophobia or racism. A 17-year-old and a 19-year-old were charged in relation to the two murders.[60]

In Kosice, **Slovakia**, on November 21, 2007, three men shouting Nazi slogans reportedly attacked a 16-year-old girl of Cuban background. The girl suffered injuries to the head, back, and right arm. A police spokeswoman said: "first they knocked the girl down to the ground. Then all the three started kicking and beating her up, shouting 'Sieg heil' and 'clear off Slovakia' at her."[61]

In the **United Kingdom**, attacks on Poles, Lithuanians, and other immigrants from the new E.U. member states became a major new component of hate crime violence, particularly in Scotland and Northern Ireland, with one racist murder reported in 2007 in Wales.

■ On February 3, 2007, in Edinburgh, Scotland, Polish construction worker Patryk Mnich was attacked and beaten in a xenophobic attack causing him severe head injuries and permanent disability. His assailant was charged with inflicting injuries causing permanent impairment and attempted murder. In September 2007, he was sentenced to seven and a half years of imprisonment; although the accused had reportedly called Mnich a "Polish bastard," a jury rejected a charge that the assault was bias-aggravated.[62]

In June 2007, police in Edinburgh said that following the attack on Patryk Mnich they were receiving an average of three reports of hate crime attacks daily, with continuing attacks on Polish and other Eastern European workers representing a high proportion of the attacks. Police said they had dealt with 1,022 racist incidents in the Lothian and Borders regions which includes Edinburgh, in the 12 months up to April 1, 2008, which was twice the rate of incidents recorded three years before. More than a third of the 900 race hate crimes in Edinburgh took place in the city center, and most of those involved Eastern European victims.[63]

■ In August, in Wales, Glasgow resident Thomas Blue killed Adam Michalski, a Polish immigrant, while shouting xenophobic and racial slurs. Blue was sentenced to life imprisonment, with a minimum 17-year term.[64]

In June 2007, Edinburgh police said that because of the rising numbers of incidents they were considering establishing a system through which Polish victims of hate crimes could report incidents to police anonymously through third parties at a Polish community center there.[65] A report drawing upon media monitoring of hate crimes in the U.K., prepared on behalf of the Federation of Poles in Great Britain, documented 50 incidents in 2007 in which Polish immigrants were assaulted. The author of the report, Wiktor Moszczynski, said the assaults occurred "primarily in small towns and in the countryside," but cited the London Metropolitan police force as having reported that "48 hate crimes against Poles were committed between December 2006 and November 2007." Many assaults, however, went unreported.[66]

In February 2007, the Lithuanian government announced that it would be establishing a consulate in Northern Ireland to respond to rising attacks on immigrants from Eastern Europe. The Lithuanian ambassador to the U.K., Vygaudas Usackas, said that 64 attacks on Lithuanians had been reported in Northern Ireland within the past year.[67]

■ On April 20, 2008, unknown attackers in Cookstown, County Tyrone, threw a petrol-bomb at the home of Lithuanian immigrants; two men and two women escaped unharmed.[68] Also in April, unknown attackers threw fireworks and bricks through the bedroom window of a Polish couple in Drumahoe, forcing them to flee.[69] In mid-May, two cars belonging to a Bulgarian family living in Portballintrae were set alight, in what was described as the latest incident in a series of "attacks on the homes, cars and businesses of newcomers."[70] On June 12, 2008, unidentified assailants threw bricks and paint at a house in which two Polish families live.[71]

An April 2007 study of new patterns of migration to Northern Ireland concludes that racism continues to rise and remains a problem "for all of the different minority ethnic and national communities in Belfast" and is continuing to increase; "while the police data provides some indication of the scale of the problem and some serious incidents get reported in the media, much of the low level and 'mundane' racism is not reported."[72]

The new patterns of anti-immigrant violence have received attention by police and policy makers in the **United Kingdom**, where detailed monitoring and statistical reporting is the norm. However, similar hate crime incidents are likely occurring elsewhere in Western Europe where governments do not make a similar effort to document and report on such incidents. Although these new immigrants do not stand out dramatically from the majority population because of skin color, their "difference" is sufficient to make them readily identifiable targets for racist violence.[73]

Anti-Immigrant Scapegoating

Politicians across Europe capitalized on growing public xenophobia, contributing to anti-immigrant rhetoric and blaming immigrants for political, economic, and social problems. In a number of countries, social and political problems were blamed with new vigor on immigrant workers, including those from within the expanded European Union, and in particular on members of the Roma minority. Anti-immigrant scapegoating in **Italy**, **Germany**, **Greece,** and **Switzerland** received national and international attention.

In **Italy**, extraordinary anti-immigrant sentiment exploded into violence toward Romanian immigrants and Roma in general in October 2007. The violence was triggered by the shocking murder of 47-year-old Giovanna Reggiani, for which a Roma man of Romanian nationality was the main suspect.[74] The government responded with roundups of Romanian immigrants and summary expulsions of some two hundred Roma migrants, in violation of E.U. immigration policy. The Mayor of Rome Walter Veltroni blamed the increase in violent crime overall on the recent immigration of Romanian Roma, asserting that "before the entry of Romania into the European Union, Rome was the safest city in the world."[75]

Racist violence in the backlash to the murder of Giovanna Reggiani included a November 2, 2007 attack on Roma living in improvised shelters in a parking lot near the scene of the murder. Up to eight attackers seriously injured three Romanians with metal bars and knives; one of the injured had deep stab wounds in his back.[76]

The violence again surged in early 2008. In May 2008, following claims that a Roma teenager had attempted to kidnapped a child, mobs targeted Roma communities for arson attacks even as police rounded up immigrants for summary deportations. Mobs burned Roma communities to the ground as police stood by in the Naples area, forcing hundreds of Roma to flee. Not only Roma were caught up in the anti-immigrant campaign. On May 23, 2008, gangs of youths armed with iron bars and baseball bats rampaged through the fashionable and multicultural Rome district of Pigneto shouting "Get out, bastard foreigners!" The attackers, wearing bandanas blazoned with swastikas and ski masks smashed the windows of Indian and Bangladeshi-owned shops and beat shopkeepers. The minority owners of shops and such establishments as launderettes and phone centers expressed fear that further assaults could be expected.[77]

In **Germany**, a heinous criminal act committed by two immigrants gave national impetus to xenophobia and racist violence. A 20-year-old Turkish man and a 17-year-old Greek immigrant were arrested for a December 20, 2007, assault on a 76-year-old German pensioner on the Munich subway. The attackers, both of whom had long police records, verbally abused and physically harmed the victim.[78]

The premier of Hesse state, Roland Koch, a leading member of Prime Minister Angela Merkel's government, seized upon the subway incident to catalyze a national debate focusing on the involvement of young noncitizens in violent crime. Koch's declaration that "we have too many criminal young foreigners" was championed by the media, while the statement that "foreigners who don't stick to our rules don't belong here" was widely reproduced by advocates of the mass deportations of

foreigners. This pointed to a key problem of integration into German society: the convention by which members of ethnic minorities in Germany "are still widely labeled 'foreigners' even if they were born in Germany, even if they have German passports, and especially if they are dark-skinned."[79]

A series of particularly severe hate crime incidents became the object of national debate and international attention in Germany in the midst of the anti-immigrant debate. Despite the attention given to serious cases involving potentially lethal mob violence, few arrests were reported, and prosecutors in the most notorious cases tended to bring charges only for minor offences resulting in fines.

On August 19, 2007, in Mügeln, Saxony, eight Indian nationals attending a town festival were severely beaten by a mob of some fifty young men shouting "Foreigners out!" and "Germany for the Germans!" Upon seeking shelter in a pizza parlor, the mob attacked the restaurant, breaking the windows, and assaulting the Indians. The incident triggered widespread outrage, with photographs of the bruised faces of Indian men appearing in all major media. Chancellor Angela Merkel said the attack was "extremely grim and shameful," adding that "it is not acceptable for people in German cities to be chased through the streets and beaten." She pledged to place the issue high on the agenda of a strategy session of the governing coalition the same day.[80]

Local officials downplayed the racist nature of the attack; both local and national officials were mostly concerned with the possible negative impact that the incident could have on the international reputation of Saxony and Germany. A government spokesman declared that racist incidents were harmful to Germany's image abroad.[81] Gotthard Deuss, the mayor, insisted that "there are no known right-wing extremists here," and questioned whether there really could be "a far-right background to this incident." He had, however, reportedly been warned in advance that neo-Nazis planned to disrupt the festival. The regional police chief, Bernd Merbitz, was slightly more open to the incident having constituted a hate crime, saying: "We are investigating all possible motives, including the possibility that this was an act aimed at foreigners."[82]

Despite the prolonged violence of the incident, and the serious injuries and damage caused, prosecutors mainly focused on hate speech in arguing the case before the court. Charges were brought against only four men. In November, an 18-year-old suspect tried in a closed hearing by a Leipzig court admitted to "xenophobic comments" during the attack and was fined €1,800. Two others were fined for shouting xenophobic slogans.[83] In December, a fourth suspect, charged with leading the mob, was convicted of racial incitement and property damage, and was sentenced to eight months imprisonment.[84] A special 16-member police task force had been set up to investigate the incident.[85]

The Mügeln incident was extraordinary because of the size of the mob involved, and the numbers of the victims. On the same night, August 19, 2007, racists attacked two other immigrants who stood out because of the color of their skin at a town festival in Guntersblum, near Mainz.[86] A Sudanese man, who was working at the festival, was hit on the head with a wine bottle and knocked to the ground; an Egyptian coworker who sought to help the victim was also cut with a broken bottle, losing one finger.[87] More blatantly racist attacks were reported in three German towns on August 24. Unknown attackers set a dog on an Iraqi man at a tram stop in Magdeberg, and beat him with a baseball bat; others attacked a Ghanaian man in Braunschweig. Also on the same night, a mob in Bützow of some 40 people attacked market stalls and a business owned by a resident of Pakistani origin.[88]

In the aftermath of the Mügeln incident, calls for increased action against extremist violence came from broad sectors of society. Stephan Kramer, the secretary

general of the Central Council of Jews, spoke out about the "apparently dangerous situation" in certain parts of Eastern Germany where foreigners were under attack, adding: "Yesterday, it was people of color, today it's foreigners, and tomorrow it could be gays and lesbians, or, perhaps, Jews."[89]

In **Greece**, senior officials in 2007 blamed Roma communities and immigrants for an overall rise in crimes. In December 2007, Supreme Court Prosecutor George Sanidas offered a generalization identifying the perpetrators of crime in one section of Athens as "foreign women of African and non-African origin" and "athinganoi" (a pejorative word for Roma). The ensuing police crackdown in central Athens led to what the Greek Helsinki Monitor group described as harassment of "African women and Roma street vendors." Robert Varenik of the Open Society Justice Initiative, which combats ethnic and racial profiling in Europe, called the chief prosecutor's accusations "unprofessional and inexcusable."[90]

In the context of official discourse blaming immigrants and Roma for crime, a series of incidents were reported in Athens, in which migrant workers were the victims of organized attacks by extremist anti-immigration militants. On December 1, 2007, some twenty-five attackers described as extreme rightists assaulted the house of a group of Pakistani migrants in the Athens suburb of Aigaleo, seriously injuring five. The attackers broke windows and gained entry by kicking down a door, and then used clubs, crowbars, and knives in the assault.[91] This was reportedly the fourth such attack on migrant housing in Athens in the last quarter of 2007. A demonstration protesting the attacks was held in Aigaleo in December. A further incident was nevertheless reported in the second week of January, 2008: attackers threw rocks at a ground-floor residence of Pakistani immigrants, breaking windows.[92]

In May 2008, a dozen or more attackers reportedly broke into a building used as an unofficial mosque by the Pakistani Community in the Rendi section of Athens, beating with sticks Pakistani worshippers and a Greek neighbor who protested. The beatings were reportedly accompanied by epithets demanding that "Pakistanis get out of Greece."[93]

The Hellenic League for Human Rights reported a steady increase in 2007 in racist attacks on immigrants and other minorities, while condemning what it said was the indifference of Greek law enforcement bodies toward the attacks.[94]

In **Switzerland**, the run-up to the October 2007 parliamentary elections was marked by a vicious anti-immigrant campaign that was denounced by human rights groups and some political leaders as blatantly racist. In August, the Swiss People's Party placed posters across the country and in the media, depicting cartoon figures of three immaculate white sheep on a Swiss map, kicking a black sheep out of the country. The poster was expressly aimed at supporting a new party platform to throw "foreign criminals" out of Switzerland. President Micheline Calmy-Rey denounced the posters and the broader campaign as "racist," and intended "to stir up hatred."[95] The Swiss Federal Commission against Racism, in a study released in December 2007, said the campaign had propagated stereotypes of foreign nationals and ethnic minorities as the perpetrators of crime, as violent, as having no respect for the law, and as incapable of integrating into Swiss society.[96] The vice president of the commission, Boël Sambuc, said the election campaign had turned into a "black-white debate."[97] In the context of the new anti-immigrant discourse, racist attacks on people of African origin rose, and refugees and asylum seekers of all origins were under renewed threat through several attacks on asylum seekers' housing.

C. Refugees and Asylum Seekers

In a range of countries, refugees and asylum and refugee seekers were among the principal targets of racist and religiously motivated violence. These immigrants often were distinguished by their appearance, language, religion and customs, particularly in largely homogenous societies. Their vulnerability increased when they were concentrated in a few cities and neighborhoods determined by the policies of national and local authorities, especially when placed in highly visible concentrations in public housing. People living in such areas were in some cases ill-protected against racist harassment and violence. Attacks on individuals and places of residence, such as refugee hostels, were recorded in various parts of Western Europe.

In **Germany**, in March, 2007, two unknown attackers in Cottbus, Brandenburg, shouted racial epithets and physically attacked two asylum seekers from Chad and Cameroon.[98]

In Asker, **Norway**, on July 18, 2008, a gunman repeatedly fired at an accommodation center for asylum seekers, which houses fifteen to eighteen youths. A 16-year-old Somali refugee was severely wounded by a projectile that penetrated the wall of the room in which he was sleeping.[99] No arrests were reported.[100]

In **Spain**, the Spanish Commission to Aid Refugees (CEAR) reported three hundred racist attacks in 2006, mostly on people of immigrant origin, and spoke out on continuing racist attacks during 2007 and 2008. The Valencia office of CEAR was attacked repeatedly in 2007 after having been vandalized three times in 2006. On February 3, 2007, unknown assailants attacked CEAR's offices with an explosive device that broke windows and damaged window frames. A similar attack took place on May 4, 2007. On May 14, 2007, employees discovered a small explosive device at the front door but managed to extinguish its fuse. On July 2,

2007, the windows in the entrance were shattered by an explosion. CEAR described the situation in Valencia as one of rising racist violence and xenophobia and a climate of impunity.[101]

In the course of 2007, at least six incidents were reported in **Switzerland** in which assailants attacked housing for asylum seekers with firebombs or gunfire. The incidents received almost no publicity in the national media, but were documented by the Swiss Foundation Against Racism and Antisemitism:

- On January 22, unidentified attackers threw Molotov cocktails at a center for asylum seekers in Birr; on June 3, 2007, gunmen fired seven shots at the same center, breaking windows.

- On March 4, 2007, in Langendorf, two men were seen driving slowly past a center for asylum seekers shortly after midnight. The same vehicle returned shortly afterward and one of its passengers was seen to fire on the building.

- Shortly after midnight on May 27, 2007, in Fällanden, two young men—aged 16 and 20—threw an incendiary device at a building housing asylum seekers. The fire was put out by residents. The following night, the men returned and threw two Molotov cocktails at the building. The attackers were detained and confessed to having intended to "frighten the residents."[102]

On June 4, 2007, the Federal Commission Against Racism expressed concern with "a changing political climate."[103] Similar attacks continued in 2008.

In **Ukraine**, refugees and asylum seekers suffered harassment and sometimes lethal violence due to racial prejudice and hatred. After the murder of a Nigerian national on May 29, 2008, the U.N. High Commissioner for Refugees (UNHCR) joined the International Organization for Migration (IOM) and other prominent groups in demanding the Ukrainian government

investigate the crime—at that time the latest of forty reported racist attacks in 2008, including four murders.

In a statement from its Geneva headquarters on June 3, 2008, UNHCR spokeswoman Jennifer Pagonis described the "increasingly violent attacks on foreigners and non-Ukrainians in Kiev and elsewhere in the country," and efforts to press Ukrainian authorities for action: "UNHCR and IOM have repeatedly expressed concern over unprovoked attacks, beatings and verbal abuse aimed at asylum seekers, refugees, migrants, foreigners and minorities in Ukraine."[104] The UNHCR had previously expressed extreme concern with "the number and seriousness of racist attacks against asylum seekers, refugees, and other foreigners in Ukraine," with reports received "on a regular basis." The UNHCR described these as "firsthand reports of racially motivated incidents, unprovoked attacks, beatings, verbal insults and other acts of xenophobia against refugees and asylum seekers in different regions of Ukraine."[105] In a February 2008 statement, the UNHCR said it had received reports from asylum seekers of seventeen incidents of beatings and other serious abuse in Kiev alone in 2007.[106]

In the **United Kingdom**, refugees and asylum seekers were the frequent object of violent assaults accompanied by racist epithets, in part because they were highly visible in their areas of placement. Asylum seekers in particular are generally assigned to public housing estates already known for high levels of criminal violence, often in high concentrations in select towns and cities.

A particularly high rate of hate violence toward refugees and asylum seekers was reported in the Strathclyde area of Glasgow, where most of Scotland's asylum seekers initially reside in public housing.[107] A Scottish Executive study labeled the levels of racial harassment there "shocking," while 60 percent of people assigned to Strathclyde leave the area once they are granted asylum.[108]

On September 28, 2007, unidentified assailants n the Cathcart area of Glasgow verbally abused and stabbed 15-year-old Christopher Ikolo, a refugee from the Democratic Republic of the Congo, on his way to school. The victim was hospitalized with a kidney injury.[109] Ikolo had been featured in a Scottish Refugee Week publication for his participation in a youth hip hop band. Police said there had been "168 race attacks perpetrated by youths" in Glasgow from mid-2006 though mid-2007.[110]

High levels of violence were also reported in England, affecting both asylum seekers and refugee settlers who had chosen a permanent place of residence. In March 2007, an unknown attacker stabbed and killed 26-year-old Afghan refugee Enayit Khalili, who had ived and worked in Oxford since 2001.[111] In May 2008, a 21-year-old man was charged with the murder.[112]

Section Endnotes

[1] Those states are: the Czech Republic, Denmark, Germany, France, Ireland, Austria, Poland, Slovakia, Finland, Sweden, the United Kingdom.

[2] European Union Agency for Fundamental Rights, *Annual Report*, 2008, TK-AG-08-001-EN-C, http://fra.europa.eu/fra/material/pub/ar08/ar08_en.pdf, pp. 32-33.

[3] European Union Agency for Fundamental Rights, *Report on Racism and Xenophobia in the Member States of the EU*, TK-AK-07-002-EN-C, August 2007, http://fra.europa.eu/fra/material/pub/racism/report_racism_0807_en.pdf, p. 118.

[4] Commission nationale consultative des droits de l'homme (CNCDH), *La lutte contre le racisme et la xénophobie: rapport d'activité 2007*, March 28, 2008, http://www.ladocumentationfrancaise.fr/rapports-publics/084000167/index.shtml.

[5] Bundesministerium des Innern, *Verfassungsschutzbericht 2007*, May 15, 2008, http://www.verfassungsschutz.de/download/SHOW/vsbericht_2007.pdf, p. 19.

[6] "Far-Right Attacks Reached New Record in Germany in 2007," *Spiegel Online*, March 10, 2008, http://www.spiegel.de/international/germany/0,1518,540550,00.html.

[7] The Swedish National Council for Crime Prevention (Brottsförebyggande rådet—Brå), *Hate crime 2007*, 2008, http://www.bra.se/extra/measurepoint/?module_instance=4&name=Hatbrott_2007_webb.pdf&url=/dynamaster/file_archive/080627/4a35a31f178 add58672ff57f0fcdb92c/Hatbrott%255f2007%255fwebb.pdf.

[8] The Ministry of Justice, *Statistics on Race and the Criminal Justice System – 2006/7*, July 2008, http://www.justice.gov.uk/docs/stats-race-criminal-justice.pdf.

[9] Wilma Riley, "Rise in race crimes linked to attacks on Poles," *the Scotsman*, June 28, 2007, http://thescotsman.scotsman.com/edinburgh/Rise-in-race-crimes-linked.3299508.jp.

[10] "Hardly an asylum seeker haven," *BBC News*, March 4, 2007, http://news.bbc.co.uk/2/hi/uk_news/scotland/6314057.stm.

[11] European Monitoring Centre on Racism and Xenophobia, *The Annual Report on the Situation regarding Racism and Xenophobia in the Member States of the EU*, EUMC 2006, http://www.ihmisoikeusliitto.fi/AR06-P2-EN.pdf.

[12] Tanja Noponen, *Poliisin tietoon tullut rasistinen rikollisuus Suomessa 2006*, Police College of Finland, http://www.poliisiammattikorkeakoulu.fi/poliisi/pakk/home.nsf/files/Tiedotteita%2062/$file/Tiedotteita%2062.pdf; and "Racist Crimes Continue to Increase," *YLE*, July 31, 2007, http://www.yle.fi/news/left/id66215.html.

[13] "Racist crime rarely leads to conviction in Finland, 175 racist crimes in Helsinki, but only six convictions," *Helsingin Sanomat*, April 26, 2007, http://www.hs.fi/english/article/Racist+crime+rarely+leads+to+conviction+in+Finland/1135226835748.

[14] European Union Agency for Fundamental Rights, *Report on Racism and Xenophobia in the Member States of the EU*, TK-AK-07-002-EN-C, August 2007, http://fra.europa.eu/fra/material/pub/racism/report_racism_0807_en.pdf, p. 116.

[15] John Lawrence, "Advisory group told of 99 alleged racist incidents," *the Irish Times*, March 21, 2008, http://www.irishtimes.com/newspaper/ireland/2008/0321/1206024699003.html.

[16] The Commission releases semiannual reports on racist incidents registered, while noting that data is primarily qualitative in nature and so useful for the identification of key issues requiring attention. The reports are not intended "to provide a comprehensive list of every racist incident in Ireland." National Consultative Committee on Racism and Interculturalism, *Reported Incidents Relating to Racism and strategic response from the NCCRI, Jul–Dec 2007*, http://www.nccri.ie/pdf/RacistIncidentsJuly-Dec07.pdf; and Louise Hogan, "Concern at 50pc rise in racist incidents," *Independent.ie*, March 21, 2008, http://www.independent.ie/national-news/concern-at-50pc-rise-in-racist-incidents-1324124.html.

[17] European Union Agency for Fundamental Rights, *Report on Racism and Xenophobia in the Member States of the EU*, TK-AK-07-002-EN-C, August 2007, http://fra.europa.eu/fra/material/pub/racism/report_racism_0807_en.pdf, p. 117.

[18] U.S. Department of Justice, Federal Bureau of Investigation, Criminal Justice Information Services Division, *Hate Crime Statistics, 2006*, Fall 2007, http://www.fbi.gov/ucr/hc2006/incidents.html.

[19] Los Angeles County Commission on Human Relations, *2007 Hate Crime Report*, http://humanrelations.co.la.ca.us/hatecrime/data/2007%20Hate%20Crime%20Report.pdf, p. 16.

[20] National Public Radio, "Latino Hate Crimes on the Rise," *All Things Considered*, December 23, 2007, http://www.npr.org/templates/player/mediaPlayer.html?action=1&t=1&islist=false&id=17563862&m=17563847.

21 Miltos Pavlou, *Annual Report 2007: Racism and Discrimination Against Immigrants and Minorities in Greece: The State of Play*, Hellenic League for Human Rights and Research Centre for Minority Groups, April 2007, http://deviousdiva.com/wp-content/uploads/hlhr-kemo-ar2007.pdf.

22 Galina Kozhevnikova, *Radical Nationalism and Efforts to Counteract it in 2007*, the SOVA Center for Information and Analysis, March 14, 2008, http://xeno.sova-center.ru/6BA2468/6BB4208/AC15D1E.

23 "August 2008. Monthly summary," the SOVA Center for Information and Analysis, September 1, 2008, http://xeno.sova-center.ru/6BA2468/6BB41EE/BA3C54A.

24 Human Rights First correspondence with Comisión Española de Ayuda al Refugiado (CEAR, the Spanish Commission to Aid Refugees), April 1, 2008.

25 Foundation against Racism and Anti-Semitism (GRA) and the Society for Minorities in Switzerland (GMS), *Zusammenfassung: 2007*, http://chrono.gra.ch/chron/chron_detail_entry.asp?jahr=2007.

26 Vyacheslav Likhachev, *Ksenofobiya v Ukraine: Materialy Monitoringa 2007-2008*, Kyiv, May 2008, p. 12.

27 European Union Agency for Fundamental Rights, *Annual Report*, 2008, TK-AG-08-001-EN-C, http://fra.europa.eu/fra/material/pub/ar08/ar08_en.pdf, pp. 32-36.

28 Galina Kozhevnikova, *Radical Nationalism and Efforts to Counteract it in 2007*, the SOVA Center for Information and Analysis, March 14, 2008, http://xeno.sova-center.ru/6BA2468/6BB4208/AC15D1E.

29 Neil Jarman and Jonny Byrne, *New Migrants and Belfast: An Overview of the Demographic Context, Social Issues and Trends*, Institute for Conflict Research, April 2007, http://www.belfastcity.gov.uk/goodrelations/docs/BelfastMigrants.doc.

30 Union of Councils for Jews in the Former Soviet Union, "Estonian Neo-Nazis Attack French Student," *the Bigotry Monitor*, vol. 7, no. 36, September 21, 2007, http://www.fsumonitor.com/stories/092107BM.shtml.

31 "Neo-Nazis attack African man in Viersen", *the Local*, May 25, 2008, http://www.thelocal.de/12075/20080525/.

32 German Woman Pushes Angolan Man in Front of Train, *Spiegel Online*, March 03, 2008, http://www.spiegel.de/international/germany/0,1518,539004,00.html.

33 U.S. Department of State, Bureau of Democracy, Human Rights and Labor, *Country Reports on Human Rights Practices 2007: Germany*, March 11, 2008, http://www.state.gov/g/drl/rls/hrrpt/2007/index.htm.

34 U.S. Department of State, Bureau of Democracy, Human Rights and Labor, *Country Reports on Human Rights Practices 2007: Germany*, March 11, 2008, http://www.state.gov/g/drl/rls/hrrpt/2007/index.htm.

35 U.S. Department of State, Bureau of Democracy, Human Rights and Labor, *Country Reports on Human Rights Practices 2007: Germany*, March 11, 2008, http://www.state.gov/g/drl/rls/hrrpt/2007/index.htm.

36 Union of Councils for Jews in the Former Soviet Union, "Man Suspected of Stabbing Cameroonian is Arrested," *the Bigotry Monitor*, vol. 7, no. 39, October 12, 2007, http://www.fsumonitor.com/stories/101207BM.shtml, citing *Jewish.Ru*.

37 Union of Councils for Jews in the Former Soviet Union, "Two Non-Slavs Attacked in St. Petersburg Metro," *the Bigotry Monitor*, vol. 7, no. 6, February 9, 2007, http://www.fsumonitor.com/stories/020907BM.shtml, citing *the St. Petersburg Times*.

38 Amnesty International, *The State of the World's Human Rights 2008: Slovakia*, POL 10/001/2008, June 2008, p. 267.

39 Foundation against Racism and Anti-Semitism (GRA) and the Society for Minorities in Switzerland (GMS), *Zusammenfassung: 2007*, http://chrono.gra.ch/chron/chron_detail_entry.asp?jahr=2007.

40 As violent hate crimes are not defined as specific penal code offenses, such crimes are not differentiated in overall statistics on common crimes such as assault or threatening behavior. Criminal justice statistics cover crimes prosecuted under Article 261bis of the Criminal Code, which defines the crime of racial discrimination, but do not cover crimes of violence or direct incitement to violence. Human Rights First, Overview: *Hate Crime Report Card: Switzerland*, December 2007, http://www.humanrightsfirst.info/pdf/071217-discrim-hc-report-card-overview-2007.pdf.

41 Molly Moore, "Swiss Fury at Foreigners Boiling Over; Grisly Attack on African Underscores Race Issue in a Harsh Campaign," *the Washington Post*, October 9, 2007, http://www.washingtonpost.com/wp-dyn/content/article/2007/10/08/AR2007100801464_pf.html.

42 Foundation against Racism and Anti-Semitism (GRA), "Rassistische Vorfälle in der Schweiz, Eine Chronologie unde eine Einschätzung," 2007, http://chrono.gra.ch/chron/chron_detail.asp?jahr=2007&monat=01.

43 Thomas Martin, "Marlon Moran killing was 'racist attack," the *Liverpool Echo*, November 16, 2007, http://www.liverpoolecho.co.uk/liverpool-news/local-news/2007/11/16/horrific-stab-killing-was-racist-attack-100252-20114898/.

44 Ben Rossington, "Marlon Moran's family endure racist threats," *the Liverpool Echo*, January 31, 2008, http://www.liverpoolecho.co.uk/liverpool-news/local-news/2008/01/31/marlon-moran-s-family-endure-racist-threats-100252-20417560/.

45 U.S. Department of Justice, Federal Bureau of Investigation, Criminal Justice Information Services Division, *Hate Crime Statistics, 2006*, Fall 2007, http://www.fbi.gov/ucr/hc2006/incidents.html.

[46] "Far-Right Attacks Reached New Record in Germany in 2007," *Spiegel Online*, March 10, 2008, http://www.spiegel.de/international/germany/0,1518,540550,00.html.

[47] National Consultative Committee on Racism and Interculturalism, *Reported Incidents Relating to Racism and strategic response from the NCCRI, Jul–Dec 2007*, http://www.nccri.ie/pdf/RacistIncidentsJuly-Dec07.pdf.

[48] "'I was thinking of what happened to those Polish men. Two guys died,'" *the Irish Times*, March 17, 2008, http://www.irishtimes.com/newspaper/ireland/2008/0317/1205706589191.html.

[49] Union of Councils for Jews in the Former Soviet Union, "Riga Racists Get Suspended Sentences," *the Bigotry Monitor*, vol. 7, no. 22, June 15, 2007, http://www.fsumonitor.com/stories/061507BM.shtml.

[50] The Council of Europe, European Commission against Racism and Intolerance, *Third Report on Latvia*, CRI(2008)2, February 12, 2008, http://www.coe.int/t/e/human_rights/ecri/1-ECRI/2-Country-by-country_approach/Latvia/Latvia_CBC_3.asp#TopOfPage.

[51] Roberto Lovato, "The Media is the (Anti-Immigrant) Message: Sen. Menendez Calls for Study of Link Between Media and Hate Crimes," *Of América*, December 13, 2007, http://ofamerica.wordpress.com/2007/12/13/the-media-is-the-anti-immigrant-message-sen-menedez-calls-for-study-of-link-between-media-and-hate-crimes.

[52] National Public Radio, "Latino Hate Crimes on the Rise," *All Things Considered*, December 23, 2007, http://www.npr.org/templates/player/mediaPlayer.html?action=1&t=1&islist=false&id=17563862&m=17563847.

[53] Brentin Mock, "Immigration Backlash: Violence Engulfs Latinos," the Southern Poverty Law Center, *Intelligence Project*, October 2007, http://www.splcenter.org/intel/news/item.jsp?site_area=1&aid=292.

[54] Amy Jackson, "New Numbers: Hate Crimes Against Latinos Have Jumped in San Diego," *KPBS News*, November 21, 2007, http://www.kpbs.org/news/local;id=10274.

[55] California Department of Justice, Division of California Justice Information Services, Bureau of Criminal Information and Analysis, *Hate Crime in California, 2007*, July 2008, http://ag.ca.gov/cjsc/publications/hatecrimes/hc07/preface07.pdf#xml=http://search.doj.ca.gov:8004/AGSearch/isysquery/30a29bbd-7222-4850-9b65-6fc40b818567/4/hilite/.

[56] Brentin Mock, "Immigration Backlash: Violence Engulfs Latinos," the Southern Poverty Law Center, *Intelligence Project*, October 2007, http://www.splcenter.org/intel/news/item.jsp?site_area=1&aid=292.

[57] Katie Fairbank and Michael J. Mooney, "Teen's suicide puzzles friends," *the Dallas Morning News*, July 8, 2007, http://www.khou.com/news/local/stories/khou070708_tnt_ritchesonsuicide.55ce8813.html.

[58] "Three Youths Charged with Racist Attack," *Prague Daily Monitor*, January 14, 2008, http://www.praguemonitor.com/en/250/czech_national_news/17037/.

[59] "Second man dies after Drimnagh attack," *the Irish Times*, February 28, 2008, http://www.irishtimes.com/newspaper/breaking/2008/0228/breaking6.html.

[60] "Family 'will never know' if attack on Pole racially driven," *the Irish Times*, February 29, 2008, http://www.irishtimes.com/newspaper/frontpage/2008/0229/1204240264139.html.

[61] "Dark-skinned girl hurt in racially motivated attack in Slovakia," *Romea.cz*, November 23, 2007, http://www.romea.cz/english/index.php?id=detail&detail=2007_646.

[62] "Polish attack victim is out of intensive care," *the Scotsman*, March 8, 2007, http://news.scotsman.com/polesinscotland/Polish-attack-victim-is-out.3352650.jp.

[63] Wilma Riley, "Rise in race crimes linked to attacks on Poles," *the Scotsman*, June 28, 2007, http://news.scotsman.com/tacklingracisminscotland/Rise-in-race-crimes-linked.3299508.jp.

[64] "Life in jail for brutal Wrexham carving knife murder," *the Daily Post*, December 5, 2007, http://www.dailypost.co.uk/news/north-wales-news/2007/12/05/life-in-jail-for-brutal-carving-knife-murder-55578-20203572/.

[65] Wilma Riley, "Rise in race crimes linked to attacks on Poles," *the Scotsman*, June 28, 2007, http://news.scotsman.com/tacklingracisminscotland/Rise-in-race-crimes-linked.3299508.jp.

[66] "Attacks on the rise against Poles in UK," *Thenews.pl*, May 20, 2008, http://www.polskieradio.pl/thenews/foreign-affairs/?id=82896.

[67] "Hate crimes prompt official visit," *BBC News*, February 2, 2007, http://news.bbc.co.uk/2/hi/uk_news/northern_ireland/6323299.stm.

[68] "PSNI to launch awareness campaign on hate crimes," *the Belfast Telegraph*, April 21, 2008, http://www.belfasttelegraph.co.uk/breaking-news/ireland/article3628380.ece.

[69] "Captain Serwiak's Polish-ed performance," *the Belfast Telegraph*, June 29, 2007, http://www.belfasttelegraph.co.uk/features/daily-features/article2720805.ece.

[70] "Committee Against Racist Attack," *North Antrim Local Interest List Blog*, May 15, 2008, http://nalil.blogspot.com/2008/05/community-against-racist-attack.html.

[71] The Alliance Party of Northern Ireland, "Hendron condemns Cregagh Road racist attack," June 13, 2008, http://www.allianceparty.org/news/003835/hendron_condemns_cregagh_road_racist_attack.html.

[72] Neil Jarman and Jonny Byrne, *New Migrants and Belfast: An Overview of the Demographic Context, Social Issues and Trends*, Institute for Conflict Research, April 2007, http://www.belfastcity.gov.uk/goodrelations/docs/BelfastMigrants.doc.

[73] European Union Agency for Fundamental Rights, *Report on Racism and Xenophobia in the Member States of the EU*, TK-AK-07-002-EN-C, August 2007, http://fra.europa.eu/fra/material/pub/racism/report_racism_0807_en.pdf.

[74] "Brutal Attack in Rome: Italy Cracks Down on Immigrant Crime Wave," *Spiegel Online*, November 2, 2007, http://www.spiegel.de/international/europe/0,1518,515008,00.html.

[75] "Sicurezza, Veltroni contro la Romania Per le espulsioni varato un decreto legge," *la Repubblica*, October 31, 2007, http://www.repubblica.it/2007/10/sezioni/cronaca/tor-di-quinto/reazioni-uccisa/reazioni-uccisa.html.

[76] John Hooper, "Violence as Italy expels migrants," *the Observer*, November 4, 2007, http://www.guardian.co.uk/world/2007/nov/04/italy.johnhooper.

[77] Richard Owen, "Mob of Nazi youths goes on immigrant rampage in 'tolerant' Rome," *Times Online*, May 26, 2008, http://www.timesonline.co.uk/tol/news/world/europe/article4004200.ece.

[78] "State Governor Wants Crackdown on 'Criminal Young Foreigners,'" *Spiegel Online*, December 29, 2007, http://www.spiegel.de/international/germany/0,1518,525734,00.html.

[79] David Crossland, "Xenophobia at the Heart of German Politics," *Spiegel Online*, January 2, 2008, http://www.spiegel.de/international/germany/0,1518,526236,00.html.

[80] "More Racist Attacks Reported Across Germany: With every attack, banning the far-right NPD rises further up the German agenda," *Deutsche Welle*, August 27, 2007, http://www.dw-world.de/dw/article/0,2144,2754348,00.html.

[81] Kate Connolly, "Jewish leader sounds alarm after racist attack," *the Guardian*, August 23, 2007, http://www.guardian.co.uk/world/2007/aug/23/germany.thefarright.

[82] Roger Boyes, "Neo-Nazi rampage triggers alarm in Berlin," *Times Online*, August 20, 2007, http://www.timesonline.co.uk/tol/news/world/europe/article2295519.ece.

[83] "Man Gets Fined for Racist Attack on Indians in Germany," *Deutsche Welle*, November 26, 2007, http://www.dw-world.de/dw/article/0,2144,2973186,00.html.

[84] "Sentence in Racist Attack Slammed for Leniency," *Spiegel Online*, November 27, 2007, http://www.spiegel.de/international/germany/0,1518,519973,00.html.

[85] David Gordon Smith, "Zero Tolerance for 'Everyday Racism,'" *Spiegel Online*, August 21, 2007, http://www.spiegel.de/international/germany/0,1518,501049,00.html.

[86] "More Racist Attacks Reported Across Germany: With every attack, banning the far-right NPD rises further up the German agenda," *Deutsche Welle*, August 27, 2007, http://www.dw-world.de/dw/article/0,2144,2754348,00.html.

[87] DPA News, 'Three Germans Given Suspended Terms: Racist Attack on African Men," *Internet Centre Anti Racism Europe*, May 30, 2008, http://www.icare.to/news.php?en#THREE%20GERMANS%20GIVEN%20SUSPENDED%20TERMS:%20RACIST%20ATTACK%20ON%20AFRICAN%20ME.

[88] "More Racist Attacks Reported Across Germany: With every attack, banning the far-right NPD rises further up the German agenda," *Deutsche Welle*, August 27, 2007, http://www.dw-world.de/dw/article/0,2144,2754348,00.html.

[89] "Attack on Indians Rekindles Racism Debate in Germany," *Deutsche Welle*, August 22, 2007, http://www.dw-world.de/dw/article/0,2144,2747458,00.html.

[90] Open Society Justice Initiative and Greek Helsinki Monitor, "Greece: Rights groups denounce Greek prosecutor's racist statement," Open Society Institute, February 5, 2008, http://www.justiceinitiative.org/db/resource2?res_id=104034.

[91] The Associated Press, "Rights Activists Say Greek Neo-Nazis Increasing Attacks on Migrants", *the International Herald Tribune*, December 5, 2007, http://www.iht.com/articles/ap/2007/12/05/europe/EU-GEN-Greece-Racist-Attack.php?WT.mc_id=rssap_news.

[92] Kathy Tzilivakis, "2007: A year of immigration reform," *Athens News*, December 28, 2007, http://www.athensnews.gr/athweb/nathens.print_unique?e=C&f=13267&m=A12&aa=1&eidos=S.

[93] "All quiet on Rendi (except for some Pakistani)," *Abravanel*, May 22, 2008, http://abravanel.wordpress.com/2008/05/22/all-quiet-on-rendi-except-for-some-pakistani/.

[94] Miltos Pavlou, *Annual Report 2007: Racism and Discrimination Against Immigrants and Minorities in Greece: The State of Play*, Hellenic League for Human Rights and KEMO (Research Centre for Minority Groups), http://deviousdiva.com/wp-content/uploads/hlhr-kemo-ar2007.pdf.

[95] "People's Party accused of 'racist' campaign," *SwissInfo*, August 30, 2007, http://www.humanrights.ch/home/en/Switzerland/Policy/Racism/Incidents/idart_5363-content.html.

[96] Commission fédérale contre le racisme, *Les étrangers et les minorités ethniques au sein de la campagne électorale—Analyse de la cou-verture médiatique lors des élections fédérales de 2007*, CFR, http://www.ekr-cfr.ch/ekr/dokumentation/00111/00245/index.html?lang=fr&PHPSESSID=0f8384403e65e48a2e798019352af444.

[97] "Election run-up made stereotypes of foreigners," *SwissInfo*, December 18, 2007, http://www.swissinfo.ch/eng/search/Result.html?siteSect=882&ty=st&sid=8546951.

[98] U.S. Department of State, Bureau of Democracy, Human Rights and Labor, *Country Reports on Human Rights Practices 2007: Germany*, March 11, 2008, http://www.state.gov/g/drl/rls/hrrpt/2007/index.htm.

[99] Sven Goll, "Young asylum seeker shot in his bed," *Aftenposten*, July 18, 2008, http://www.aftenposten.no/english/local/article2548303.ece.

[100] The Associated Press, "Group Armed With Bats, Iron Bars Attacks Norway Center for Political Asylum-Seekers," *Fox News*, July 25, 2008, http://www.foxnews.com/story/0,2933,391161,00.html.

[101] Human Rights First correspondence with Comisión Española de Ayuda al Refugiado (CEAR, the Spanish Commission to Aid Refugees), April 1, 2008.

[102] Foundation against Racism and Anti-Semitism (GRA), "Rassistische Vorfälle in der Schweiz, Eine Chronologie unde eine Einschätzung," 2007, http://chrono.gra.ch/chron/chron_detail.asp?jahr=2007&monat=01.

[103] Commission fédérale contre le racisme, "Incendie d'une synagogue, coups de feu contre un centre de requérants d'asile et norme pénale contre le racisme," Press Release, June 4, 2007, http://www.ekr-cfr.ch/ekr/themen/00104/00656/index.html?lang=fr.

[104] The Office of the UN High Commissioner for Refugees, "Ukraine: UNHCR condemns murder of Nigerian," Press Briefing, June 3, 2008, http://www.unhcr.org/news/NEWS/484563402.html.

[105] The Office of the UN High Commissioner for Refugees, "Ukraine: UNHCR concerned by rise in attacks on asylum seekers, refugees," Press Briefing, June 8, 2007, http://www.unhcr.org/news/NEWS/4669266f2.html.

[106] The Office of the UN High Commissioner for Refugees, "UNHCR concerned over the murder of an asylum seeker in Ukraine," Press Briefing, February 1, 2008, http://www.un.org.ua/en/news/2008-02-01/.

[107] Richard Elias, "Incidents of Racism Rise by One-Fifth," *the Scotsman*, January 20, 2008, http://news.scotsman.com/tacklingracisminscotland/Incidents-of-racism-rise-by.3691602.jp.

[108] Stephen Stewart, "Asylum seekers targeted by gangs", *BBC News*, March 2, 2007, http://news.bbc.co.uk/2/hi/uk_news/scotland/6292747.stm.

[109] The 2007 Retrospective Project, "15-year-old Christopher Ikolo seriously injured in racist attack," http://www.2007retrospective.org/september/christopher_ikolo_seriously_injured_in_racist_attack.htm.

[110] Neil Mackay, "Talented teenage immigrant stabbed in racist attack," *the Sunday Herald*, September 30, 2007, http://www.sundayherald.com/news/heraldnews/display.var.1724307.0.talented_teenage_immigrant_stabbed_in_racist_attack.php.

[111] Arifa Akbar, "Tribute to 'modern Muslim' murdered at home," *the Independent*, March 31, 2007, http://www.independent.co.uk/news/uk/crime/tribute-to-modern-muslim-murdered-at-home-442557.html.

[112] Jason Collie, "Man charged with murdering Enayit, *Oxford Mail*, May 18, 2008, http://www.oxfordmail.net/search/display.var.2279653.0.update_man_charged_with_murdering_enayit.php.

Antisemitic Violence

Table of Contents

Executive Summary

Ant semitic violence continued to rise across many parts of Europe and North America in 2007, despite improvements in some countries where there nevertheless remain historically high levels of violence motivated by anti-Jewish prejudice. But even in these places, there is pressure on people to conceal their Jewish identity. The decline in levels of antisemitic incidents in some countries coincided with an alarming trend toward an increasing number of violent personal assaults.

In 2007, overall levels of violent antisemitic attacks against persons increased in **Canada**, **Germany**, the **Russian Federation**, **Ukraine**, and the **United Kingdom** according to official statistics and reports of nongovernmental monitors. In the **United Kingdom**, violent antisemitic attacks rose while the overall incident level declined moderately. The proportion of antisemitic incidents involving violent attacks on persons held steady in **France**, even as overall levels of antisemitic incidents there dropped significantly. In **Belgium**, the **Netherlands** and the **United States**, antisemitic crimes of violence declined.

There are undoubtedly a number of other European countries where antisemitic violence is also problematic, but where information on attacks—either from official or unofficial sources—is much less readily available.

Between 2000 and 2005, levels of antisemitic violence had fluctuated significantly in direct relation to events in the Middle East, which provide new impetus for those already predisposed to antisemitism in Europe. Since 2005, this pattern has to some extent changed, with month-by-month levels of antisemitic violence showing little change. These more uniform rates show little correlation with specific events involving Israel and the Middle East. This does not mean however, that the threat of antisemitic violence has diminished. In fact,

the new norm is for very high levels of antisemitic violence, still estimated in a number of countries to be several times higher than that of the 1990's.

In some countries, the frequency and severity of attacks on Jewish places of worship, community centers, schools, and other institutions has resulted in a need for security measures by representatives of both the Jewish community and local or national government. Enhanced security can be credited for a reduction in attacks on Jewish sites and property in **France**, **Germany**, and the **United Kingdom**, where successive governments have made a strong commitment to protect the Jewish community. However, the need for such security is a powerful indicator of the revival of antisemitism in recent years.

Monitoring, a vigorous law enforcement response to individual incidents, cooperation between the police and affected communities, and attention to prevention, including through education, are all needed to combat antisemitism and its violent manifestations. Although some governments in Europe and North America have instituted effective systems of monitoring and reporting on antisemitic hate crimes, most have not. And, while local nongovernmental organizations and community leaders provide information on such crimes, as well as insights into the response of the communities affected to those crimes, these initiatives are no substitute for state authorities addressing the problem directly.

I. Antisemitic Violence Still Rising

As the country-by-country overview below illustrates, antisemitic violence continued to rise in **Canada**, **Germany**, the **Russian Federation**, and **Ukraine** in 2007. The proportion of incidents involving violent attacks on persons continued to rise in the **United Kingdom** and remained at high levels in **France**, even as overall levels of anti-Jewish crimes decreased in those two countries.[1] Available data had shown an increase in antisemitic incidents in all of these countries in 2006.

These country-by-country assessments are echoed by data collected on a region-wide basis as well. Global data from the Stephen Roth Institute for the Study of Contemporary Antisemitism and Racism shows a 6.6 percent rise in incidents overall, from 593 to 632 in 2007—with most reported incidents coming from Europe and North America. There were 352 reported from Europe (up from 326), 78 in the former Soviet Union (up from 76), and 140 from North America (up from 103).

Most significantly, there were 35 "major attacks" in Europe (up from 8 in 2006), 8 in the former Soviet Union (up from 4), and 8 in North America (up from 5) in the Stephen Roth data. Major attacks were defined as incidents involving weapons, arson, or an intent to kill. Overall, this represented a nearly four-fold rise in Europe and North America in the most serious incidents from 2006 levels, from 13 to 51.[2] Although the report registered a decline in overall incidents in **Belgium**, **France**, **Germany**, the **United Kingdom** and the **United States**, there was a rise in more significant antisemitic violence in **France**, **Germany**, and the **United Kingdom**.

In some countries, the frequency and severity of attacks on Jewish places of worship, community centers, schools, and other institutions resulted in a need for security measures by representatives of both the Jewish community and local or national government. In **Germany**, special security was provided by police to synagogues and Jewish schools, and even to Jewish book stores and kosher grocery shops. In the **United Kingdom**, constant police protection was required for synagogues, Jewish schools, and Jewish institutions.

Enhanced security was credited for the reduction of serious attacks on Jewish sites in **France**, **Germany**, and the **United Kingdom**, where a strong commitment to such protection has been made by successive governments. The reality in which such protection is required on an everyday basis is, however, perhaps the truest indicator of just how far the revival of antisemitism has progressed since 2000.

The Organization for Security and Cooperation in Europe (OSCE) has been an important source of leadership in this area. In recent years, the OSCE has hosted international conferences on the issue, appointed a personal representative to the Chairman-in-Office on combating antisemitism, announced commitments to practical measures to address the phenomenon, and developed commitments for member states to implement institutional mechanisms to fight discrimination.

The Office for Democratic Institutions and Human Rights (OSCE/ODIHR) produces an annual report on hate crime incidents and responses. The 2006 publication acknowledged that antisemitic incidents and crimes continued to threaten stability and security in the OSCE.[3] The ODIHR also maintains a tolerance and nondiscrimination web-based information system that includes a section on international commitments and practical initiatives undertaken by states to combat antisemitism.

Professor Gert Weisskirchen, the current Personal Representative of the Chairman-in-Office of the OSCE on Combating Antisemitism, publishes a separate annual report, outlining the goals and activities of his office.[4] The Personal Representative has been productive in putting a spotlight on the issue, engaging and advising political leaders, investigating incidents, and participating in coordination activities. On January 29, 2008, Professor Weisskirchen testified in a United States Helsinki Commission Hearing on combating antisemitism in the OSCE region, noting that "there have been recurrent manifestations of antisemitism in many countries despite the considerable efforts that have been undertaken in many participating states."[5]

The institutions of the Council of Europe and the European Union have also worked to promote standards, compile and publish data, and to make urgent recommendations for action to their member states. European institutions continue to make important public commitments in support of continuing efforts in this regard. For example, on June 27, 2007, the Parliamentary Assembly of the Council of Europe resolved that it "remains deeply concerned about the persistence and escalation of antisemitic phenomena" and noted that "no member state is shielded from, or immune to, this fundamental affront to human rights." The resolution further stated the unacceptability of antisemitism, while warning that it continued to be on the rise, "appearing in a variety of forms and becoming relatively commonplace, to varying degrees, in all Council of Europe member states."[6]

The E.U.'s Fundamental Rights Agency (FRA) has regularly reported on the response of E.U. states to antisemitic crime and has paid special attention to the importance of data collection to those efforts. In its 2008 annual report (for the year 2007) the FRA reported that only five countries—**Austria**, **France**, **Germany**, **Sweden**, and the **United Kingdom**—collect data on antisemitic crime in such a way that allows for a trend analysis over time. Of those that do, **France**, **Sweden**, and the **United Kingdom** experienced a general upward trend in recorded antisemitic crime between 2001–2006.[7]

In the sections below detailing various forms of antisemitic violence against both people and property, representative cases are provided. Nongovernmental monitors have captured a much larger range of incidents in their reporting than can be included in this report. We have created an online *Annex* to this report that includes a fuller range of cases with, in some instances, a greater level of detail than provided below. It can be accessed at www.humanrightsfirst.org/discrimination/index.asp.

II. Antisemitic Violence Against Individuals

Throughout much of the region, antisemitic incidents increasingly took the form of physical attacks on individuals. Since 2005, the statistical findings of both official and nongovernmental monitors have identified a pattern in which such attacks constitute a growing proportion of incidents overall. Even in the absence of detailed statistical data, the evidence from incident reports and NGO analyses provide equally compelling evidence of the increase of personal assaults within a larger environment of burgeoning antisemitic and racist discourse.

A. "Visibly Jewish" Persons

The targets of personal attacks were frequently identified as Jewish because they wore a kippah (yarmulke), distinctive clothing or jewelry. Others were targeted as "visibly Jewish"—a term commonly used by Jewish community monitors of antisemitism—because they followed the customs of Orthodox Jewry. In many cases of physical assaults, attackers targeted people attending or going to or from Jewish schools, community centers, and synagogues.

- In **France**, on September 6, 2007, in Garges-lès-Gonesse, an unknown attacker punched a man, who was leaving a synagogue, several times and smashed the rear window of his car.[8]

- In the **United Kingdom**, on July 21, 2007, a group of teenage youths shouting antisemitic epithets attacked a man leaving a synagogue in Salford, Manchester after evening services. They punched him in the head and threw bricks at him.[9]

- In **Ukraine**, on September 27, 2007, a group of four youths attacked a worshipper as he left a synagogue in Zhytomyr after evening prayers; the

target of the attack, an Israeli Jew, responded with mace and drove off the attackers.[10]

In many cases, physical violence appeared to represent spontaneous acts of prejudice and hatred against individuals who were considered to be visibly Jewish.

- In **Germany**, on December 12, 2007, two inebriated young men in their twenties harassed two Jews traveling on a bus in Berlin, spitting on one and pushing him. The attackers, who shouted antisemitic slurs, were subsequently arrested.[11]

- In the **Russian Federation,** men described as skinheads assaulted two Jewish men on June 11, 2007, in Ivanovo, northeast of Moscow, while shouting antisemitic epithets. The victims were wearing "traditional Jewish clothes" when attacked. Two 21-year-olds were detained, and a prosecutor said they would be charged with incitement to racial and religious hatred. [12]

B. Religious Leaders and Their Families

In a disturbing number of cases, Jewish religious leaders were singled out for violence. Among the examples of assault were:

- In **France**, on April 19, 2007, Rabbi Elie Dahan was attacked by a young man at the Paris Nord railway station. Onlookers sought to detain the attacker, but failed to do so. Rabbi Dahan's glasses were broken, causing an eye injury.

- In **Germany**, a man attacked 42-year-old Rabbi Zalman Gurevitch on September 7, 2007, in Frankfurt, stabbing him in the stomach and shouting antisemitic expletives.[13]

■ In **Ukraine**, on November 29, 2007, a group shouting antisemitic epithets attacked Rabbi Binyamin Wolf, the chief rabbi of Sevastopol and Chabad representative, as he left his home for a synagogue. Wolf suffered serious injuries and was subsequently hospitalized.[14]

■ In the **United States**, on October 9, 2007, Orthodox Rabbi Mordechai Moskowitz was brutally beaten with an aluminum baseball bat in Lakewood, New Jersey. Witnesses told police they saw a man walk by Rabbi Moskowitz and turn on the rabbi, beating him in the head and body with the baseball bat."[15]

C. Schools and Students

Jewish children and young people were frequent victims of assaults and threatening behavior in the street, in public spaces, on public transport, and in and around their schools. Jewish schools had their windows broken, were daubed with threatening antisemitic graffiti, and were subjected to bomb threats and arson. Children in school playgrounds were pelted with stones. Human Rights First is aware of cases in which school students were physically assaulted in **France**, **Germany**, the **Russian Federation**, the **United Kingdom**, and the **United States**. Representative examples include:

■ In **France**, on October 8, 2007, a group of young people attacked a 14-year-old student of a Jewish school in Paris, kicking him and hitting him with a stick; he reportedly suffered an eye injury and scratches.[16]

■ In **Germany**'s capital, Berlin, on January 16, 2007, four attackers accosted five students of the city's nonreligious Jewish high school, insulting them with antisemitic screeds and setting a dog on them.[17]

■ In the **Russian Federation**'s Moscow Oblast, on February 19, 2007, a group of young people harassed three pupils from the Torat Chaim Jewish

School after classes, demanded they confirm they were Jewish and physically assaulted them, leaving one with a concussion.[18]

In a number of incidents, schools, from kindergarten to high school, suffered stone-throwing, bomb threats, arson, and serious acts of vandalism:

■ In **Canada**, the Jewish People's and Peretz School in Montreal was forced to evacuate 500 students after a telephoned bomb threat on February 2, 2007.[19] A further threat was received on February 6.[20]

■ In **Germany**, in February 2007, attackers threw a smoke bomb through the window of a Jewish kindergarten in Berlin, which failed to go off. The same individuals were reported to have sprayed swastikas, other racist symbols, and antisemitic slogans on school walls and playground equipment.[21]

Violent manifestations of antisemitism were also present on university campuses, with assaults on Jewish students and student centers, dormitories, and Jewish fraternity houses. Jewish university students were under threat off campus. In one widely reported incident in the **United States**, a group of four college students on a New York City subway train became the target of antisemitic epithets and physical assault on December 11, 2007. The victims may have been saved from more serious injuries thanks to 20-year-old Hassan Askari, a Muslim of Bangladeshi origin, who intervened to protect them and was subsequently attacked as well.[22]

D. Living with Harassment and Violence

An overwhelming number of assaults reported involved incidents of harassment and intimidation involving relatively minor, but nevertheless threatening acts of violence. These incidents, in which antisemitic taunts and threats were accompanied by the throwing of objects, spitting, slapping, or jostling, were the everyday actions that challenge many members of Jewish communities with a constant reminder of hatred and prejudice.

In many incidents, people described as visibly Jewish were assaulted as they walked on city sidewalks: pelted with eggs or trash, spat upon, or doused with unknown liquids while being subjected to antisemitic slurs. In Montreal, **Canada**, for example, a customer at a gas station spat upon a Jewish patron there after identifying him as a Jew.[23]

In the **United Kingdom**, a small sampling of the reported incidents represents a virtual map of Jewish London and the Midlands, covered in egg splatter, trash, and broken bottles. The recurrent incidents leave the Jewish community angered, irritated, frustrated, and worried about what might come next. A number of representative cases from 2007 involving debris throwing, including the following:

- On June 9, in Ilford, the occupants of a passing vehicle threw white paint over visibly Jewish pedestrians who were walking home from synagogue.[24]

- On April 3, a person who was visibly Jewish was pelted with eggs as he walked home from a Passover meal in Ilford.[25]

- On January 30, in Wood Green, London, youths approached a visibly Jewish teenager and his mother on the upper deck of a bus, and knocked off his hat. When the two got up and went to find seats below, one of the youths followed and spat on the boy.[26]

Similar everyday harassment and violence was reported elsewhere in the region. In the **United States**, in Howell, New Jersey, seven teenagers were arrested after having traveled through a Jewish neighborhood to throw eggs at an Orthodox Jewish resident while screaming antisemitic epithets and obscenities.[27]

E. Constant Pressure to Conceal a Jewish Identity

Attackers have targeted and identified victims based on distinctive clothing and jewelry, or facial features, such as beards or sidecurls associated with Orthodox Jewish men. A result is a constant pressure to conceal one's identity. But for many Jews, and in particular those of Orthodox faith, a concealment of identity is neither possible nor desirable.

The constant threat of harassment or physical attack prompts some Jewish men to conceal their religious identity by wearing baseball caps or other hats over their skull-caps. In **France**, Jewish men have been under pressure to conceal their religious affiliation as a matter of safety, with several religious leaders acknowledging the need to wear concealing hats themselves over their kippahs.[28] A March 2008 Jewish Telegraph Agency story reported that "covering their yarmulke-clad heads with baseball caps and tucking away their Stars of David, French Jews who once advertised their Jewishness are keeping a low profile in an environment where Jews remain targets."[29]

In **Poland**, a 31-year-old Swedish rabbi, now a resident of Wrocław, described his feelings after an incident in which he was threatened on a train in an antisemitic harangue. Rabbi Icchak Rapaport told the *European Jewish Press* that he had not previously been the target of an antisemitic attack, and that there was a "wonderful atmosphere" in his neighborhood. But the attack changed everything: "Now I am really scared. From this day on I will wear a hat instead of a yarmulke outside my city. Once such a thing has happened I am not going to tempt my fate again. This is the sad reality. One cannot publicly wear a kippah."[30]

III. Vandalism and Attacks on Property

Antisemitic vandalism communicates a message cf hatred and exclusion to the Jewish community and other communities as well. The swastika remains the main graphic symbol of antisemitism, used to deface homes, community centers, synagogues, gravesites, Jewish-owned businesses, and public spaces.

Graffiti was frequently used to intimidate specific individuals, families, and communities. Hate messages on Jewish homes, schools, and places of worship were often personal and explicit, threatening particular families or groups, such as students or members of a congregation. Alternatively, antisemitic graffiti in public places—along public highways or in city centers or even in rural areas—was targeted in a more general way These messages to the general public aim to gain adherents, display the "reach" of the advocates of hatred and exclusion, and to broaden the scope of antisemitic threats beyond individual families or local communities.

While posing a direct threat to all Jews, the antisemitic Nazi symbols often include a more generalized message of racism, with slogans denigrating and threatening violence toward Jews accompanied by attacks on other minorities. The swastika is now used by racial supremacists and hate mongers across Europe and North America, daubed on graves; synagogues, churches and mosques; schools and universities; refugee hostels and immigrant homes.

The swastika is a symbol recalling the dehumanization and genocidal murder of the Holocaust. The swastika's display is often accompanied by slogans that expressly invoke the Holocaust, threatening its renewal and attempting both to offend and to offer a tangible threat to Jews as individuals and as a people. The Holocaust is often *celebrated* in antisemitic graffiti, while Holocaust denial provides a backdrop to the demagoguery of antisemitic propagandists and political movements.

A. Threats and Vandalism at Home

Perpetrators of antisemitic violence and threats often targeted Jewish families in their homes or in communal areas, vandalizing automobiles, breaking windows, daubing threatening graffiti, or smearing doors with excrement. Everyday harassment included epithets directed at family members as they went to and from their houses, being pelted with missiles, and aggressive pounding on the doors and windows of family homes. *Mezuzahs* (cases holding parchments inscribed with Hebrew verses that are fixed to the doors of many observant Jews) were also vandalized.

The majority of reports of incidents involving vandalism of homes and personal property came from Western Europe and North America, where official and community-based monitoring and reporting systems were available. Human Rights First is aware of incidents in which families were targeted for harassment and vandalism in their homes in **Canada**, **France**, the **Netherlands**, the **Russian Federation**, the **United Kingdom**, and the **United States.** Representative examples include:

- In **Canada**, in June 2007, attackers broke into the home of a Jewish family in Bowmanville, Ontario, and daubed swastikas and other antisemitic graffiti on the walls.[31]

- In the **Russian Federation**, on June 13, 2007 vandals sprayed graffiti on the home of a Jewish woman in Murmansk.[32]

- In the **United Kingdom**, on April 1, 2007, vandals attacked a Jewish home in London, identifiable by a mezuzah, and smeared excrement on the front door.[33]

B. Centers of Jewish Life and Memory

Jewish institutions have been particularly susceptible to attacks. Centers of Jewish life became the main targets for those seeking to express their hatred and strike a symbolic blow against Jews as a people. Places of worship, burial grounds, and Jewish community centers were the usual sites of antisemitic violence. Vandals and arsonists attacked synagogues, cemeteries, and Holocaust memorials throughout the region.

Human Rights First is aware of over 40 attacks on synagogues in **Belgium**, **Canada**, **Denmark**, **France**, **Latvia**, **Poland**, the **Russian Federation**, **Switzerland**, **Serbia**, **Ukraine**, **United Kingdom**, and the **United States** in the period covered by the report. Examples include:

- In **Belgium**, the Machsike Hadass Synagogue in Antwerp was pelted with stones in a series of incidents beginning on December 4, 2007. The stone-throwers, who gathered on a nearby railway embankment, broke numerous windows.[34]

- In Copenhagen, **Denmark**, the Krystalgade Synagogue was vandalized on the night of January 21, 2007, with two windows smashed by rocks.[35]

- In Daugavpils, **Latvia**, vandals on February 2, 2007, threw a large stone through the window of a synagogue that opened there in 2006.[36]

- In **Serbia**, vandals sprayed a swastika on the façade of the Novi Sad Synagogue on March 17, 2007.[37]

- In **Switzerland**, on May 24, 2007, arsonists set alight Geneva's modern Hekhal Haness Synagogue, seriously damaging the building.[38]

The desecration of Jewish graves and memorials continued to occur on a widespread basis. Grave markers and memorials to the war dead and victims of the Holocaust were smashed, daubed with graffiti, or fouled with excrement. Hundreds of tombstones marking Jewish graves were defaced with graffiti, toppled, or shattered. Attackers caused wholesale destruction in Jewish cemeteries, singling out the graves marked with a Jewish star in public burial places. Human Rights First has reviewed over 60 attacks on cemeteries and Holocaust memorials, in **Armenia**, **Belarus**, **Belgium**, **Bulgaria**, **Canada**, the **Czech Republic, Denmark**, **France**, **Georgia, Germany, Greece, Hungary, Italy**, **Lithuania**, **Moldova**, the **Netherlands**, **Poland**, **Portugal**, **Romania**, the **Russian Federation**, **Switzerland**, **Serbia**, **Ukraine**, the **United Kingdom**, and the **United States.** Examples include:

- In **Armenia**, on December 23, 2007, in the capital, Yerevan, vandals desecrated a memorial to Jewish victims of the Holocaust in the city's Aragast Park, daubing it with a swastika and black paint.[39]

- In **Belarus**, several attacks were reported in 2007. In February, vandals in Minsk smashed the cenotaph that is part of the monument marking the site of the murder of Jews from Bremen in the Minsk ghetto.[40] In June, vandals damaged four Jewish gravestones in a cemetery in Mahilyow, where previous attacks had been reported.[41] In October, vandals damaged fifteen graves in Babruysk, and daubed antisemitic graffiti and a swastika on cemetery gates.[42]

- In the **Czech Republic**, in February, unknown attackers in Česká Lípa vandalized a memorial to Jews who died there in a death march to the Schwarzheide concentration camp in 1945. Bronze plaques and Jewish stars, as well as a bronze menorah commemorating the dead were stolen.[43]

- In **Hungary**, in September 2007, vandals in Gödöllő, outside Budapest, sprayed antisemitic slogans on a Hungarian memorial to the Holocaust; the train carriage established as a mobile memorial in April 2006 had been on display throughout Hungary.[44]

- In Arezzo, **Italy**, vandals described as neo-Nazis chose January 25, 2007, International Holocaust Memorial Day, to mutilate a hilltop olive tree that memorializes the site of an 18th century Jewish cemetery. Vandals cut all the branches from the tree and left posters with swastikas.[45]

- In **Moldova,** a guard was assaulted after witnessing the daylight desecration of the Jewish cemetery in Chisinau by five young people. Police said they had initiated an investigation.[46]

- In **Poland**, in August 2007, vandals at the Jewish Cemetery in Częstochowa daubed 100 tombstones with antisemitic graffiti. Police said at the time that a criminal investigation had been opened.[47]

- In **Portugal**, on September 26, 2007, vandals spray-painted 12 gravestones in a Lisbon Jewish cemetery with swastikas and antisemitic epithets and disturbed a fresh grave that had no marker. Two young men described as skinheads were detained by police who were alerted by a cemetery guard.[48] It is not known whether the two were charged and tried for the crime.

- In **Romania**, vandals on February 10 and 11, 2007 desecrated dozens of tombstones and graves at the Cimitirul Mozaic Jewish cemetery in Bucharest.[49]

IV. The Causes and Sources of Antisemitic Violence

The dramatic rise of antisemitic violence since 2000 has been in part attributed to anti-Jewish sentiment triggered by the Second Palestinian Intifada. Antipathy toward Israeli policies sometimes translated into racist hostility toward all Jews, regardless of their political views or nationality. In countries where detailed statistics are provided, the number of antisemitic incidents increased several times over 1990's levels.

Between 2000 and 2005, levels of antisemitic violence fluctuated significantly in direct relation to events in the Middle East, which provided a new impetus for those already predisposed to antisemitism in Europe. Since 2005, this pattern has to some extent changed, with month-by-month patterns of antisemitic violence leveling off, with more uniform rates that show little correlation with events involving Israel and the Middle East. But this does not mean the threat has diminished. In fact, the new norm is for very high levels of antisemitic violence throughout the year.

In the 2007 annual report on global antisemitic incidents, the Stephen Roth Institute for the Study of Contemporary Antisemitism and Racism wrote that "the rate of violent antisemitic activities in 2007 proved once again that contrary to former assumptions, Middle East events are not the underlying cause. Some community reports, such as those of France, Canada and the UK, have already questioned this supposition."[50]

Analysts have variously attributed particular patterns and acts to the adherents of traditional antisemitism, including groups of the extreme right; and, since 2000, to a "new antisemitism" that is linked to the Middle East conflict. Ongoing violence tied to organized racial supremacist groups in Western Europe illustrates aspects of traditional antisemitism, as does the creation of a series of nationalist paramilitary organizations in Eastern Europe—for example, in Bulgaria—that are founded on ancient antisemitic screeds. In tracking the "new antisemitism," in contrast, monitors have focused on members of largely Muslim sectors of immigrant origin who have been influenced by a fusion of antipathy for Israel with the ancient tenets of European antisemitism.

In **Bulgaria**, the extreme nationalist Bulgarian National Union (BNU) announced the formation of a party militia to provide a means of "self-defense" against national minorities. Jewish community leaders voiced concerns that the measure seized upon an anti-Roma sentiment while pursuing a broader agenda of hatred and exclusion. In an open letter to Bulgaria's president and prime minister, the chairmen of Bulgaria Shalom and members of the Central Israeli Spiritual Council wrote that "formations such as the national guard could threaten the ethnic peace in the country. Today this guard will 'protect' Bulgarians from the Roma, tomorrow from the Jewish people, and then probably from Armenians and Muslims."[51]

In **Canada**, B'nai Brith Canada's annual audit of antisemitism for 2007 provides information on the ethnic origin of known perpetrators. Of the 1,042 incidents registered, there were 24 cases in which perpetrators "self-identified as of Arab origin,"—a threefold decrease in the number of perpetrators of such background since 2006; others included 4 Germans, 4 Polish, 4 Hungarians, and 1 Romanian.[52] B'nai Brith Canada further observed that in 2007 extreme right- and left-wing extremists found a common ground, with some on far left "borrowing Holocaust imagery" in their attacks on Israel, while the extreme right adopted "anti-Israel rhetoric to mask their anti-Jewish animosity."[53]

In **France,** some of the most serious reported crimes involved attacks by nationalistic unemployed youth, often described as skinheads. On the morning of February 22, 2008, a group of six young men kidnapped and tortured a 19-year-old man in Hauts-de-Seine. The victim, Mathieu Roumi, whose father is Jewish, was handcuffed and beaten while subjected to antisemitic and homophobic epithets. The six perpetrators, aged 17 to 25 and of French, African, and North African origin, were arrested in the following days. Police said they acknowledged the crime.[54]

In January 2008, Roger Cukierman, the outgoing head of the Representative Council of Jewish Institutions in France (CRIF), said that changing patterns of antisemitism were "a part of a general change in French society that is becoming more violent, in which values are wavering and sometimes lapsing into barbarity." He added that this was a matter for the nation as a whole, and in particular required attention to those who feel excluded:

> This does not concern only the Jews. But it is clear that antisemitism has touched a new public, that it is no longer the exclusive domain of the extreme right. It is now something for those who feel excluded from society and who are looking for a scapegoat. This situation will improve only if integration progresses, which really implies the involvement of the State, but also the owners of residences, the entrepreneurs. [55]

The new president of CRIF, Richard Prasquier, responding to the February 2008 incident described above, said the incident showed that "antisemitism remains profoundly present," and—despite the decline in overall numbers of incidents—"the aggressors are young people, and in this generation, violence can very quickly take an antisemitic connotation, as its part of their cultural background."[56]

CRIF also suggested that "traditional antisemitism" was on the rise in both public discourse and as a motive in

antisemitic violence, including what has been described as the "banalization of the antisemitic insult." In the annual hate crime report, CRIF noted "a return to the most traditional antisemitic formulations, bearing on religion, the notion of race, the collusion of Jews, power, and money." Since 2004, the organization found that "references to the Israel-Palestine conflict have almost disappeared from the forms of expression that have accompanied or motivated antisemitic acts." While the mode of expression accompanying antisemitic acts may have changed in this regard, the report cautions that the identified perpetrators of these acts have not.[57]

France's official antidiscrimination body, the National Consultative Commission on Human Rights (CNCDH), noted that "international affairs and particularly the tensions in the Middle East had no appreciable influence on the pattern of antisemitism in 2007, in contrast to previous years." At the same time, in line with the findings of other European monitors, CNCDH cited a resurgence of traditional antisemitism, with its expression founded in references "to race, religion, money and the extermination of the Jews during the Shoah." This, in turn, was held to demonstrate the urgency of measures of public authorities to put into place "preventative measures and education oriented more specifically toward the fight against prejudice and stereotypes."

The CNCDH report for 2007 noted that the perpetrators could not be identified in 54 percent of reported antisemitic incidents. In 27 cases (33 percent) those identified were from "the Arab-Muslim milieu," a rise of 5 percent from 2006, while the "extreme right" attackers remained at 11 percent of the total. Despite a 32.5 percent decline in documented antisemitic incidents, the report concluded that there was a need to remain vigilant, and that the statistical record since 2000 showed both "that such violence had become deeply rooted and a certain banalization of the phenomenon." This notwithstanding, there was a concern that trigger events, international or domestic, still had the potential to provide surges of antisemitic violence.[58]

In **Germany**, where public security measures to combat antisemitism fall within the framework of laws and policies to suppress right-wing extremism as a threat to the Constitution, preliminary statistics showed a rise in violent acts of antisemitism, from 43 in 2006 to 59 in 2007.[59]

Germany's national leaders continued to condemn antisemitic acts in the course of the year. On January 25, 2008, in advance of an annual memorial day commemorating the victims of Nazi Germany, Chancellor Angela Merkel spoke out against both the prejudice commonly ascribed to economically poorer parts of German society, and "a more disguised form of antisemitism, that is not so readily defined." Merkel observed that "there is, in broad parts of the population, an awful silence when faced with all the historical images, with our own history, and this silence is always a danger" and "a form of middle-class antisemitism."[60]

In the **Netherlands**, the Racism and Extremism Monitor observed that the contribution of extreme right-wing participants to racial violence as a whole (including antisemitism) has risen sharply (from 38 incidents in 2005 to 67 in 2006). While the group of extreme right political parties has since 2006 "receded further and further in importance," new significance was gained by "more loosely organized extreme right-wing groups." The latter includes informal movements of extreme right-wing young people (often termed "Lonsdale youth" or skinheads), and neo-Nazi groups characterized by "the absence of formal organizational elements such as a legal personality, statutes and an administrative board."

The Monitor also provided some information on the ethnic background of perpetrators, noting that in the overall survey of cases for 2006, "information was sufficiently available in 123 (of 265) cases to enable us to identify the (alleged) perpetrators as native Dutch or ethnic minorities: 97 native Dutch and 26 ethnic minorities." In the case of antisemitic violence, they found that "four of the 35 incidents had ethnic minority perpetrators."[61]

The adoption of language demonizing Israel by extreme right organizations that are both antisemitic and anti-Muslim, and more broadly racist and anti-immigrant, has been observed in a number of countries. B'nai Brith **Canada**, for example, cites a bulletin of the neo-Nazi website *Stormfront* in the annual report on antisemitism for 2007, showing that the old antisemitism is alive and well and seeking a new gloss—substituting Zionists for Jews—for its ancient hatreds:

> Reproduced here in the original, spelling mistakes and all, is the advice Stormfront gives to its supporters: "Remember to say 'Zionists' ... or 'Israel Firsters' instead of 'Jews' when making public speeches or writing articles. ... It is entirely possible to stay within the bounds of the law and still promote our cause."[62]

Similarly, a 2006 report on the **Netherlands** by the Tel Aviv-based Stephen Roth Institute observed that antisemitic adherents of the far right increasingly sought to portray their views as anti-Zionist or anti-Israeli, on the grounds that this is more politically acceptable than open advocacy of Nazi positions. The same report added that this political overlay applied broadly to acts of generalized hatred and intolerance, ranging from desecration of Holocaust monuments to arson attacks on synagogues.[63] In a November 2007 report, the Dutch monitoring organization Centre Documentation and Information on Israel (CIDI) expressed concern with the numerous incidents reported on May 4 and 5 (the anniversary of the German surrender in 1945), in which monuments to victims of the Holocaust were defaced or destroyed. These actions were seen to be directly related to "the rise of the extreme right," with monuments scrawled with swastikas and neo-Nazi slogans.[64]

Extreme nationalist parties in some countries used antisemitism as a central tenet of their campaigning, while combining anti-Jewish slogans and epithets with a broader message of hatred and exclusion. Increasingly, public appeals of extremist parties have centered on a message of hatred toward immigrants, including demands for mass expulsions, while still professing a virulent antisemitism as a core organizing principle. Nationalist literature and statements to the media have been accompanied by public demonstrations in which this message of broad spectrum intolerance and hatred was taken to the streets, often accompanied by violence.

The extreme right threat also evolved in other ways. In **Ukraine**, on December 8, 2007, supporters of the Freedom Party and the Patriots of Ukraine organization took part in a torchlight march through Kyiv, chanting antisemitic, ant-immigrant, and pro-white power slogans, including "one race, one nation, one motherland."[65]

V. Review of Select Countries

Only a handful of governments in the OSCE have instituted effective systems of detailed monitoring and reporting on antisemitic violence and other hate crimes. These official monitoring systems and the data they provide are supplemented by information collected by community-based monitors, nongovernmental organizations, and the media. Among the countries discussed below, systematic governmental and/or nongovernmental monitoring has been established in **Canada**, **France**, **Germany**, **Netherlands**, **United Kingdom**, and the **United States**, and provides important insights into antisemitic violence there and elsewhere in the region. This section of the report describes the situation in those countries and the important measures to combat antisemitism undertaken by governments and civil societies there.

In other countries, local nongovernmental organizations and community leaders provide fundamental insights into changing situations, while a collation of press reports can provide a general view of more serious incidents. The situation of antisemitism in the **Russian Federation** is of particular concern, even while largely overlooked in lieu of the enormous scale of racist assaults and murders of members of other minorities and Russia's immigrant populations. Human Rights First is also concerned about rising antisemitic violence in **Ukraine**. In these and other situations where government statistics are nonexistent, we have used the available information on individual cases of antisemitic violence and reviewed the analysis of NGO and Jewish community partners with a view to identifying new developments and trends.

What follows below is an analysis of the statistics and trends in those countries where monitoring and reporting systems are sufficiently comprehensive to allow such a review. There are undoubtedly a number of

other European countries where antisemitic violence is also problematic, but where information on attacks— either from official or unofficial sources—is much less readily available.

Belgium

Jewish community-based monitors in Belgium have tracked a modest but persistent rise in antisemitic incidents since 2003, growing from 60 in 2005, to 66 in 2006, and 69 in 2007. Only a small percentage of these incidents involved acts of violence. In 2007 those defined as "violent" dropped by 75 percent. Monitors registered one case of personal assault in 2007: an attack on a young Jewish man in Brussels.

The 2007 annual report from *antisemitisme.be*, the principle monitoring group supported by Jewish community organizations, identified as a particular problem the rising level of incidents involving the Orthodox Jewish community in Antwerp and a tendency of members of this community not to submit complaints about abuses. This community "stands out and is easily recognizable as Jewish because they wear distinctive clothing, is a priority target." Notwithstanding efforts by both the Jewish community and Antwerp police to encourage victims and witnesses to come forward, these abuses tend to be underreported.[66] In one series of incidents in Niel, vandals damaged some forty vehicles and a dozen stores, scratching swastikas into cars and storefronts. Police sought witnesses and encouraged victims to make formal complaints.[67]

Canada

The annual audit of antisemitism by B'nai Brith's League for Human Rights for 2007 found an overall rise of 11.4 percent in the number of antisemitic incidents, with levels of violent incidents remaining much the same. A high incidence of antisemitic crimes was reported in both rural and urban areas, but the survey found that the highest rises affected "the small centers of Jewish presence" outside the major urban centers of Montreal, Toronto, and Ottawa. Antisemitic incidents were also reported in new situations: in "union settings, medical facilities, retail outlets and other usually benign places where one would not normally expect antisemitism to manifest."

Canadian cases are categorized as vandalism, harassment, and violence. The levels of violence remain largely unchanged from 2006, with 2.7 percent of the overall reported antisemitic incidents (there were 28 cases in 2007 compared to 30 in 2006). The report expressed concern at "a growing public acceptance of a certain level of hate activity as 'tolerable' to society."[68]

The total number of incidents rose to 1,042, nearly double the 584 mark of 2003, and continuing an almost uninterrupted upward trend since 1998, when 240 cases were reported. Levels of vandalism, representing 32 percent of the total incidents, dropped slightly, from 317 in 2006 to 315 cases in 2007. These included 22 incidents involving synagogues, down from 42 in 2006, and 6 involving Jewish community centers. There were 9 cases of cemetery desecration, compared with 1 in 2006 and 2 in 2005. An Ottawa cemetery was vandalized three times over three months, with 66 graves damaged or defaced. Vandals attacked Canadian Jewish homes in 132 cases, up from 118 in 2006.[69]

While B'nai Brith's annual audit remains the most comprehensive tracking of antisemitic incidents nationwide, and the only source that allows for an analysis of trends over time, official data has also become a useful source of information. On June 9, 2008, the government released national hate crime statistics for the first time. This report consists of data reflecting 892 hate-motivated cases from the year

2006. Police-reported data found that approximately 137 incidents (15 percent) represent anti-Jewish hate crimes. Of those, 32 incidents (23 percent) involved violence. Within the category of religious-motivated offenses (220 total), anti-Jewish hate crimes constitute 62 percent.[70] The Canadian Centre for Justice Statistics—the body responsible for producing these hate crime statistics—anticipates publishing hate crime statistics on an annual basis with 2007 hate crime statistics to be published in spring 2009.[71] This should provide a new source of valuable information on incidents and trends going forward.

France

In France, 2007 data on antisemitic offences from the Interior Ministry and the National Consultative Commission on Human Rights (CNCDH) show a 32.5 percent decline since 2006, a finding with which Jewish community monitors largely concur.[72] The Representative Council of French Jewish Communities (CRIF), documented a 30 percent drop in total incidents in 2007, even while reporting a steady level of violent physical attacks as a percentage of overall incidents.

CRIF reported 146 acts of antisemitic violence in 2007, a decline of about 32 percent from the 213 in 2006, while registering 115 threats (contrasted to 158 in 2006), a decline of 27.5 percent. CRIF found an overall decline in the figures for most categories of incidents, such as harassment, although the proportion involving violence held steady at high levels. Of the 261 incidents in 2007, 56 percent were acts of violence, compared to the 371 cases in 2006, of which 213, or 57 percent, were of a violent nature.[73]

Official figures on antisemitic, racist, and xenophobic violence in France for 2007 reflect a similar trend in anti-Jewish violence. This data, drawn primarily from the Interior Ministry, is compiled in the annual report on racism and xenophobia of the CNCDH. The CNCDH report, which used the statistics compiled by CRIF and its overall findings, highlights a continuing trend toward increased personal violence, even as overall numbers of incidents decline.

The CNCDH study reported 707 racist, antisemitic, and xenophobic acts in 2007 (down 23.5 percent from 923 in 2006). Antisemitic acts, which CNCDH reports on separately, declined by 32.5 percent (386 in 2007, down from 571 in 2006) from 2006 levels (after rising 6 percent in 2006). The report concluded, however, that the levels of racist and antisemitic violence, taken together, continued to be significantly higher than those recorded during the previous decade; in 2000, for example, fewer than 250 antisemitic and racist incidents were reported.

The CNCDH study notes that while cases of antisemitic violence declined in 2007 by 22 percent over the previous year, cases of threats declined by 35 percent. The report states that "acts of antisemitism have retained a violent character, which elicits the concern of the CNCDH." CNCDH reported 64 personal assaults on French Jews registered in 2007. Six victims were minors. Assaults represented more than 60 percent of the 106 incidents registered as "antisemitic acts" (in contrast to threats). The trend of high levels of personal violence continued, though not matching the extraordinary 45 percent rise in acts of violence in 2006 (with 97 incidents in contrast to 54 in 2005). Five synagogues were reported desecrated, and two were the objects of arson attacks. Six cemeteries or monuments were defiled. Twenty homes and private vehicles were vandalized. One school was attacked by arsonists, and another vandalized. The report stresses, moreover, that its coverage is far from comprehensive.[74]

Adding to concerns about the level of violence is the 2007 report of the Stephen Roth Institute for the Study of Contemporary Antisemitism and Racism which cited 8 incidents of "major antisemitic attacks" in France, up from just 2 such attacks, using the same methodology, in 2006.[75]

Germany

In Germany, the official Committee for the Defense of the Constitution figures showed a 25 percent rise in the number of victims of far-right violence in Germany in the first nine months of 2007 and a similar rise in violent antisemitic crime.[76] The Federal Interior Ministry said there had been more than 700 anti-Jewish crimes as of October, including 125 in Berlin. Subsequent statistics for the whole of 2007, which may be subject to further updating, indicated a rise in antisemitic crimes of violence, but an overall decline of 5.8 percent in "right-wing politically motivated offences with an extremist and antisemitic background," from 1,636 in 2006 to 1,541.

Official year-end statistics reported a 37 percent rise in "right-extremist antisemitic crimes of violence," from 43 in 2006 to 59 in 2007. This contrasted with a 6 percent decline in right-wing extremist crimes of violence overall, from 1,047 in 2006 to 980 in 2007. Similarly, violent xenophobic or "antiforeigner" crime dropped from 484 in 2006 to 414 in 2007. Antisemitic offences defined as major crimes of violence represented a relatively small proportion when compared to the overall toll of violent crimes attributed to the extreme right in Germany; just 6 percent of the 980 reported incidents. At the same time, these figures show only the most serious crimes of violence, excluding vandalism and the combination of desecration and often violent property damage of attacks on Jewish cemeteries and memorials to victims of the Holocaust.[77]

Netherlands

In the annual report on antisemitism in the Netherlands for 2006 and the first quarter of 2007, the monitoring group Center for Information and Documentation on Israel demonstrated a significant decline in incidents of violence, with just 8 acts defined as "physical violence" and "physical threats," down from 23 in 2005 and the lowest reported since 2001. Data from the period

January 1 to May 5, 2007, covered in the same report, showed a similar rate of violence.[78]

CIDI contrasted the decline in violent crimes with a 64 percent rise in the number of cases of overall antisemitic incidents, from 159 in 2005 to 261 in 2006. Registered cases included threatening and abusive statements made on the Internet and in electronic correspondence and specific mailings of antisemitic pamphlets that came to the organization's attention.[79] It cited just 8 cases of violent attacks and 7 instances of "violent behavior." CIDI's director, Ronny Naftaniel, noted that the highest number of incidents was reported in Amsterdam, with some cases involving "shouting and insults at people wearing a skull-cap," while others included email threats and harassment.[80]

The annual report of the Monitoring Racism and Extreme Right Violence project for 2006 drew similar conclusions on antisemitic violence within the broader spectrum of extremism. The report, produced under the auspices of the Anne Frank House and the University of Leiden, notes that racially motivated violence, including antisemitic incidents, decreased in 2006, with the total number of violent incidents reduced by about 10 percent over 2005.

In a separate report in December 2007, the Racism and Extremism Monitor assessed the record of investigations and prosecutions of racist violence. In 2004, the Monitor had concluded that police response to racist violence was "increasingly inadequate." In contrast, the 2007 report's headline stressed "the priority now being given to discrimination by the Dutch police and the Public Prosecution Service has been shown to be of help. Never before have so many cases been dealt with."[81]

Norway

In Norway, Oslo's Jewish Museum was repeatedly vandalized, even as overall levels of antisemitic violence remained low. On the night of August 2, 2007, vandals smashed a dozen of the museum's windows; another was broken on August 5. On August 7, a stone broke a window and narrowly missed a museum employee.[82] Norway's Department of Justice and Police announced in March 2007 a determination to require police to record all incidents of hate crime. Norway's Equality and Antidiscrimination Ombudsman told Human Rights First in October, 2007, that his office was working with police to implement the decision, that registration procedures had been developed, and that "police will begin recording bias motivations based on ethnic origin, sexual orientation, and religion."[83]

Russian Federation

The Moscow-based SOVA Center for Information and Analysis reported a significant increase in incidents in which Jews were targeted for violent assaults in the Russian Federation. These attacks occur in the context of extraordinary levels of violence targeting visible minorities, in particular those of immigrant origin. While the SOVA Center had said in the past that Jews were rarely targeted by racist violence because "in most cases they are not easily identifiable in the crowd," a new pattern appeared to be emerging. Three Jews were attacked in 2004, and four in 2005. In 2006, nine worshippers were injured in an attack on a Moscow synagogue, while four others suffered from personal assaults. In 2007, violent incidents targeting Jews "increased dramatically," as nine crimes affecting at least thirteen individuals were reported.[84]

In some cases, attacks on Jews appeared to have been tied to the larger pattern of violence in which individuals were targeted because they did not appear to be ethnic Russians. On December 5, 2007, in Saint Petersburg, a

Jewish man was hospitalized after being repeatedly stabbed; an Uzbek and a Moldovan were also attacked in the same area on that day.[85]

In October 2007, a drunken Russian passenger on a flight from Moscow to Munich attacked another traveler and insulted passengers he believed to be Jewish. The perpetrator, who claimed to be a "Cossack of the Don," was subdued on the plane and arrested by German authorities.[86]

Ukraine

Ukraine has experienced a rise in reported incidents of antisemitic violence, including both violent personal assaults and attacks on synagogues, memorials, and Jewish institutions. Among the reported cases of violence against individuals include the following:

- On January 24, 2008, a rabbi was severely beaten on a main street in Dnipropetrovsk. Rabbi Dov-Ber Baitman, a teacher at the Jewish educational center Shaarei Torah, was assaulted by four men who shouted antisemitic epithets.[87]

- On September 29, 2007, a group of men attacked a rabbi and two yeshiva students in Cherkasy. Rabbi Yosef Rafaelov came with the students from Israel to join the local community in celebrating a holiday. On Saturday evening, they were attacked near the synagogue by a group of men who beat them and kicked them repeatedly.[88]

- On September 27, 2007, four youths attacked an Israeli citizen near a synagogue in Zhytomyr. A few months earlier, in July, Rabbi Shlomo Vilgen was accosted by a mob of around twenty people shouting antisemitic slogans near the synagogue.[89] On August 6, 2007, two young skinheads attacked Nochum Tamarin, director of the local branch of the Federation of Jewish Communities, and his wife Brocha. The youths hit the victims several times in the face.[90]

- In August, one of Ukraine's chief rabbis, Rabbi Ariel Chaikin, issued an open letter to Ukrainian officials decrying the fact that Jews "feel that they are in danger" in Zhytomyr. "They are constantly threatened, they are insulted on the street, and people throw things at them," he wrote, further charging that "officials in Zhytomyr either don't have the desire to or are incapable of preserving security and interethnic and interreligious peace in the city." He said the police who now patrol the area near the synagogue "are unable to seriously resist antisemitic gangs" and that the state security agency refuses to investigate the incidents or the antisemitic and xenophobic gangs in Zhytomyr.[91]

Despite the rise in anti-Jewish violence in Ukraine, little attention was given to particular incidents by mainstream media in the country, and public officials tended to downplay the severity of the problem. In the few cases in which antisemitic incidents led to arrests and prosecutions, monitors observed the tendency to charge the defendants with "hooliganism."[92]

President Viktor Yushchenko on April 12, 2007 called upon top security officials to stop vandalism of Jewish cemeteries and other memorial sites, acknowledging for the first time a rise in such attacks, as well as the growth of extremist groups.[93] In a speech made during a visit to Israel, on November 15, 2007, however, Yushchenko said these incidents were few in number and that "we are dealing with them," while declaring that "we must treat this unemotionally and remember that they are marginal."[94]

United Kingdom

The number of violent attacks on individuals rose, even as antisemitic incidents dropped. There were 114 personal assaults in 2007, a reported all time high, rising from 13 percent of the total incidents to 21 percent.[95]

The annual survey of antisemitism, produced by the Community Security Trust (CST), found 2007 to have been the worst year on record for violent assaults since monitoring began in 1984, with a 2 percent rise over the previous record high level reported in 2006. It was the second worst year, after 2006, for incidents overall, with 547 registered, 47 fewer than the previous year. The chair of the United Kingdom's All-Party Parliamentary Group against Antisemitism, John Mann MP, commented on the overall decline, while declaring that "the base level of antisemitism in the UK is too high." The CST's annual survey reported a total of 114 assault cases, the highest on record, while noting that in a survey twenty years before it had recorded just 17. It reported on one incident from 2007 that was clearly life-threatening:

> An elderly rabbi in Northeast England was walking along a pavement when a car mounted the kerb, knocked him over, then reversed and tried to run him over again. The rabbi required hospital treatment for injuries to his head, arms and legs. The driver has never been identified.[96]

In at least six other incidents of assault, victims required hospital treatment. Fourteen of the recorded attacks targeted schoolchildren. In May 2008, the United Kingdom published a progress report on the implementation of the thirty-five recommendations of the 2006 All Party Parliamentary Inquiry on Antisemitism. The progress report included an Action Plan to address the low number of prosecutions for antisemitic crimes; a commitment to ensure police data collection on all hate crimes, including antisemitism; and new funding provisions to ensure security for schools confronting hate crimes.[97]

United States

The Anti-Defamation League (ADL), a longstanding monitor of antisemitism in the United States and a leader of efforts to combat all forms of hate crime, reported a decline for the third consecutive year in antisemitic incidents in the annual report for 2007. The ADL registered 1,460 incidents, a 6 percent decline from 1,554 in 2006, and down from a peak of 1,821 in 2004. There were 699 incidents of vandalism (including cemetery desecration, graffiti, and other forms of property damage), and 761 of harassment (which in the ADL typology includes "physical or verbal assaults directed at individuals or institutions").[98]

Official Federal Bureau of Investigation (FBI) statistics showed a somewhat different trend. While hate crime statistics for 2007 were not available as of the end of August 2008, the FBI hate crime report shows a rise in anti-Jewish offenses, from 900 in 2005 to 1,027 in 2006. Anti-Jewish hate crimes in both years represent a large majority of hate crimes falling in the category of "religious bias."[99]

Section Endnotes

[1] Anshel Pfeffer and Asaf Uni, "Anti-Semitic incidents rise in Germany, Australia, U.S. in 2007," *Haaretz*, January 27, 2008, http://primage.tau.ac.il/asm/000197956.pdf.

[2] The Stephen Roth Institute for the Study of Contemporary Antisemitism and Racism, *Antisemitism Worldwide 2007, General Analysis*, April 2008, http://www.tau.ac.il/Anti-Semitism/asw2007/gen-analysis-07.pdf.

[3] OSCE Office for Democratic Institutions and Human Rights, *Hate Crimes in the OSCE Region: Incidents and Responses - Annual Report for 2006*, September 18, 2007, OSCE http://www.osce.org/odihr/item_11_26296.html.

[4] Gert Weisskirchen, *Report to the Permanent Council of the OSCE*, Personal Representative of the Chairman-in-Office of the OSCE on Combating Antisemitism, CIO.GAL/171/07, November 13, 2007, http://www.osce.org/documents/pc/2007/11/28073_en.pdf.

[5] U.S. Commission on Security and Cooperation in Europe, "Taking Stock: Combating Antisemitism in the OSCE Region," Briefing, January 29, 2008, http://www.csce.gov/index.cfm?Fuseaction=ContentRecords.ViewDetail&ContentRecord_id=409&ContentType=H,B&ContentRecordType=H&CFID=9292 32&CFTOKEN=70697758.

[6] The Council of Europe, "Combating anti-Semitism in Europe," Parliamentary Assembly, Resolution 1563 (2007), http://www.assembly.coe.int/Mainf.asp?link=/Documents/AdoptedText/ta07/ERES1563.htm.

[7] European Union Agency for Fundamental Rights, *Annual Report*, 2008, TK-AG-08-001-EN-C, http://fra.europa.eu/fra/material/pub/ar08/ar08_en.pdf, pp. 34-35.

[8] The Coordination Forum for Countering Antisemitism, "Assault of a Jewish man in Garges-les-Gonesses," September 6, 2007, http://www.antisemitism.org.il/eng/events/26540/France%E2%80%93_Assault_of_a_Jewish_man_in_Garges-les-Gonesses.

[9] The Coordination Forum for Countering Antisemitism, "Jew violently assaulted in Manchester," July 23, 2007, http://www.antisemitism.org.il/eng/events/24096/Britain-_Jew_violently_assaulted_in_Manchester.

[10] Chicago Action Yad L'yad, "Where in the world is Lida," *Tekiah*, January 2008, http://www.chicagoaction.org/CurrentII.pdf.

[11] The Coordination Forum for Countering Antisemitism, "Two Jews harassed on a bus in Berlin," December 12, 2007, http://www.antisemitism.org.il/eng/events/26825/Germany_%E2%80%93_Two_Jews_harassed_on_a_bus_in_Berlin.

[12] The Anti-Defamation League, "Global Anti-Semitism: Selected Incidents Around the World in 2007," http://www.adl.org/Anti_semitism/anti-semitism_global_incidents_2007.asp.

[13] "German authorities charge 22-year-old man with stabbing rabbi," *Haaretz*, January 31, 2008, http://www.haaretz.com/hasen/spages/950056.html.

[14] The Coordination Forum for Countering Antisemitism, "Habad Representative Attacked in Sebastopol," September 29, 2007, http://www.antisemitism.org.il/eng/events/25128/Ukraine%E2%80%93_Habad_Representative_Attacked_in_Sebastopol.

[15] Deborah Garcia, "Rabbi Beaten With Bat In Possible Bias Attack," *CBS*, October 10, 2007 http://wcbstv.com/local/lakewood.rabbi.attacked.2.341832.html.

[16] The Coordination Forum for Countering Antisemitism, "A Jewish Pupil Attacked," October 9, 2007, http://www.antisemitism.org.il/eng/events/25251/France_%E2%80%93_A_Jewish_Pupil_Attacked.

[17] The Associated Press, "Berlin Mayor Condemns Attack on Jewish High-School Students," *the Jerusalem Post*, January 17, 2008, http://www.jpost.com/servlet/Satellite?cid=1200572478642&pagename=JPost%2FJPArticle%2FShowFull.

[18] Interfax, "Jewish children attacked in Moscow region," *Interfax-Religion*, February 19, 2007, http://www.interfax-religion.com/?act=news&div=2621.

[19] The Coordination Forum for Countering Antisemitism, "A Threatening Phone Call to a Jewish School in Montreal," February 2, 2007, http://www.antisemitism.org.il/eng/events/22921/Canada%E2%80%93_A_Threatening_Phone_Call_to_a_Jewish_School_in_Montreal.

[20] The Coordination Forum for Countering Antisemitism, "Threats to Jewish Schools in Montreal," February 6, 2007, http://www.antisemitism.org.il/eng/events/22922/Canada%E2%80%93_Threats_to_Jewish_Schools_in_Montreal.

[21] Oliver Bradley, "Smoke bomb thrown into Jewish kindergarten in Berlin," *European Jewish Press*, February 26, 2007, http://www.ejpress.org/article/14511.

[22] The Associated Press and Haaretz Service, "ADL commends N.Y. police for arrests in anti-Semitic subway attack," *Haaretz*, December 12, 2007, http://www.haaretz.com/hasen/spages/933597.html.

[23] Ruth Klein and Anita Bloomberg, *2007 Audit of Antisemitsic Incidents: Patterns of Prejudice in Canada*, League for Human Rights of B'nai Brith Canada, 2008, http://www.bnaibrith.ca/publications/audit2007/audit2007.pdf, p. 8.

[24] The Coordination Forum for Countering Antisemitism, "Paint thrown at Jews in Ilford," June 9, 2007, http://www.antisemitism.org.il/eng/events/23306/Britain-_paint_thrown_at_Jews_in_Ilford.

[25] The Coordination Forum for Countering Antisemitism, "Violent incident in Essex," April 3, 2007, http://www.antisemitism.org.il/eng/events/23800/Britain-Violent_incident_in_Essex.

[26] The Coordination Forum for Countering Antisemitism, "Mother and son assaulted on bus in London," January 30, 2007, http://www.antisemitism.org.il/eng/events/20855/Britain_%E2%80%93_Mother_and_son_assaulted_on_bus_in_London.

[27] The Coordination Forum for Countering Antisemitism, "7 teens charged with drive-by bias crimes," *Asbury Park Press*, June 19, 2007, http://www.antisemitism.org.il/eng/events/22877/USA_-_7_teens_charged_with_drive-by_bias_crimes.

[28] Human Rights First, *Companion Survey on Antisemitism*, September 2007, http://www.humanrightsfirst.info/pdf/07601-discrim-hc-antisemitsm-web.pdf.

[29] Devorah Lauter, "With baseball caps and discretion, French Jews hide their Jewishness,"*JTA*, May 20, 2008, http://jta.org/cgi-bin/iowa/news/article/2008021220080205kippas.html.

[30] Piotr Łukasz, "Polish rabbi attacked in a train," *European Jewish Press*, October 28, 2007, http://www.ejpress.org/article/news/eastern_europe/21256.

[31] Ruth Klein and Anita Bloomberg, *2007 Audit of Antisemitsic Incidents: Patterns of Prejudice in Canada*, League for Human Rights of B'nai Brith Canada, 2008, http://www.bnaibrith.ca/publications/audit2007/audit2007.pdf, p. 9.

[32] The Coordination Forum for Countering Antisemitism, "Antisemitic Graffiti in Murmansk," June 13, 2006, http://www.antisemitism.org.il/eng/events/22862/Russia_%E2%80%93_Antisemitic_Graffiti_in_Murmansk.

[33] The Coordination Forum for Countering Antisemitism, "Excrement smeared on door in London," April 1, 2007, http://www.antisemitism.org.il/eng/events/23791/Britain-_Excrement_smeared_on_door_in_London.

[34] "Antwerp synagogue vandalized," *JTA*, December 6, 2007, http://jta.org/cgi-bin/iowa/breaking/105737.html.

[35] The Coordination Forum for Countering Antisemitism, "A synagogue was vandalized," January 22, 2007, http://www.antisemitism.org.il/eng/events/20576/Denmark_%E2%80%93_A_synagogue_was_vandalized.

[36] The Coordination Forum for Countering Antisemitism, "A Stone Tossed at a Synagogue in Daugavpils," February 2, 2007, http://www.antisemitism.org.il/eng/events/23569/Latvia%E2%80%80%93_A_Stone_Tossed_at_a_Synagogue_in_Daugavpils.

[37] Tanjug News Agency, "Vandals deface Novi Sad synagogue," *B92*, March 20, 2007, http://www.b92.net/eng/news/crimes-article.php?yyyy=2007&mm=03&dd=19&nav_id=40228.

[38] The Associated Press, "Geneva synagogue damaged by fire," the *International Herald Tribune*, May 24, 2007, http://www.iht.com/articles/2007/05/24/europe/swiss.php.

[39] Michael Freund, "Vandals deface Holocaust memorial in Armenia," the *Jerusalem Post*, December 23, 2007, http://www.jpost.com/servlet/Satellite?cid=1196847408736&pagename=JPost%2FJPArticle%2FShowFull.

[40] The Coordination Forum for Countering Antisemitism, "Desecration of a Memorial in Minsk," February 28, 2007, http://www.antisemitism.org.il/eng/events/23565/Belarus%E2%80%93_Desecration_of_a_Memorial_in_Minsk.

[41] "Jewish tombstones knocked down in Belarus," *JTA*, June 29 2007, http://jta.org/cgi-bin/iowa/breaking/102763.html',595,700).

[42] Union of Councils for Jews in the Former Soviet Union, "Jewish Cemetery Vandalized in Belarus," the *Bigotry Monitor*, vol. 7, no. 25, July 6, 2007, http://www.fsumonitor.com/stories/101707Belarus.shtml.

[43] "Czech Memorial to Jewish victims of death march vandalized," *European Jewish Press*, February 6, 2007, http://www.ejpress.org/article/13822.

[44] DPA News, Anti-Semitic slogans sprayed on Hungarian Holocaust memorial, *Haaretz*, September 27, 2007, http://www.haaretz.com/hasen/spages/907681.html.

[45] The Coordination Forum for Countering Antisemitism, "Desecration of a Memorial Tree in Arezzo," January 25, 2007, http://www.antisemitism.org.il/eng/events/21837/Italy%E2%80%93_Desecration_of_a_Memorial_Tree_in_Arezzo.

[46] The Coordination Forum for Countering Antisemitism, "Desecration of a Jewish Cemetery in Chisinau," April 23, 2007, http://www.antisemitism.org.il/eng/events/21894/Moldova_%E2%80%93_Desecration_of_a_Jewish_Cemetery_in_Chisinau_%28Kishinev%29.

[47] Agence France-Presse, Jewish cemetery desecrated in Poland, *European Jewish Press*, August 06, 2007, http://www.ejpress.org/article/18974.

[48] The Anti-Defamation League, "Global Anti-Semitism: Selected Incidents Around the World in 2007," http://www.adl.org/Anti_semitism/anti-semitism_global_incidents_2007.asp.

[49] Attila Somfalvi, "Jewish cemetery in Bucharest desecrated," *Israel News*, February 13, 2007, http://www.ynetnews.com/articles/0,7340,L-3364863,00.html.

[50] The Stephen Roth Institute for the Study of Contemporary Antisemitism and Racism, *Antisemitism Worldwide 2007, General Analysis*, April 2008, http://www.tau.ac.il/Anti-Semitism/asw2007/gen-analysis-07.pdf.

[51] Petar Kostadinov, "Hand of Bulgaria's Law," *the Sofia Echo*, August 27, 2007, http://www.sofiaecho.com/article/hand-of-the-law/id_24553/catid_5.

[52] Ruth Klein and Anita Bloomberg, *2007 Audit of Antisemitsic Incidents: Patterns of Prejudice in Canada*, League for Human Rights of B'nai Brith Canada, 2008, http://www.bnaibrith.ca/publications/audit2007/audit2007.pdf, p. 2.

[53] Ruth Klein and Anita Bloomberg, *2007 Audit of Antisemitsic Incidents: Patterns of Prejudice in Canada*, League for Human Rights of B'nai Brith Canada, 2008, http://www.bnaibrith.ca/publications/audit2007/audit2007.pdf, p. 2.

[54] S. Pouzet, "Séquestration et torture pour un jeune homme à Bagneux," *20Minutes.fr*, May 13, 2008, http://www.20minutes.fr/article/217067/France-Sequestration-et-torture-pour-un-jeune-homme-a-Bagneux.php.

[55] Cécilia Gabizon, "Cukierman: '*L'antisémitisme a touché un public nouveau*,'" *le Figaro*, January 23, 2007, http://www.lefigaro.fr/france/20070123.FIG000000018_cukierman_l_antisemitisme_a_touche_un_public_nouveau.html.

[56] Thomas Prouteau, "*Un jeune d'origine juive séquestré et agressé à Bagneux*," *RTL.fr*, March 05, 2008, http://www.rtl.fr/fiche/60774/un-jeune-d-origine-juive-sequestre-et-agresse-a-bagneux.html.

[57] Le Service de Protection de la Communauté Juive, *Rapport sur l'Antisémitisme en France, 2007*, February 2008, http://www.jean-jaures.org/NL/299/Rapport_Antisemitisme_2007.pdf, p. 9.

[58] Commission nationale consultative des droits de l'homme (CNCDH), *La lutte contre le racisme et la xénophobie: rapport d'activité 2007*, March 28, 2008, http://www.ladocumentationfrancaise.fr/rapports-publics/084000167/index.shtml.

[59] Bundesministerium des Innern, *Verfassungsschutzbericht 2007*, May 15, 2008, http://www.verfassungsschutz.de/download/SHOW/vsbericht_2007.pdf.

[60] Sylvia Westall, "Germany's Merkel attacks 'middle-class anti-Semitism,'" *Reuters*, January 25, 2008, http://in.reuters.com/article/worldNews/idINIndia-31598120080125.

[61] Jaap Van Donselaar and Willem Wagenaar, *Racial violence and violence incited by the extreme right in 2006*, Racism and Extremism Monitor, Anne Frank House and the University of Leiden, August 27, 2007, http://www.annefrank.org/upload/Downloads/RacialViolence2006.pdf.

[62] Ruth Klein and Anita Bloomberg, *2007 Audit of Antisemitsic Incidents: Patterns of Prejudice in Canada*, League for Human Rights of B'nai Brith Canada, 2008, http://www.bnaibrith.ca/publications/audit2007/audit2007.pdf, p. 17.

[63] The Stephen Roth Institute for the Study of Contemporary Antisemitism and Racism, *Netherlands 2006*, http://www.tau.ac.il/Anti-Semitism/asw2006/netherland.htm.

[64] Centre Information and Documentation on Israel, *Anti-Semitism 2006—January though May 2007*, Summary, http://www.cidi.nl/dossiers/an/rapporten/report2006.pdf.

[65] Union of Councils for Jews in the Former Soviet Union, "Antisemitic Rally in Kiev," *the Bigotry Monitor*, vol. 4, no. 40, November 12, 2007, http://www.fsumonitor.com/stories/111204Bigotry.shtml.

[66] Antisemetisme.be, *Rapport sur l'antisémitisme en Belgique pour l'année 2007*, February 14, 2008, http://www.antisemitisme.be/site/event_detail.asp?eventId=676&catId=36&language=FR.

[67] Antisemetisme.be, *Croix gammées et voitures endommagées à Niel*, November 11, 2007, http://www.antisemitisme.be/site/event_detail.asp?eventId=624&catId=30&language=FR.

[68] Ruth Klein and Anita Bloomberg, *2007 Audit of Antisemitsic Incidents: Patterns of Prejudice in Canada*, League for Human Rights of B'nai Brith Canada, 2008, http://www.bnaibrith.ca/publications/audit2007/audit2007.pdf, p. 2.

[69] The Stephen Roth Institute for the Study of Contemporary Antisemitism and Racism, *Antisemitism Worldwide 2007, General Analysis*, April 2008, http://www.tau.ac.il/Anti-Semitism/asw2007/gen-analysis-07.pdf.

[70] Mia Dauvergne, Katie Scrim and Shannon Brennan, *Hate Crime in Canada 2006*, Canadian Centre for Justice Statistics Profile Series, 2006, http://www.statcan.ca/english/research/85F0033MIE/85F0033MIE2008017.pdf.

[71] Human Rights First correspondence with a senior analyst at the Policing Services Program, Canadian Centre for Justice Statistics, Statistics Canada, August 18, 2008.

[72] Commission nationale consultative des droits de l'homme (CNCDH), *La lutte contre le racisme et la xénophobie: rapport d'activité 2007*, March 28, 2008, http://www.ladocumentationfrancaise.fr/rapports-publics/084000167/index.shtml.

[73] Le Service de Protection de la Communauté Juive, *Rapport sur l'Antisémitisme en France, 2007*, February 2008, http://www.jean-jaures.org/NL/299/Rapport_Antisemitisme_2007.pdf.

[74] Commission nationale consultative des droits de l'homme (CNCDH), *La lutte contre le racisme et la xénophobie: rapport d'activité 2007*, March 28, 2008, http://www.ladocumentationfrancaise.fr/rapports-publics/084000167/index.shtml.

[75] The Stephen Roth Institute for the Study of Contemporary Antisemitism and Racism, *Antisemitism Worldwide 2007, General Analysis*, April 2008, http://www.tau.ac.il/Anti-Semitism/asw2007/gen-analysis-07.pdf.

[76] Sylvia Westall, "Germany's Merkel attacks 'middle-class anti-Semitism,'" *Reuters*, January 25, 2008, http://in.reuters.com/article/worldNews/idINIndia-31598120080125.

[77] Bundesministerium des Innern, *Verfassungsschutzbericht 2007*, May 15, 2008, http://www.verfassungsschutz.de/download/SHOW/vsbericht_2007.pdf.

[78] The Stephen Roth Institute for the Study of Contemporary Antisemitism and Racism, *Netherlands 2006*, http://www.tau.ac.il/Anti-Semitism/asw2006/netherland.htm.

[79] Centre Information and Documentation on Israel, *Anti-Semitism 2006—January though May 2007*, Summary, http://www.cidi.nl/dossiers/an/rapporten/report2006.pdf.

[80] Chaan Liphshiz, "Jewish group says anti-Semitic incidents in Holland up by 64 percent," *Haaretz*, November 17, 2007, http://www.haaretz.com/hasen/spages/924989.html.

[81] Marija Davicovi and Peter R. Rodrigues, *Monitor racisme & extremisme: opsporing en vervolging in 2006*, Racism and Extremism Monitor, Anne Frank House and the University of Leiden, December 12, 2007, http://www.annefrank.org/content.asp?PID=817&LID=2.

[82] The Coordination Forum for Countering Antisemitism, "Violent Incidents at the Jewish Museum in Oslo," August 2, 2007, http://www.antisemitism.org.il/eng/events/23835/Norway%E2%80%93_Violent_Incidents_at_the_Jewish_Museum_in_Oslo.

[83] Human Rights First, *Hate Crime Report Card, Country-by-Country: Norway*, September 2007, http://www.humanrightsfirst.org/discrimination/hate-crime/country/count_a.asp.

[84] Galina Kozhevnikova, *Radical Nationalism and Efforts to Counteract it in 2007*, the SOVA Center for Information and Analysis, March 14, 2008, http://xeno.sova-center.ru/6BA2468/6BB4208/AC15D1E.

[85] The Coordination Forum for Countering Antisemitism, "Antisemitic and racist violence in St. Petersburg," December 5, 2007, http://www.antisemitism.org.il/eng/events/26576/Russia_-_Antisemitic_and_racist_violence_in_St._Petersburg.

[86] The Anti-Defamation League, "Global Anti-Semitism: Selected Incidents Around the World in 2007," http://www.adl.org/Anti_semitism/anti-semitism_global_incidents_2007.asp.

[87] Vyacheslav Likhachev, *Ksenofobiya v Ukraine: Materialy Monitoringa 2007-2008*, Kyiv, May 2008, p. 18.

[88] Nickolai Butkevich, "Jew-Hatred Is on The Rise in the Land of Pogroms," Forward, October 17, 2007, http://www.forward.com/articles/11836/.

[89] Nickolai Butkevich, "Jew-Hatred Is on The Rise in the Land of Pogroms," Forward, October 17, 2007, http://www.forward.com/articles/11836/.

[90] "V Zhitomire snova izbili evreev," *Zhitomir City Journal*, August 8, 2007, http://zhzh.info/news/2007-08-08-1547.

[91] Union of Councils for Jews in the Former Soviet Union, "New incident in Zhitomir; Chief Rabbi Publicly Complains," *the Bigotry Monitor*, vol. 7, no. 32, August 24, 2007, http://www.fsumonitor.com/stories/082407BM.shtml.

[92] Union of Councils for Jews in the Former Soviet Union, "Antisemitic and Racist Violence in Ukraine and the Russian Federation," 2007, http://www.fsumonitor.com/stories/012708KirkSummary.pdf.

[93] Union of Councils for Jews in the Former Soviet Union, "Yushenko Asks for Measures to Stop Vandalism," *the Bigotry Monitor*, vol. 7, no. 15, April 13, 2007, http://www.fsumonitor.com/stories/041307BM.shtml.

[94] Anshel Pfeffer, "Ukraine President defends posthumous honor to alleged head of pogrom," *Haaretz*, November 15, 2007, http://www.haaretz.com/hasen/spages/924553.html.

[95] The Community Security Trust, *Antisemitic Incidents Report 2007*, 2008, http://www.thecst.org.uk/docs/Incidents_Report_07.pdf.

[96] Leon Symons and Yaakov Wise, "Last year 'the second worst' for hate crime," *the Jewish Chronicle*, February 2, 2008, http://www.thejc.com/home.aspx?AId=58085&ATypeId=1&search=true2&srchstr=antisemitism&srchtxt=1&srchhead=1&srchauthor=1&srchsandp=1&scsrch=0.

[97] The Parliamentary Committee Against Antisemitism, *Report of the All-Party Parliamentary Inquiry into Antisemitism: Government Response*, March 29, 2007, http://www.thepcaa.org/responses.html.

[98] The Anti-Defamation League, "Anti-Semitic Incidents Decline For Third Straight Year In U.S., According To Annual ADL Audit," Press Release, March 19, 2008, http://www.adl.org/PresRele/ASUS_12/5246_12.htm.

[99] U.S. Department of Justice, Federal Bureau of Investigation, *Uniform Crime Reports*, http://www.fbi.gov/ucr/ucr.htm.

Violence Against Muslims

Table of Contents

Executive Summary

Acts of bias-driven violence against Muslims and their places of worship continued in 2007 and 2008. The more serious of these offenses included assaults—sometimes deadly—against Muslim religious leaders, ordinary Muslims, and those perceived to be Muslim. Documented and reported offenses also included cases of harassment and attacks on places of worship.

While attacks on Muslims may often be motivated by racist or ethnic bias, intolerance is increasingly directed at Muslim immigrants and other minorities expressly because of their religion. The complexity of the problem of anti-Muslim violence is further intensified by the multiple dimensions of discrimination that may occur in a single incident, with overlays of intolerance often based on the victim's religion, ethnicity, and gender. Women who wear the hijāb—a highly visible sign of a woman's religious and cultural background—are particularly vulnerable to harassment and violence by those who wish to send a message of hatred. While law enforcement officials have responded to some of the more serious cases in several countries, underreporting remains a key problem, as most victims refrain from reporting attacks to the police.

Acts of aggression against Muslim individuals and places of worship are being committed in the context of a longstanding strain of political discourse in Europe that has projected immigrants in general and Muslims in particular as a threat not only to security but to European homogeneity and culture. The situation has worsened in recent years in the context of terrorist attacks and the response of governments to them.

Anti-Muslim prejudice and violence occur throughout the Organization for Security and Cooperation in Europe (OSCE) region, although the context differs from one country or region to another. Moreover, certain international and domestic events—such as the terrorist

attack in Scotland in June 2007—continue to provoke backlash attacks on Muslims and those perceived to be Muslims.

There is a lack of official statistics on the incidence of violent hate crimes against Muslims, as only a few countries engage in official monitoring of this form of bias. This data deficit proves a challenge to comprehensive and well thought-out policy decisions to address the problem. The **United States** has long been systematically monitoring anti-Muslim crimes, while such monitoring and public reporting has been conducted for the past two years in **Sweden**. In the **United Kingdom** monitoring and reporting on "Islamophobic" hate crimes is most developed in London. Authorities in the United States reported an increase in the level of violence against Muslims between 2005 and 2006—the last time period for which data is available. Statistics from Sweden and from the London Metropolitan Police have shown a slight decline in the incidence of such crimes between 2006 and 2007.

In two other countries, data on hate crime targeting Muslims was reported for the first time in 2008. In June, **Canada** released the first national hate crime statistics, which included data on hate crimes perpetrated against Muslims. Previously, official data from Canada had been limited to several police jurisdictions. **Austria** has begun to monitor "Islamophobic crimes" within the framework of its reporting on right-wing extremism, releasing data for the first time on two such cases in the 2007 reporting.

Authorities in **France** do not report explicitly on violence against Muslims, but their reporting of racist and xenophobic hate crimes offers a window into the problem of anti-Muslim violence, with over 60 percent of reported incidents perpetrated against people of North African origin, who are predominantly Muslim. No other government in the OSCE region reports crimes motivated by hatred toward Muslims.

Comprehensive data from nongovernmental sources is also generally unavailable, as very few NGOs across the region monitor and publicly report specifically on violent anti-Muslim hate crimes. Overall, the lack of reporting makes it difficult to assess the official responses to such incidents by the police and in the courts.

I. The Facets of Anti-Muslim Violence

There is an everyday pattern of racially and religiously motivated violence against Muslims and those perceived to be Muslims in many parts of Europe and North America that is tied to longstanding racism, intolerance, and exclusion in communities where Muslims live. Intolerance, discrimination, and violence have been exacerbated in recent years by the reaction to terrorism and extremism in the name of Islam. Since September 11, 2001, in particular, this reaction has included the perpetuation of negative stereotypes and generalizations about Muslims, and the idea—advanced by the proponents of discrimination and violence—of collective responsibility of all Muslims for the acts of others who claim to share the same faith.

Although only a few NGOs across the region report regularly and systematically on the problem of violent anti-Muslim hate crime, there is a growing body of reporting from intergovernmental bodies that has contributed to an improved understanding of the nature of discrimination and violence against Muslims.

According to Ambassador Ömür Orhun, the Personal Representative of the OSCE Chairman-in-Office on Combating Intolerance and Discrimination against Muslims, the environment in which Muslims live has deteriorated considerably since September 11, with Muslims and Muslim communities becoming "victims of negative stereotyping and manifestations of prejudice."[1] The OSCE's Office for Democratic Institutions and Human Rights (OSCE/ODIHR) has similarly noted such trends. In the most recent annual report (covering 2006), the ODIHR documents a wide range of incidents across the OSCE region, identifying the firebombing of mosques and other property as a particularly disturbing trend.[2]

Other European institutions also address this issue. The Council of Europe Commissioner for Human Rights

Thomas Hammarberg highlighted the problem of violence against Muslims in a June 2008 article, noting that

> a mixture of Islamophobia and racism is also directed against immigrant Muslims or their children. This tendency has increased considerably after 9/11 and government responses to such terrorist crimes. Muslims have been physically attacked and mosques vandalised or burnt in a number of countries. In the United Kingdom no less than eleven mosques were attacked after the London terrorist bombings on 7 July 2005 and in France five mosques were attacked with explosives or put alight in 2006.[3]

On an earlier occasion, in January 2007, Hammarberg wrote that "manifestations of Islamophobia within European societies have taken the form of persisting prejudice, negative attitudes, discrimination, and sometimes violence."[4] The Council of Europe's antiracism body, the European Commission Against Racism and Intolerance (ECRI) has also raised concern about the problem of discrimination and violence against Muslims in individual country reports, as well as in the 2007 annual report:

> ECRI is concerned by the continuing climate of hostility towards persons who are Muslim or are perceived to be Muslim, and deplores the fact that Islamophobia continues to manifest itself in different guises within European societies. Muslim communities and their members continue to face prejudice, negative attitudes, and discrimination. The discourse of certain political figures or some of the media contributes to this negative climate, which can sometimes lead to acts of violence against Muslim communities.[5]

The European Monitoring Centre on Racism and Xenophobia (EUMC)—the predecessor to the European Union's Fundamental Rights Agency (FRA), produced several reports in recent years analyzing challenges faced by Muslim communities in Europe, most comprehensively in the report on *Discrimination and*

Islamophobia against Muslims in the European Union in 2006. The report showed the disadvantaged position of Muslim minorities in key areas of social life, such as employment, education and housing. It also documented manifestations of "Islamophobia" in all E.U. member states, including cases of racist violence and crime.[6]

Numerous other reports—both intergovernmental and nongovernmental—as well as statements by advocates of human rights, including Orhun and Hammarberg, have raised concerns in regard to the discrimination that Muslims face in several aspects of life, from finding employment to building mosques. Many Muslims, particularly young people, "face limited opportunities for social advancement, social exclusion and discrimination." They are also often confined to poor housing conditions, worse jobs, and limited opportunities for educational advancement than other citizens.[7] Muslims find themselves in an environment of hostility, "characterized by suspicion and prejudice; negative or patronizing imaging; discrimination and stereotyping; lack of provision, recognition and respect for Muslims in public institutions; and attacks, abuse, harassment and violence directed against persons perceived to be Muslim and against mosques, Muslim property and cemeteries."[8]

The geographic scope of anti-Muslim violence encompasses the entire OSCE region, although the specific forces driving it may vary from one country or region to another.

In the **United States**, anti-Muslim prejudice arises largely out of the perceived security threat posed by Muslims. Attacks against Muslims and those perceived to be Muslims have risen sharply immediately following terrorist attacks, most notably in the aftermath of September 11, 2001, and remain at historically high levels. A report by the American-Arab Anti-Discrimination Committee (ADC) documented incidents of violence between 2004 and 2007 against Arab

Americans of all faiths, including death threats, vandalism, and at least one murder. ADC also highlighted a number of trends in hate crimes against Arab-Americans, and those perceived to be of Middle Eastern descent, including Muslims:

- during the period of 2003-2007, the rate of violent hate crimes continued to decline from the immediate post-9/11 surge, yet still remained at a higher rate than in the five years leading up to the 2001 attacks;

- surges in reported hate crimes have been observed following international events such as the July 2005 London bombings as well as terrorist attacks against American targets in Iraq.

- hate crimes have especially targeted mosques and Islamic centers around the country, in the form of vandalism and destruction of property.[9]

In many European countries, acts of aggression against individuals and places of worship are committed in the context of a longstanding strain of political discourse that has projected immigrants in general and Muslim immigrants in particular as threats to European security, homogeneity, and culture. Terrorist incidents lead to further strains and, typically, an increase in violent attacks targeting Muslims, those perceived to be Muslims, and mosques.

In **Finland**, interlocutors of Ambassador Orhun confirmed the rise in incidents of physical attacks and harassment against Muslims during a December 2007 visit, noting that such violence is rarely reported or is misrepresented as racist violence by the authorities, who have nevertheless stepped up their response to hate crimes in recent years.[10]

In **France**, according to official statistics, people of North African origin—largely of Muslim background—are the object of the majority of hate crimes classified as "racist" by the authorities. One French NGO, the Collectif contre l'Islamophobie en France, reported a

20 percent rise in hate-motivated acts (including violent incidents) against Muslims: in 2007, there were 65 such acts, compared with 54 and 53 incidents in 2006 and 2005, respectively.

In the **United Kingdom**, Muslim minorities have expressed increasing concern about their security, even as official figures suggest a decline in the number of crimes motivated by hatred toward Muslims. Inayat Bunglawala, spokesman for the Muslim Council of Britain, confirmed incidents of attacks against mosques and Islamic schools and noted that British Muslims generally consider anti-Muslim prejudice to be increasing. Britain's first Muslim minister, Shahid Malik, criticized what he described as growing hostility to Muslims in the U.K.[11]

The rise of racist and religious violence against Muslims in Europe has occurred in tandem with the adoption of anti-immigrant political platforms by both fringe and mainstream political movements. Public debates on immigration and the status of Europe's minorities can have a racial cast and be dominated by aggressive "us versus them" discourse. The resulting anti-Muslim rhetoric has also in many countries become embedded in mainstream political debate, its rise to prominence illustrated by the influence of extremist political figures. Radical political leaders have sought to legitimize xenophobia and have contributed to the growth of popular anti-Muslim sentiment and intolerance across Europe.

In the **Czech Republic**, Muneeb Hassan Alrawi, chairman of the Brno-based Islamic Foundation, reported that intolerance and hatred against Muslims has increased over the past several years, blaming politicians, certain interest groups, and the media. He stated: "We are afraid of the day when this venomous campaign against Islam and Muslims results in physical attacks, which creates an atmosphere of fear and instability in society."[12]

In **Denmark**, the Danish People's Party used a poster of a burqa-clad woman wielding a judge's gavel as part of its initiative to ban public employees from wearing Islamic headscarves. The Muslim community reacted with outrage, while Birthe Rønn Hornbech, Denmark's Immigration Minister, denounced the campaign as "fanatically anti-Muslim."[13]

According to the latest ECRI report on the **Netherlands**, anti-Muslim hostility in Holland has increased dramatically since 2000. This has been influenced by the terrorist attacks of 9/11 and the murder of Dutch filmmaker Theo van Gogh in September 2004. ECRI noted that "Muslims of the Netherlands have been the subject of stereotyping, stigmatizing and sometimes outright racist political discourse and of biased media portrayal and have been disproportionately targeted by security and other policies. They have also been the victims of racist violence and other racist crimes and have experienced discrimination."[14]

In many countries in Eastern Europe, current violence against Muslims is intimately linked to anti-immigrant sentiment as well as historical developments. In the **Russian Federation**, people from the Caucasus and Central Asia—both Russian citizens and foreigners—suffer the highest proportion of bias motivated violence. Incidents of personal violence have in some cases been a response to the war in Chechnya and associated terrorist attacks.

At the same time, comprehensive reporting on attacks against migrants from these areas remains unavailable, as the victims tend to fear police abuse or arrest and are least likely to report bias-motivated attacks. Attacks on immigrants from these regions are generally perceived to be motivated by racism, but sometimes have an overlay of religious hatred and intolerance: many people from the Caucasus and Central Asia are Muslims.

In a particularly horrific case in August 2007 that seemed to bridge these different aspects of intolerance and prejudice, perpetrators circulated video-taped murders of two men allegedly of Dagestani and Tajik origin. The video footage of the execution-style killings showed the beheading of one and the shooting of the other, with a Nazi flag in the background. The video was posted on the Internet in the name of a previously unknown Russian neo-Nazi group with a demand for the expulsion from Russia of all Asians and people from the Caucasus.

In **Ukraine**, bias-motivated attacks on Crimean Tatars—who are Muslim—and their property are largely thought to be motivated by ethnic hatred, although there is undoubtedly an element of religious intolerance in those acts as well. In a recent report on Ukraine, European Commission against Racism and Intolerance (ECRI) noted that "the situation in the Crimea is particularly worrying as there has been a rise in ethnic clashes and racially motivated violence in that region between skinheads and Cossacks (vigilante groups) on the one hand and members of the Crimean Tatar community on the other. Three such major clashes involving several hundred people occurred in July and August 2006." ECRI also referred to cases of physical attacks against Crimean Tatars as well as destruction of property and desecration of cemeteries by skinhead groups. ECRI further expressed concern over reports "according to which the local police's response to these types of incidents is generally inadequate as they often deny the involvement of neo-Nazi groups."[15]

II. Assaults on Individuals

In 2007 and early 2008, discrimination and violence against Muslims frequently took the form of assaults on ordinary people in their shops, schools, or homes often accompanied by racist and/or anti-Muslim epithets. While attacks on Muslims may often be motivated primarily by racial or ethnic bias, intolerance is increasingly directed at Muslim immigrants and other minorities expressly because of their religion.

The complexity of the problem of anti-Muslim violence is further intensified by the multiple dimensions of discrimination that may occur in a single incident, as there can be an overlay of intolerance based on such characteristics as the victim's religion, ethnicity, and gender. Women who wear the hijāb—a highly visible sign of a woman's religious and cultural background—are particularly vulnerable to harassment and violence by those who wish to send a message of hatred.

On February 7, 2008, in **Belgium**, in Liège, two young women, described as being of "Maghreb origin," were attacked by three men in the city center. The victims were verbally abused and physically threatened with a firearm. One of the perpetrators was described as having right-wing extremist affiliations. Following a trial, the two primary offenders were sentenced to jail sentences of fifteen and twelve months respectively (of which six were suspended). Jozef De Witte, director of the Belgian Centre for Equal Opportunities and Opposition to Racism, pointed to the quick and powerful response of the court, stating that "their exemplary decision and sentence is an encouragement to all who fight for a tolerant society in which equality is possible."[16]

On March 19, 2008, in **Denmark**, Deniz Özgür Uzun, a 16-year-old teenager of Turkish origin, was distributing newspapers in the Amager district of Copenhagen. He was verbally harassed by three Danish teenagers aged fifteen, seventeen and eighteen, who then began assaulting him with a baseball bat and a hammer. Deniz died the following day after having sustained severe brain damage.[17] One eyewitness reported the use of a racist slur.[18] The Turkish press immediately labeled the offence a racist attack, while the mainstream Danish press speculated whether or not the attack was racially motivated. The Danish police did not qualify the attack as a hate crime. Ove Dahl, the chief murder investigator of the Copenhagen police department, said: "I can fully refute that this murder has anything to do with racism or religion. It is purely violence for the sake of violence."[19] The three boys were arrested and faced charges of either murder or nonnegligent manslaughter. Two of the defendants, due to the fact that they were minors, were put in juvenile facilities.[20]

On the night of July 24, 2008, Nouredine Rachedi, a 30-year-old French-born statistician, was beaten by two men in Yvelines, **France**. An official medical examination diagnosed head injuries and bruising to the face and body. As of the end of August 2008, an 18-year-old was in custody under investigation for assault motivated by religious hatred. Despite Rachedi's detailed account of the attack, the anti-Muslim motivation of the assault was not initially reflected in the police report or charges. In an interview, the victim explained the attack: "They came towards me because I look like someone from the Maghreb. It is because I answered that I was Muslim that they attacked me. [This is a reflection of] the routinization of Islamophobia."[21]

The anti-Muslim bias reported in the assault on Nouredine Rachedi was reflected in criminal charges only after the victim, on the advice of his lawyer, approached the media and antidiscrimination bodies regarding the case. On August 10, an 18-year-old was in custody and under investigation for the crime of assault, "aggravated by having been committed with others and by reason of religious bias." Police said a search of his residence had found a large quantity of neo-Nazi literature. A second suspect was being sought by police.[22]

On April 26, 2007, in Kostroma in the **Russian Federation**, two youths assaulted Imam Ulugbek Abdullaev and his wife, both of whom were dressed in distinctive Islamic clothing. When one of the attackers pushed imam's wife Nadira, Abdullaev stepped in and was beaten by the two minors. Police subsequently detained the suspected attackers.[23] The imam said that the attackers shouted "go back to your Muslim country," and investigators from the Department of the Interior Ministry of the Kostroma Oblast also reported that the attackers were shouting nationalistic slogans.[24] However, the assault charges did not include a reference to the anti-Muslim motive.[25]

In **Serbia**, Mufti Muamer Zukorlić, the leader of Serbia's Muslim community, reported five death threats between December 2006 and March 2007. Zukorlić opted to hire a private bodyguard, because he reportedly could not get enough police protection at the time.[26]

On August 23, 2007, in the **United Kingdom**, in Southampton, a driver attempted to hit a 30-year-old woman wearing traditional Islamic dress and a head scarf. According to police, the man drove up to her and verbally abused her. He then left, turned the car around, and drove toward her. The woman escaped unharmed, although badly shaken by the incident.[27]

On or around May 15, 2007 in Meersbrook, Isma Din, a 23-year-old Muslim woman was repeatedly punched in the face and head while her 15-year-old female assailant screamed racial obscenities. The victim, who sustained cuts to her face and a fractured eye socket, suffered blurred and double vision and required surgery. She believed the motivation for the attack was the head scarf she was wearing.[28]

In Scotland, on September 10, 2007, a 32-year-old woman stabbed 17-year-old Tarik Husan while he was standing at a bus stop. As she stabbed him in the chest and arm, the perpetrator told the victim: "You're all terrorists." In the trial that followed, the presiding judge called the attack "completely unprovoked" and sentenced the perpetrator to six years in prison.[29]

In April 2007, in North Wales, a young man approached a Muslim woman, shouted racial slurs at her and then yanked off her veil. He was subsequently apprehended, brought before a court and charged with racially aggravated assault. The trial judge said that the offender's behavior in grabbing the hijāb had been "deplorable, despicable and quite disgraceful." After a public apology to the victim, the perpetrator was sentenced to an 18-week prison sentence suspended for two years.[30]

In April 2008, a sentence was handed down in the case of Amjid Mehmood, who was subjected to racial harassment and abuse by co-workers over a period of nine months in 2005-2006. During that time, he was publicly humiliated and threatened, force-fed bacon, set on fire, and tied to railings along a public motorway. In a subsequent trial, Mehmood told the court the abuse had "left him very depressed, suicidal and unable to sleep." The court sentenced three perpetrators, who were charged for nine separate incidents of racial harassment, to three years imprisonment. In handing down the sentence, Judge John Warner said that this was "an appalling example of racial harassment that will not be tolerated in a civilized society."[31]

On January 14, 2007, in the **United States**, in Lackawanna, New York, a 26-year old man of Yemeni ethnicity was physically assaulted by attackers who used a racist and anti-Muslim epithet during the incident. The victim was thrown to the ground, sustaining a fracture under one eye, a broken nose, and cuts requiring six stitches on his face and staples to the back of his head.[32]

On September 15, 2007, in a particularly violent anti-Muslim act in Locust Valley, New York, two men attacked 52-year-old Zohreh Assemi, a naturalized citizen from Iran who had been living and working n the United States for over twenty years. Assemi was attacked in her nail salon in an upscale neighborhood. The two attackers forced the victim into her store at gunpoint, "slammed her head on a counter, shoved a towel in her mouth, smashed her hand with a hammer and sliced her face, neck, back and chest with a knife and a box cutter" while calling her a terrorist and cursing at her. After having scrawled anti-Muslim messages on the mirrors and vandalizing the shop, they robbed Assemi. The police investigation yielded no suspects.[33]

The American-Arab Anti-Discrimination Committee (ADC) has been generally positive concerning police and prosecutorial follow-up to anti-Muslim hate crimes in the United States. In the 2008 report it concludes that "hate crimes have for the most part been thoroughly investigated by law enforcement authorities, particularly the civil rights division of the Department of Justice (DOJ). ADC commends local, state and federal law enforcement for their efforts to ensure that Arab Americans and those perceived to be Arab Americans are protected from hate crimes."[34]

III. Violent Backlash to Terrorist and Other Attacks

While incidents of violence and harassment of Muslims have become an everyday occurrence in many countries, certain events exacerbate the situation. Since 2001, foreign and domestic events have repeatedly led to periods of violent backlash against Muslims and those perceived to be Muslim in North America and Europe. In the **United States**, the Arab and South Asian communities suffered a surge in hate incidents in the immediate aftermath of the September 11 terrorist attacks. In Europe, too, terrorist attacks prompted a significant increase in hate incidents against Muslims and those perceived to be Muslim.

In 2004, the **Netherlands** was shaken when the filmmaker Theo Van Gogh was murdered in Amsterdam by a young man of immigrant origin, a Muslim who invoked the name of Islam in the killing. In the immediate aftermath of the murder, hate crime monitors at the Anne Frank House and the University of Leiden registered a dramatic rise in anti-Muslim incidents.[35]

The July 2005 bombings in London similarly served as a powerful trigger event of anti-Muslim violence in the **United Kingdom**. Nongovernmental organizations and police agencies reported a surge in anti-Muslim incidents in the immediate aftermath of the attack.

Two events in 2007 and early 2008 have served as similar trigger events. Although smaller in terms of the scale of the backlash, the terrorist acts nevertheless are a reminder of the link between domestic and international events and spikes of hate crimes against Muslims.

On June 29, 2007, in the **United Kingdom**, two cars containing homemade bombs made of gasoline, gas cylinders, and nails, failed to explode in central London.[36] The following day, two men rammed a jeep packed with propane gas canisters into the main terminal of the Glasgow International Airport. An Iraqi doctor and an Indian engineer were arrested at the airport following the failed car bombing. The attack in Glasgow and the subsequent arrest of numerous suspects of Asian and Middle Eastern descent resulted in a backlash of anti-Muslim violence. Statistics released by Scottish authorities showed a surge in anti-Muslim abuse, harassment, and violence in the four weeks following the attempted airport bombing. In the region of Strathclyde, officials recorded 258 incidents in July, up from 201 in June, "of which more than 10 percent were directly linked to the airport attack on June 30."[37] Violent incidents linked to the bombings included the following:

- In the early morning of June 30, 2007, four men reportedly jumped from a car in Blackley and attacked and stabbed Ghulam Mustafa Naz, a Muslim religious teacher, leaving him seriously wounded.[38]

- On July 3, the shop belonging to Ashfaq Ahmed was attacked. A vehicle was driven into the store's shutters but, when it failed to enter the shop, the driver attempted to set fire to the vehicle and finally threw a gas canister into the shop. The massive blast destroyed the store.[39]

- On August 3, a mosque in Bradford was seriously damaged in an arson attack.[40]

- On August 9, assailants attacked the 58-year-old imam of the Central Mosque in London's Regents Park. The victim required emergency surgery on both eyes as a result.[41]

On June 2, 2008, a car bomb exploded outside the Danish Embassy in Islamabad, Pakistan, killing six people and wounding dozens, in an attack thought to be linked to al Qaeda threats in connection to the reprinting of caricatures of the prophet Muhammad. The bombing appears to have sparked threats and acts of violence against Muslims in **Denmark**. On June 2, 2008, in Copenhagen, Kasem Said Ahmed, the former spokesperson of the Islamic Faith Society (IFS), was punched in the face after being asked if he was an imam. The victim believed the attack may have been a backlash response to the bombing of the Danish Embassy in Pakistan. That same day, the IFS reported that two women were threatened by hooded men on the way to a mosque in the Norrebro section of Copenhagen. The Islamic Faith Society says it also received hate mail demanding that it leave Denmark. In response to these attacks and threats, Per Larsen of the Copenhagen police vowed to deal with such attacks before the situation "gets out of hand and develops into something unstoppable."[42]

IV. Attacks on Places of Worship and Cemeteries

Mosques, religious buildings, and cemeteries were particular targets of vandalism and arson in 2007 and early 2008. In some incidents, religious texts were also desecrated and destroyed.

- In Graz, **Austria**, on February 5, 2008, the local police reported that close to sixty tombstones of Muslims had been desecrated. It was unclear when the attack occurred and the police have not ruled out the involvement of right-wing extremists.[43]

- In **Bulgaria**, in early April 2008, offensive graffiti was smeared on the walls of the building of the Chief Mufti's Office. Hussein Hafyzov, the Chief Secretary of the Chief Mufti's Office in Bulgaria, explained that other shrines and mosques around the country have been desecrated in the same fashion: "It has happened many times in Kazanlak, Pleven, and Varna. Our statistics reveal that our buildings—administrative ones and mosques in all twelve regional Mufti's Offices—have been desecrated over fifty times in the last ten years." Vandalism of mosques and religious buildings in Bulgaria rarely results in arrests or prosecution. Hafyzov reported that vandals were caught in only two or three occasions, and "the very few perpetrators who were caught were not convicted."[44]

- In **France**, on April 20, 2008, the Al-Salam Mosque was destroyed after it was set alight in Toulouse. Investigators and rescue officials quickly concluded that it was a deliberate act of arson. Interior Minister Michèle Alliot-Marie called it an "odious act" and stated that "all efforts will be exerted to identify the perpetrators and bring them to justice."[45] In late May, French police arrested eight people in connection with the attack.

Earlier in April 2008, 148 Muslim graves were desecrated at the country's largest war cemetery, Notre Dame de Lorette in Pas-de-Calais. The act was widely condemned by French officials, including President Nicolas Sarkozy, who has vowed to step up the fight against "Islamophobia in France."[46]

- On December 10, 2007 in Lauingen, **Germany**, an incendiary device was ignited outside a mosque. The fire was quickly extinguished, causing no damage. The following day, a mosque in the town of Lindau was defaced with neo-Nazi graffiti and swastikas. No arrests were reported in either incident.[47]

- On October 24, 2007, in **Italy**, a masked man on a motorcycle reportedly threw a firebomb into the courtyard of the Alif Baa Islamic Centre, in Abbiategrasso, near Milan, although no major damage or injuries were reported. The center experienced similar attacks earlier this year, on July 25 and August 10. This was reportedly the eighth attack on Islamic centers in the region of Lombardy in recent months. On August 5, a mosque in the nearby city of Segrate was attacked and the imam's car was destroyed.[48]

In June 2008, two handmade bombs were thrown at the Islamic Center in Milan, damaging the main gate. This was the second such attack in less than two weeks. No arrests were reported in the immediate aftermath of the incident.[49]

- In **Kosovo (Serbia)**,[50] on August 7, 2007, a mosque in the town of Shkabaj was damaged in an apparent arson attack. The previous day, two graves at a cemetery in the town of Gazimestan were desecrated. No arrests were reported in the immediate aftermath of the incident.[51]

■ On November 28, 2007, in the **Russian Federation**, a mosque was attacked in Vladimir. According to eyewitnesses, four unidentified men threw stones at windows. The mosque had been attacked several times during the past several years. Windows were broken on three occasions, and there was a case of attempted arson.[52] With regard to this latest incident, the police opened an investigation into hooliganism.[53] On January 1, 2008, in Sergiyev Posad, Moscow Oblast, a Muslim prayer house was attacked with Molotov cocktails, marking the second attack in two months. In spite of significant damage to the building as a result of the attack, the police reportedly did not open an investigation.[54]

■ On February 9, 2008, in the **United States**, members of the right-wing extremist Christian Identity Movement used Molotov cocktails to firebomb the Islamic Center in Columbia, Tennessee.[55]

V. Official Statistics on Violence Against Muslims

There continue to be few official statistics on violent hate crimes against Muslims. The **United States** is the only country that has been systematically monitoring anti-Muslim crimes over the course of many years, while such monitoring and public reporting has been conducted for the past two years in **Sweden**. In the **United Kingdom**, monitoring and reporting on "Islamo-phobic" hate crimes is most developed in London. Such statistics have been particularly useful in documenting the periodic spikes in incidents that have accompanied terrorist attacks. On June 9, 2008, the government of **Canada** released the first nationwide hate crime statistics that also included hate crimes against Muslims. Similarly, in 2007 the government of **Austria** reported on the number of crimes motivated by hatred toward Muslims. Hate crime statistics in **France** provide information about violence against Muslims through reporting on crimes targeting people of North African origin. Anti-Muslim hate crime data is not collected expressly.

While these efforts to collect data are important, the extent to which these and other hate crime statistics reflect the actual levels of bias-motivated violence against Muslims is questionable. Because hate crime against Muslims frequently contains a combination of racist and anti-religious sentiment, anti-Muslim hate crimes are not always registered as such. Instead, they may be registered as "racist," "xenophobic," or under other similar categories. For example, following the June 2008 release of the first national hate crime statistics in Canada, Imam Mohamed Elmasry, national president of the Canadian Islamic Congress, said that hate crimes against Muslims are often misfiled by police. "A Somali family who reports a hate crime, they might put it under black when it's supposed to be under Muslim. That Somali family should be under Muslim and not under black, because the motivation is really because the woman is wearing a ḥijāb. It is easier for the hate crime unit to put the report under black because it's a visible minority," reiterated Dr. Elmasry.[56]

Another problem—that of underreporting—persists throughout the region, including in countries where systems for data collection and police outreach to vulnerable communities are well-established. For example, in the aftermath of the attempted bombing at the Glasgow International Airport and subsequent backlash against Muslims, Sohaib Saeed of the Islamic Centre of Edinburgh Trust indicated that the real number of attacks was likely considerably higher than the official figures.[57]

Nonetheless, official efforts are being made in a number of countries to publicly report on anti-Muslim incidents in their countries.

In **Austria**, the Federal Agency for State Protection and Counter Terrorism of the Ministry of the Interior produces an annual security report.[58] Within the framework of right-wing extremism, the government reported 371 criminal incidents or acts. For the first time in 2007, the organization registered anti-Muslim hate crimes as a separate category, citing two incidents.[59]

On June 9, 2008, the government of **Canada** released the first national hate crime statistics for 2006. Overall, there were 892 hate-motivated crimes, of which 46 were against Muslims, including 19 classified as violent crimes. The Canadian police register crimes based on ethnicity; therefore religious motivation may have been overlooked in crimes committed against people of Arab and Western Asian descent. Of the 61 cases in this category, 30 were registered as incidents of violence.[60] In addition to the national data, a number of individual police jurisdictions have been reporting on hate crimes. For example, the Toronto Police Department reported nine registrations of hate crimes against Muslims; incidents included a bomb threat, three cases of mischief, a personal threat, and four cases of willful promotion of hatred. The number of registered incidents decreased from fifteen in 2006 to nine in 2007.[61]

In **France**, official statistics for 2007 registered 707 offenses of racist, xenophobic, or antisemitic nature, a 23.5 percent decline in comparison to 2006. Racist and xenophobic offences, which exclude those motivated by antisemitism, experienced a decline in total numbers, with a 9 percent reduction.

Although the data does not specifically refer to anti-Muslim crimes, the findings identify people of North African origin—who are largely Muslim—as the most affected by racist and xenophobic offenses, accounting for nearly 68 percent of racist violence and 60 percent of racist threats.[62]

In **Sweden**, in 2006, out of a total of 3,259 reported hate crimes, there were 252 reports of crimes with an Islamophobic motive.[63] In 2007, there was a decrease to 206 in the number of such crimes reported.[64]

In the **United Kingdom**, the London Metropolitan Police Service (MET) began registering "Islamophobic" crimes separately from "faith" hate crimes in 2006/2007. This followed a directive in 2006 by the Association of Chief Police Officers (ACPO) requesting that U.K. police start recording the religion of the victims of faith-motivated hate crimes. ACPO wanted to obtain a clear picture of community tensions nationwide after reports surfaced of attacks on Muslims after the September 11, 2001 attack and the London bombings in July 2005.[65]

From April 2007 to March 2008, the MET registered 106 Islamophobic incidents and 89 crimes. This marked a significant decrease from the previous year, when the MET registered 206 incidents and 188 crimes.[66] This dramatic decrease appears to follow an overall trend in declining faith hate crimes over the past three years (1,103 crimes in 2005/2006; 823 crimes in 2006/2007 and 521 crimes in 2007/2008).[67]

As concerns prosecutions, the Crown Prosecution Service (CPS), which covers England and Wales, reported that 27 cases were recorded as religious-aggravated incidents in 2006/2007. This represents a 37.2 percent decrease from the 2005/2006 period, when 43 defendants were charged with religious-aggravated crimes. Of these, 22 defendants (81.5 percent) were prosecuted, compared to 95.3 percent in the previous year. In 17 of the 27 cases, the victim was identified as Muslim.[68]

In the **United States**, in 2006, the FBI reported 156 incidents and 191 offenses of anti-Islamic nature, involving 208 victims.[69] The offenses included 24 aggravated assaults, 30 simple assaults, 79 cases of intimidation, 1 robbery, 5 burglaries, 51 cases involving destruction or damage to property, and 1 "other" offense. Among the 1,750 victims of hate crimes motivated by religious hatred, the 208 people who were victims of anti-Islamic prejudice represented about 12 percent of the overall number.[70]

These figures represent an increase over the figures reported by the FBI in 2005. In that year, the organization reported 128 incidents and 146 offenses involving 151 victims. These offenses included 8 aggravated assaults, 27 simple assaults, 64 cases of intimidation, 4 robberies, 3 burglaries, 2 cases of larceny-theft, 36 cases involving destruction or damage to property, and two "other" offenses. An increase could be seen in all categories except that of robbery.[71]

Comprehensive data from nongovernmental sources is generally unavailable, as very few NGOs across the region monitor and publicly report specifically on violent anti-Muslim hate crimes. Overall, the lack of reporting by either official or private sources makes it difficult to assess the official responses to such incidents by the police and in the courts.

Section Endnotes

[1] Ömür Orhun, "Incitement to Racial and Religious Hatred–Islamophobia," Cojep International Colloquium, Strasbourg, Council of Europe, Personal Representative of the OSCE Chairman-in-Office on Combating Intolerance and Discrimination Against Muslims, July 3 2007, http://www.osce.org/documents/pr/2007/07/26907_en.pdf.

[2] The OSCE Office for Democratic Institutions and Human Rights, *Hate Crimes in the OSCE Region: Incidents and Responses, Annual Report for 2006*, September 26, 2007, http://www.osce.org/publications/odihr/2007/09/26296_931_en.pdf.

[3] Thomas Hammarberg, "Hate crimes–the ugly face of racism, anti-Semitism, anti-Gypsyism, Islamophobia and homophobia," *Viewpoints*, the Council of Europe Commissioner for Human Rights, July 21, 2008, http://www.coe.int/t/commissioner/Viewpoints/080721_en.asp.

[4] Thomas Hammarberg, "Muslims are discriminated against in Europe," *Viewpoints*, the Council of Europe Commissioner for Human Rights, January 22, 2007, http://www.coe.int/t/commissioner/Viewpoints/070122_en.asp.

[5] European Commission against Racism and Intolerance, *Annual Report on ECRI's Activities: covering the period from 1 January to 31 December 2007*, May 6, 2008, http://www.coe.int/t/e/human_rights/ecri/1-ecri/1-presentation_of_ecri/4-annual_report_2007/Annual%20report%202007.pdf.

[6] European Monitoring Centre on Racism and Xenophobia, *Muslims in the European Union: Discrimination and Islamophobia*, December 18, 2006, http://eumc.europa.eu/eumc/material/pub/muslim/Manifestations_EN.pdf.

[7] European Monitoring Centre on Racism and Xenophobia, *Muslims in the European Union: Discrimination and Islamophobia*, December 18, 2006, http://eumc.europa.eu/eumc/material/pub/muslim/Manifestations_EN.pdf.

[8] Ömür Orhun, "Intolerance and Discrimination Against Muslims," Personal Representative of the OSCE Chairman-in-Office on Combating Intolerance and Discrimination Against Muslims, remarks at Mannheim Conference on Antisemitism and Islamophobia, March 15, 2007, http://www.osce.org/documents/pr/2007/03/26904_en.pdf.

[9] American-Arab Anti-Discrimination Committee, *Report on Hate Crimes and Discrimination Against Arab Americans: 2003-2007*, ADC-RI, Washington, DC: 2008, p. 10.

[10] Ömür Orhun, "Report on visit to and contacts in Finland," Personal Representative of the OSCE Chairman-in-Office on Combating Intolerance and Discrimination Against Muslims, January 25, 2008, http://www.osce.org/documents/cio/2007/12/30140_en.pdf.

[11] Nigel Morris, "Huge rise in number of racist attacks", *the Independent*, July 9, 2008, http://www.independent.co.uk/news/uk/home-news/huge-rise-in-number-of-racist-attacks-862944.html.

[12] "Czech Muslims say intolerance growing, call for reconciliation," *České Noviny*, March 29, 2008, http://www.ceskenoviny.cz/news/index_view.php?id=304700.

[13] "Covering up," *the Economist*, May 29, 2008, http://www.economist.com/world/europe/displaystory.cfm?story_id=11461714.

[14] European Commission against Racism and Intolerance, *Third Report on the Netherlands*, CRI(2008)3, February 12, 2008, http://www.coe.int/t/e/human_rights/ecri/1-ECRI/2-Country-by-country_approach/Netherlands/Netherlands_CBC_3.asp.

[15] European Commission against Racism and Intolerance, *Third Report on Ukraine*, February 12, 2008, CRI(2008)4, http://www.coe.int/t/e/human_rights/ecri/1-ecri/2-country-by-country_approach/Ukraine/.

[16] Centre for Equal Opportunities and Opposition to Racism, "Gewelddadig geval van racisme: 15 maanden gevangenis Belgium," http://www.diversiteit.be/index.php?action=artikel_detail&artikel=41.

[17] Hadi Yahmid, "Danish Islamophobia Kills Muslim Teen," *IslamOnline.net*, March 24, 2008, http://www.islamonline.net/servlet/Satellite?c=Article_C&cid=1203758361910&pagename=Zone-English-News/NWELayout.

[18] "Racistisk overfald, siger øjenvidne," *DR Nyheder*, March 21, 2008, http://www.dr.dk/Nyheder/Indland/kriminalitet/2008/03/21/190000.htm.

[19] Frederik Roed, "Islamisk Råd: Had til islam dræbte avisbud," *Avisen.dk*, March 28, 2008, http://avisen.dk/islamisk-raad-had-til-islam-draebte-avisbud_9168.aspx.

[20] Rasmus Karkov, "Drengen der måtte slå ihjel," *Avisen.dk*, April 1, 2008, http://avisen.dk/drengen-der-maatte-slaa-ihjel_7261.aspx; and Niels Kvale, "Hjemmeside: Dansk islamofobi dræbte avisbud," *DR Nyheder*, March 12, 2008, http://www.dr.dk/Nyheder/Indland/2008/03/27/061038.htm.

[21] Caroline Vigoureux, "Nouredine Rachedi, 'tabassé parce que musulman,'" *Rue89*, August 9, 2008, http://www.rue89.com/2008/08/09/nouredine-rachedi-tabasse-parce-que-musulman.

[22] Luc Bronner. "Un jeune proche de l'extrême droite mis en examen pour une agression antimusulmane," *le Monde*, August 13, 2008, http://www.lemonde.fr/cgi-bin/ACHATS/acheter.cgi?offre=ARCHIVES&type_item=ART_ARCH_30J&objet_id=1047031&clef=ARC-TRK-G_01.

[23] Union of Councils for Jews in the Former Soviet Union, "In Kostroma, Youths Assault Imam and Pregnant Wife," *the Bigotry Monitor*, vol. 7, no. 18, May 4, 2007, http://www.fsumonitor.com/stories/050407BM.shtml.

[24] Olga Verner, "Zamechanie Zametili," *Kasparov.Ru*, March 5, 2007, http://www.kasparov.ru/material.php?id=463A23B303E76.

[25] "Prokuratura ne nashla priznakov natsionalizma v dejstviyah podrostkov, izbivshih imama," *IA Regnum*, April 5, 2007, http://www.regnum.ru/news/823198.html?forprint.

[26] Drasko Djenovic, "Serbia: Violence continues against religious communities," Forum 18, October 9, 2007, http://www.forum18.org/Archive.php?article_id=1030.

[27] "Driver Attempts to Run Woman Over," *BBC News*, August 21, 2007, http://news.bbc.co.uk/2/hi/uk_news/england/hampshire/6972201.stm.

[28] Sarah Dunn, "Isma beaten by racist, 15," *the Star*, May 16, 2007, http://www.thestar.co.uk/news?articleid=2878108.

[29] "Stab woman made terrorist claim," *BBC News*, February 13, 2008, http://news.bbc.co.uk/2/hi/uk_news/scotland/glasgow_and_west/7242727.stm.

[30] "Thug who ripped off Muslim's veil spared jail," *Daily Post*, November 2, 2007, http://www.dailypost.co.uk/news/north-wales-news/2007/11/02/thug-who-ripped-off-muslim-s-veil-spared-jail-55578-20051330/.

[31] "Colleagues jailed for race abuse", *BBC News*, 17 April 2008, http://news.bbc.co.uk/2/hi/uk_news/england/west_midlands/7352935.stm.

[32] "Hate crimes against Arabs and Muslims surge nationwide," *the Arab-American News*, January 27, 2007, http://www.arabamericannews.com/newsarticle.php?articleid=7457.

[33] "Police probe anti-Muslim attack at Long Island salon; woman beaten," *the International Herald Tribune*, September 16, 2007, http://www.iht.com/articles/ap/2007/09/16/america/NA-GEN-US-Bias-Attack.php

[34] American-Arab Anti-Discrimination Committee, *Report on Hate Crimes and Discrimination Against Arab Americans: 2003-2007*, ADC-RI, Washington, DC: 2008, p. 10.

[35] Categories of incidents registered include targeted graffiti, threats, bomb threats, confrontations between groups of Dutch-origin and non-Dutch-origin minority youths, destruction of property, arson, assault, bomb attacks and homicide. See Michael McClintock, *Everyday Fears: A Survey of Violent Hate Crimes in Europe and North America*, Human Rights First, September 13, 2005, http://www.humanrightsfirst.org/discrimination/pdf/everyday-fears-080805.pdf.

[36] "Friday 29 June: Failed Car Bomb Attacks in London," *BBC News*, June 29, 2007, http://news.bbc.co.uk/2/hi/uk_news/6260626.stm.

[37] Richard Elias, "Race Attacks Soar After Terror Strike," *Scotland on Sunday*, August 12, 2007, http://scotlandonsunday.scotsman.com/latestnews/Race-attacks-soar-after-terror.3315991.jp.

[38] James Rush, "Mosque fire treated as arson," *Telegraph and Argus*, August 4, 2007, http://www.thetelegraphandargus.co.uk/mostpopular.var.1596062.mostviewed.mosque_fire_treated_as_arson.php.

[39] Richard Elias, "Race Attacks Soar After Terror Strike," *Scotland on Sunday*, August 12, 2007, http://scotlandonsunday.scotsman.com/latestnews/Race-attacks-soar-after-terror.3315991.jp.

[40] Henry Lee and Marisa Lagos, "Muslim leaders call Antioch mosque fire 'act of terror,'" *San Francisco Chronicle*, August 13, 2007, http://www.sfgate.com/cgi-bin/article.cgi?f=/c/a/2007/08/13/BAGKRRHRLH9.DTL.

[41] Nigel Morris, "Imam Attacked as Anti-Muslim Violence Grows," *the Independent*, August 14, 2007, http://news.independent.co.uk/uk/crime/article2861744.ece; and Karima Hamdan, "The Tragic Consequences of Demonizing Muslims," *Umma Pulse*, August 13, 2007, http://ummahpulse.com/index.php?option=com_content&task=view&id=181&Itemid=37.

[42] "Denmark: Three Muslims attacked after embassy bombing," *Islam in Europe*, June 4, 2008, http://islamineurope.blogspot.com/2008/06/denmark-three-muslims-attacked-after.html.

[43] "Vandals Destroy Dozens of Muslim Graves in Southern Austrian City of Graz," *Fox News*, February 5, 2008, http://www.foxnews.com/story/0,2933,328627,00.html.

[44] Emil Cohen, "Following another desecration of a Muslim building the institutions remain silent," *Obektiv*, Issue 153, April 2008, http://www.bghelsinki.org/obektiv/2008/153/153-07.pdf.

[45] Hadi Yahmid, "Who Burned Toulouse Mosque," *IslamOnline.net*, April 21, 2008, http://www.islamonline.net/servlet/Satellite?c=Article_C&cid=1203759225407&pagename=Zone-English-News%2FNWELayout.

[46] "France arrests 8 over mosque attack," *Press TV*, May 28, 2008, http://www.presstv.ir/detail.aspx?id=57720&sectionid=351020603.

[47] "Neo-Nazi graffiti defaces mosque in Germany," *the Earth Times*, December 11, 2007, http://www.earthtimes.org/articles/show/156694.html.

[48] "Italy: Eighth mosque attacked in northern region of Lombardy," *Adkronos International*, October 25, 2007, http://www.adnkronos.com/AKI/English/Religion/?id=1.0.1472225001.

[49] "Attacks against Islamic Center in Italy," *Islamouna*, June 16, 2008, http://www.islamouna.info/English/Default.aspx?tabid=806.

[50] Kosovo unilaterally declared independence in February 2008 and gained recognition by many European states; see the United Nations Security Council Resolution 1244.

[51] Radio Free Europe/Radio Liberty, "Mosque Attacked In Kosovo," *RFE/RL Newsline*, vol. 11, no. 147, August 10, 2007, http://www.rferl.org/newsline/2007/08/4-SEE/see-100807.asp.

[52] Interfax, "Vladimir mosque attack is not pre-election provocation—Council of Muftis," *Interfax-Religion*, November 29, 2007, http://www.interfax-religion.com/?act=news&div=4003.

[53] "Natsionalisty zakidali kamnyami mechet' vo Vladimire," *Novye Izvestiya*, November 11, 2007, http://www.newizv.ru/lenta/80692.

[54] Union of Councils for Jews in the Former Soviet Union, "Muslim Prayer House Near Moscow Firebombed," *the Bigotry Monitor*, vol. 8, no. 2, January 11, 2008, http://listserv.shamash.org/cgi-bin/wa?A2=ind0801&L=BIGOTRYMONITOR&P=711.

[55] Chris Ecehgaray, "Officials: Men admit to varied roles in mosque fire," *the Tennessean*, February 28, 2008, http://archive2.newsfeeds.com/soc/Officials__Men_admit_to_varied_roles_in_mosque_fire12746608.html.

[56] Becky Rynor and Amy Husser, "Hate crime study wrong, says Muslim leader," *Canwest News Service*, June 9, 2008, http://www.canada.com/topics/news/national/story.html?id=0fd82f6a-9dde-4cd6-9f1a-a8c9da0f0647.

[57] Richard Elias, "Race Attacks Soar After Terror Strike," *Scotland on Sunday*, August 12, 2007, http://scotlandonsunday.scotsman.com/latestnews/Race-attacks-soar-after-terror.3315991.jp.

[58] The Federal Ministry for the Interior of Austria, *Verfassungschutzbericht 2007*, Bundesamt für Verfassungsschutz und Terrorismusbekämpfung (Federal Agency for State Protection and Counter Terrorism), http://www.bmi.gv.at/staatsschutz.

[59] Human Rights First Correspondence with Austrian Interior Ministry, August 22, 2008.

[60] Canadian Centre for Justice Statistics, *Hate Crime in Canada 2006*, June 9, 2008, http://www.statcan.ca/english/research/85F0033MIE/85F0033MIE2008017.pdf.

[61] Toronto Police Service, Hate Crime Unit, Intelligence Division, *2007 Annual Hate/Bias Crime Statistical Report*, http://www.torontopolice.on.ca/publications/files/reports/2007hatecrimereport.pdf.

[62] Commission Nationale Consultative des Droits de l'Homme, *La Lutte Contre le Racisme et la Xénophobie: Rapport d'activité 2007*, Paris: 2008, http://lesrapports.ladocumentationfrancaise.fr/BRP/084000167/0000.pdf.

[63] The Swedish National Council for Crime Prevention, (Brottsförebyggande rådet - Brå), *Hate Crime*, http://www.bra.se/extra/pod/?action=pod_show&id=53&module_instance=11.

[64] The Swedish National Council for Crime Prevention (Brottsförebyggande rådet - Brå), *Hate crime 2007*, http://www.bra.se/extra/measurepoint/?module_instance=4&name=Hatbrott_2007_webb.pdf&url=/dynamaster/file_archive/080627/4a35a31f178add58672ff57f0fcdb92c/Hatbrott%255f2007%255fwebb.pdf.

[65] Tom Harper and Ben Leapman, "Jews far more likely to be victims of faith hatred than Muslims," *the Sunday Telegraph*, December 17, 2006, http://www.telegraph.co.uk/news/main.jhtml?xml=/news/2006/12/17/nislam117.xml.

[66] Human Rights First Correspondence with David McNaghten, Detective Sergeant, Violent Crimes Directorate of the Metropolitin Police Service, United Kingdom, June 4, 2008.

[67] Metropolitan Police Service, "Hate Crime," *Communities Together*, No. 112, January 16, 2008, http://www.met.police.uk/communities_together/docs/bulletin_112.pdf.

[68] Crown Prosecution Service, *Racist and Religious Incident Monitoring Annual Report 2006-2007*, December 2006, http://www.cps.gov.uk/publications/docs/rims06-07.pdf.

[69] U.S. Department of Justice, Federal Bureau of Investigation, Criminal Justice Information Services Division, *Hate Crime Statistics, 2006*, Fall 2007, http://www.fbi.gov/ucr/hc2006/table1.html.

[70] U.S. Department of Justice, Federal Bureau of Investigation, Criminal Justice Information Services Division, *Hate Crime Statistics, 2006*, Fall 2007, http://www.fbi.gov/ucr/hc2006/victims.html.

[71] U.S. Department of Justice, Federal Bureau of Investigation, Criminal Justice Information Services Division, *Hate Crime Statistics, 2005*, Fall 2006, http://www.fbi.gov/ucr/hc2005/table4.htm.

Violence Based on Religious Intolerance

Table of Contents

Executive Summary

Violence motivated by religious intolerance continued to be reported in many countries in Europe and North America in 2007 and 2008. Members of religious minorities throughout the region were subjected to numerous physical assaults causing serious injury or death. Adherents of religions deemed by governments to be nontraditional in Eastern Europe and the former Soviet Union, including Jehovah's Witnesses, Roman Catholics, Seventh Day Adventists, Evangelical Protestants, minority Orthodox Christians, and members of the Church of Jesus Christ of Latter-day Saints, were among those targeted for violence, sometimes in the context of government restrictions on religious activities and official rhetoric that vilifies such groups. In the United States, violent attacks on religious institutions sometimes combined antipathy toward particular confessions with hatred motivated by the racial makeup of their congregations.

High levels of violent attacks against Jews synagogues, and other Jewish sites continue across Europe and North America, combining both religious intolerance and racism. Antisemitic hate crimes are addressed in a separate section of the *2008 Hate Crime Survey*: ***Antisemitic Violence***.

Anti-Muslim violence, which includes violence motivated by religious intolerance as well as racist and anti-immigrant bias, was also present in many of the countries covered in this report. These and other patterns of violence towards Muslims are discussed in another section: ***Violence Against Muslims***.

This section addresses violence against adherents and property of other vulnerable religious minorities. In some countries, members of minority religions are subject to violent attacks, reflecting longstanding tensions between minority religious groups and the majority religious community. In other cases, adherents of religions that are new or are perceived to be new in a particular area are the targets of violence.

Government officials are not always neutral with regard to such tensions and disputes, and may exacerbate them or create the atmosphere in which violent acts take place, as well as influencing the way such violent acts are addressed by the authorities. In several countries discussed here, governments have enforced restrictions on religious activity, specifically targeting minority religious groups and beliefs. In extreme cases, religious activities that are not approved by the authorities are criminalized, while official approval of religious activities by some groups is arbitrarily withheld. Government security forces and law enforcement officials have harassed or committed other abuses against persons engaged in religious activities, forcefully breaking up religious services, confiscating property, and fining or detaining religious leaders and other participants.

With or without such government action, officials at times condone or fail to refute vilification against some religious minority groups in the state or private media. In particularly egregious cases, law enforcement officials participate in attacks or fail to intervene and provide protection to members of religious minorities.

I. Violence Based on Religious Intolerance

A. Violence Against Individuals

In many countries of Eastern and Southeastern Europe and in the Russian Federation, nationalists promote the view of a people united by its ethnic origins and its unitary Church. The fusion of a religious identity with nationalist ethnic ideals has led to the exclusion of those who do not share this identity. As a consequence, the so-called nontraditional religions are under attack by governments and extreme nationalists alike. Government officials and extremist groups often use the same rhetoric against nontraditional religious groups, accusing the latter of being dangers to the nation's future and even agents of foreign powers. This view can be heightened by the presence of religious groups that are new, or perceived to be new, to a particular place, especially as a result of the new freedoms following the fall of communism in Eastern Europe and the former Soviet Union.

In a climate of xenophobia and religious chauvinism, the pastors, priests, rabbis, or imams of minority religious congregations are particularly susceptible to threats and physical attacks in some countries, as they face, in some countries, official harassment or even imprisonment. Visiting religious workers of foreign nationality, if permitted access, may also be subject to the same harassment, threats, and violence to which citizens are subjected, as well as summary deportation and the denial of visas.

Many individuals were particularly vulnerable because they were readily identified as members of minority religions: some were attacked during religious services, or en route to and from places of worship. Others included religious minority children in state schools. People who stood out because of distinctive dress, religious headgear, or other characteristics were attacked in the street by strangers shouting epithets. Members of religions for which missionary work is integral to their faith were also particularly vulnerable to attack:

- In **Armenia**, on March 29, 2007, a Jehovah's Witness was reportedly attacked and choked at his workplace after a coworker learned of his religious adherence.[1]

- In **Azerbaijan**, four men on April 17, 2007, broke into a building Jehovah's Witnesses rented for religious meetings in Baku and attacked two members of the congregation and property; although witnesses identified the attackers, police reportedly refused to investigate.[2]

- In the **Russian Federation**, on July 5, 2007, unidentified young men attacked worshippers in a Baptist church with pepper gas during a service in Kirovo-Chepetsk (Kirov Oblast); the same church was repeatedly vandalized during the year.[3]

- In Malatya, **Turkey**, on April 18, 2007, a group of young men claiming to be defending Islam and Turkish nationalism bound, tortured, and killed Necati Aydın, Uğur Yüksel, and Tillman Geske—who were employees of a Christian publishing house.

- In the **United States**, on May 24, 2007, a fellow student attacked 16-year-old Harpal Vacher, a Sikh, at Newtown High School in New York City. The attacker dragged Vacher into a bathroom, pulled off his turban, and sheared off his waist-length hair.[4] In June, the New York-based civil rights organization Sikh Coalition said that at least 60 percent of Sikh students "suffered harassment in one form or another because of their religious symbols."[5]

Members of majority religions were also the object of attacks motivated by religious hatred:

■ On March 12, in London, **United Kingdom**, two young people described as of Asian origin attacked 57-year-old Anglican priest Canon Michael Ains-worth, at St. George-in-the-East Church, in what police described as a "faith hate" crime. The two reportedly "jeered at the priest for being a church-man," while inflicting bruises and cuts in severe beating.[6]

B. Vandalism and Attacks on Property

The perpetrators of violent hate crimes motivated by religious hatred have also targeted places of worship, community centers, schools, and other community institutions. They also routinely targeted burial sites.

In several countries of Europe and North America attackers painted threatening graffiti and smashed windows in churches, temples, and other religious assembly halls, thereby expressing hatred and prejudice toward minority religions. These centers of religious activity are easily targeted and are often the most visible signs of a religious congregation's presence in a particular area. These attacks echo similar incidents targeting Jewish and Muslim religious property that are discussed in sections of the *2008 Hate Crime Survey* on *Antisemitic Violence* and *Violence Against Muslims*.

In **Greece,** on February 20, 2007, in Menidi, Athens, vandals threw three Molotov cocktails at a Jehovah's Witnesses Kingdom Hall. A police investigation led to no arrests.[7]

In the **Russian Federation**, places of worship were attacked during services or targeted at night for vandalism and arson:

■ On July 11, 2008, arson completely destroyed a Jehovah's Witnesses' place of worship in Chekhov, Moscow Oblast. According to a member of the

congregation, who led the efforts to salvage the building at four o'clock in the morning, the fire started with an explosion, and the flame spread rapidly through the entire building because the foundation was soaked with a flammable liquid. Jehovah's Witnesses' representatives were dissatis-fied with the hesitant response by police and firefighters. Local police have reportedly refused to open an official investigation following the inci-dent.[8]

■ In March 2007, attackers partially destroyed an Assembly of God Church in Moscow, setting off a blaze that destroyed the roof and much of the inte-rior with an explosive device. The congregation had received numerous threats and local authorities had refused to register the property as belonging to the church.[9]

■ In February 2007, a young man firebombed a Jehovah's Witnesses center in Kuybyshev, Novosi-birsk Oblast.[10]

■ Attackers twice set fire to a Catholic chapel in the Krasnodar region during 2007.[11]

In **Serbia**, on January 8, 2007, in Stapar, arsonists attacked an Adventist Church with a Molotov cocktail, causing serious damage to the interior; the fire department took action in time to save the building. President Boris Tadić mentioned the incident in his national address, saying that such acts must be stopped.[12]

In the **United States**, in attacks in April, 2007, vandals in Stafford, Virginia broke windows at the Union Bell Baptist Church and daubed racial slurs on its walls; vandals also defaced the Strong Tower Ministries Church with racist and antireligious graffiti. Police investigated the incidents as hate crimes and detained four students as suspects.[13]

C. Desecration of Burial Sites

The desecration of graves and cemeteries of religious minority communities was also reported throughout Europe and North America. Bias-driven vandals painted slogans on tombstones monuments and smashed them with hammers or explosives. Dozens of examples of such vandalism and desecration of graves and memorials are documented in sections of this *Survey* on ***Antisemitic Violence*** and ***Violence Against Muslims***. Some additional examples of acts of vandalism against the property of minority religious groups include the following:

In the **Russian Federation**, in early March, 2007, vandals shattered some 30 Jewish and Lutheran gravestones at Ekaterinburg's city cemetery.[14] In May 2007, vandals daubed swastikas on some 40 Armenian gravestones in Krasnokumsky, Russia (Stavropol Krai). Police detained four suspects, accused of "mocking the bodies of the dead and their places of burial."[15]

In **Kosovo**[16] **(Serbia)**, members of the Orthodox Serbian minority required the protection of the U.N. and Kosovo police military escorts to visit cemeteries in Albanian majority areas. Serb grave markers were routinely toppled or smashed. Serbs, who visited family graves in the cemetery in the Albanian part of Mitrovica in March 2008, said an estimated 80 percent of the Orthodox tombstones there—numbering more than 500—had been vandalized since 1999.[17] On May 30, 2007, in a rare official acknowledgement, police confirmed that gravestones had been damaged at an Orthodox cemetery in Prizren.[18]

Minority Armenian communities in Eastern Europe have suffered similar attacks—with gravestones identified with the Armenian Apostolic Church singled out for graffiti or destruction.

II. Government Hostility Toward Targets of Violence

Patterns of religiously motivated violence and prejudice often occur against a backdrop of official policies of discrimination and intolerance. Governments in some countries deny religious communities legal status, bar the construction or rental of places of worship, deny permits for cemeteries, and place restrictions on freedom of assembly, while subjecting members of religious minorities to harassment, public vilification by state officials or in the state media, arrests, beatings, and imprisonment.

Intolerance toward minority religions has, in some countries, been endorsed by local or national officials, and may be accompanied by violent police actions suppressing religious freedom. In some cases, police have actively collaborated with violent mobs to harm members of minority religions.

In several countries government officials deny the right to freedom of assembly and the right to build a place of worship to members of minority religious communities, while local authorities bar groups from renting premises for worship. Thus, religious minorities, notably Jehovah's Witnesses and evangelical Christian churches, find obstacles to finding a place for their religious practices. Often the result is that worship services must be held in private homes. But such arrangements—not always legal—make individuals from these congregations vulnerable to attacks by their neighbors, as well as police harassment and raids.

■ In the **Russian Federation**, national and local officials have encouraged public antipathy toward nontraditional religions, which are sometimes characterized as harmful "cults" and denounced as foreign-supported representatives of external interests. In August 2007, for example, Governor Vyacheslav Dudka of Tula Oblast described adherents of the Church of Jesus Christ of Latter-day Saints and Jehovah's Witnesses as part of a "religious expansion into Russia, stimulated by foreign intelligence agencies."[19]

■ In **Serbia**, monitors reported an increase in vandalism at Baptist, Adventist, and other Protestant churches, in the context of news media campaigns characterizing these faiths as malicious sects.[20] The Council of Europe's European Commission against Racism and Intolerance (ECRI), in a 2008 report, concludes that Serbia's Law on Churches and Religious Communities "helps create a negative climate for the so-called untraditional religious communities, such as Jehovah's witnesses and certain Evangelical groups," which is exacerbated by some leaders of the dominant church.[21]

In some countries, religious majorities have played a role in the exclusion of minority religious groups, including by stigmatizing minority faith and belief communities and by pressing governments for measures to restrict their activities.

■ In **Armenia**, a number of incidents were reported in which clergy of the majority Armenian Apostolic Church assaulted members of minority religious groups with impunity. On June 1, 2007, in Lusarat, an Armenian Church priest reportedly harassed and physically assaulted two Jehovah's Witnesses in a public square. On August 21, 2006, a priest reportedly assaulted two female Jehovah's Witnesses, breaking the arm of one of them; police reportedly suspended a criminal investigation into the assault on the grounds that the priest had expressed remorse.[22]

- In **Serbia**, ECRI's 2008 country report noted that government hostility toward minority religions had been exacerbated by leaders of the majority Serbian Orthodox Church, noting that some dignitaries of the church "have had a part in fostering hostility towards these groups, which they refer to as 'cults,' accusing their followers of being 'satanists.'"[23]

III. Review of Religious Intolerance in Select Countries

Kyrgyzstan

In Kyrgyzstan, the government does not officially support any religion. However, a May 6, 2006 decree recognized Islam, the religion of the majority, and Russian Orthodoxy as traditional religious groups.[24] Members of some minority—nontraditional—religions have been denied the right to bury their dead in cemeteries controlled by local administrations, where burials are permitted in accord with Islamic ritual alone. Protestant families seeking to bury relatives in local cemeteries have been attacked by mobs and denied access to cemeteries by public authorities.

Protests were made by Protestant leaders over an incident in May 2008, in the village of Kulanak (Ysyk-Kol Oblasty). A mob armed with farm implements halted the funeral of a 14-year-old boy from a Baptist family and refused to allow his burial at the local cemetery. The mob subsequently went to the dead boy's home to threaten and beat mourners. Police arrived, but, according to one witness, stood by as a member of the mob "was hitting the believers and the father." Police then broke into the house and "took away the body of the boy despite the tears and crying in despair of the family members." Police reportedly took the boy's body and buried him in a shallow grave some 40 kilometers from the village. The family said it was subsequently under pressure to leave the community.[25] Representatives of the Russian Orthodox Church reportedly assured Protestant representatives at a meeting on July 2, 2008, that Baptists and members of other Christian denominations could bury their dead in Orthodox cemeteries. However, most local cemeteries banned the burials of non-Muslims.[26]

Russian Federation

While adherents of officially designated traditional religions in Russia—Orthodox Christianity, Islam, Judaism, and Buddhism—continue to be victimized by violent ultranationalists, an increasingly high level of violence was directed toward nontraditional religions.[27] In many regions of Russia, attacks targeted representatives of minority Christian denominations associated with the West. Frequent victims included members of various Protestant churches including Evangelical and Reformed Christians, Roman Catholics, and the Church of Jesus Christ of Latter-day Saints. The SOVA Center for Information and Analysis reported six attacks on Protestant churches, two on Catholic churches, as well as one attack on a Jehovah's Witnesses meeting hall and one on a Mormon church in 2007.[28]

Harassment and violence against members of minority religions and faith communities in Russia occurred in the context of public policies and pronouncements restricting the freedom of religion of those professing so-called nontraditional faiths. These included often arbitrary and overly burdensome registration requirements, restrictions on building permits for places of worship, formal or informal bans on the rental of places of assembly for religious services, and sporadic public statements by political leaders denouncing minority faiths.

The SOVA Center observed in a March 2008 report that government and law enforcement officials frequently made negative statements "about representatives of Protestant churches and new religious movements," the latter usually described by officials, media, and the public as nontraditional religions or "totalitarian sects."

In official rhetoric against these "new movements" and nontraditional faiths—including Baptists, Roman Catholics, and Pentecostals—the public officials emphasized their "alien nature" and foreign funding, while accusing these groups of espionage. The public discourse of hostility toward minority religions, official discrimination that limits the rights of freedom of religion, and the government's failure to protect religious minorities combines to send a message throughout Russian society that, in the SOVA Center's view, "religious inequality is a norm of public life," further encouraging religious intolerance and violence.[29]

The SOVA Center has also suggested that violence against religious minorities was exacerbated by an expectation of impunity for such crimes. For example, on the night of January 6, 2007, young people stormed the headquarters of a Latter-day Saints church in Samara, smashing windows and throwing smoke bombs.[30] The SOVA Center argued that the incident showed that extremist groups were confident they could act with impunity: a statement of the extreme nationalist Eurasian Union of Youths (ESM) took credit for the attack, as well as an assault on the office of the Russian Family Planning Association in Orenburg. The statement declared that ESM would continue to bring pressure against the "sectarians," and that "acts of vandalism are extremely important for the building of a sovereign democracy and a healthy civil society in Russia." No investigation into the organization's role in the incidents was reported by law enforcement agencies.[31]

A number of incidents were reported in 2007 and 2008 in which members of other minority religions and their places of worship and assembly were the targets of hate-motivated violence:

■ In September 2007 in the Voronezh Oblast, classmates beat David Perov, a first grade school student whose father is a pastor at the local Christ Community Protestant Church, "for refusing to take part in an Orthodox prayer led by a priest whose son was David's classmate."[32]

■ In August 2007, three young men attacked the Orthodox Cultural and Educational Center in Istrinskiy District (Moscow Oblast), assaulting the building supervisor and breaking windows after apparently mistaking the building for a Jehovah's Witness facility. "The Center staff tried to convince the attackers to stop the destruction, but the young men said that they had come from Moscow specifically to beat the 'Jehovists.'"[33]

Arson attacks, in addition to those already cited, included the setting on fire in November 2007 of the home of the rector of a Roman Catholic church in Arkhangelsk—St. Elijah's Cathedral—and, in December, the burning of a Catholic chapel in the village of Stanitsa Leningradskaya in the Krasnodar Krai.[34]

Vandals also targeted cemeteries and monuments in the Russian Federation, with antireligious hatred motivating attacks on minority faiths as well as on Russian Orthodox churches and sites. For example, vandals in Saint Petersburg twice damaged crosses at the construction site of an Orthodox cathedral, in June and September 2007. Incidents of antireligious vandalism were reported at six Orthodox churches and a number of Orthodox cemeteries across Russia during the year.[35]

Limited progress in police investigations into the types of incidents described above was reported in the Russian Federation, with prosecutions going forward in a number of arson attacks on places of worship in past years. In Novgorod, in February, a man accused of burning down a Seventh-day Adventist Church in September 2003 was convicted on charges of "intentional destruction of a property." He was sentenced to two years imprisonment.[36]

Serbia

In the annual survey of attacks on religious communities in Serbia, covering September 2006 to September 2007, the monitoring group Forum 18 said attacks were more violent and increasingly directed at individuals, although the overall number of attacks declined. It said police "continue to be apparently unwilling to protect members of religious minorities or religious sites at risk of attack—even if they have already been attacked.' The report found that, notwithstanding a number of robberies of places of worship of the Serbian Orthodox Church, "the vast majority of attacks have been on Protestant, Catholic, Muslim, Jewish, Jehovah's Witness, and other religious minority individuals and property." There are seven traditional religious communities in Serbia: the Serbian Orthodox Church, the Muslim community, the Roman Catholic Church, the Slovak Evangelical Church, the Jewish community, the Reform Christian Church, and the Evangelical Christian Church. Additionally, six nontraditional religious groups received legal status from the Religion Ministry: the Seventh-day Adventists, United Methodist Church, Church of Jesus Christ of Latter-day Saints (Mormons), Evangelical Church of Serbia, Church of Christ's Love, and Christ's Spiritual Church.[37]

Forum 18 stressed reluctance by many religious communities to report attacks to the police or to make public the fact of such attacks. In some cases, smaller traditional communities that have been attacked have denied being victims of bias-motivated violence—with a view to avoiding the stigma of a church under attack. A new religion law categorizes religious communities either as traditional or nontraditional, and some smaller communities classified as traditional have told monitors "they want to follow the lead of the Orthodox and Catholics in not often publicly discussing attacks."

A number of incidents in Serbia in 2007 included physical assaults:

- On March 28, 2007 a resident of Stari Banovci (Srem District) held at gunpoint two Jehovah's Witness missionaries, Austrian Wolfgang Hrdina and American Christopher Kunicki, threatening and insulting them for 45 minutes. The same individual reportedly smashed the windshield of Hrdina's car, and on April 10 he beat Hrdina about the head and kicked him until passersby came to the victim's aid. It is not known whether prosecutors have investigated the case.[38]

In its 2008 annual report, Amnesty International criticized Serbia for continued "ethnically and politically motivated attacks." The report cited an attack on Života Milanović, a member of the Hare Krishna religious community in Jagodina:

> [Milanović] who had been assaulted five times since 2001, was in June 2007 stabbed in the stomach, arms and legs. In November, the NGO Youth Initiative for Human Rights applied on his behalf to the European Court of Human Rights in respect of Serbia's failure to protect the right to life, provide an efficient legal remedy, and ensure freedom from torture and discrimination.[39]

Other incidents in Serbia in 2007 cited by Forum 18, apart from those in Kosovo, included arson attacks and vandalism of places of worship and the homes of religious leaders:

- On September 23, in Batajnica, the façade and entrance door of a new Jehovah's Witness Kingdom Hall was damaged by vandals immediately after it opened. One day later, a police inspector began a series of public lectures sponsored by the local Serbian Orthodox Church about dangerous "sects."

- On the night of September 16, in Kraljevo, vandals daubed the slogan "Stop Sects" on an Evangelical (Pentecostal) church and an Adventist church.

- On May 29, unknown attackers threw stones at an Adventist church in Novi Sad, breaking two windows and shutters. There were also traces of fire damage.

- On March 29, unknown attackers threw stones at the Vojvodina headquarters of an Adventist church in Novi Sad, breaking four windows.

- On the night of March 18, in Sombor, attackers smashed windows at the home of the Adventist pastor, with one stone landing "near the bed of two of his young sons." Police said the attacker was identified, but he was not charged with committing a religiously motivated crime.

- Vandals in early January attacked a Brethren church, in Sremska Mitrovica, breaking windows and damaging a door and an interior wall.

- On January 8, in Stapar, arsonists attacked an Adventist Church with a Molotov cocktail, causing serious damage to the interior; the fire department took action in time to save the building.[40]

Other reported incidents of vandalism at Adventist churches included a July 9, 2007, case in which an Adventist Church in Belgrade was plastered with stickers with the slogan "Sects are Death for the Serbian nation." Adventist churches in Sombor, Stapari, Kikinda, and Ruma were reportedly the object of attacks by vandals prior to the Belgrade incident.[41]

Kosovo[42]

Attacks on Serbian Orthodox religious sites occurred in **Kosovo**, which unilaterally declared independence in February 2008 and gained recognition by many European states. Attacks were made on Orthodox churches and cemeteries associated with the Serbian minority as well as ethnic Serbs participating in Orthodox religious rites.

- On March 2, 2007, two juveniles were detained on suspicion of involvement in vandalism at the Orthodox cemetery in Obliliq.

- On August 17, 2007, vandals defaced the cross on the gate of Orthodox Church in Gjilan, and wrote racist slogans on its walls, including "Death for all Serbs."

- On May 30, 2007, five young teenagers were detained for damaging an Orthodox church in Prizren; Kosovo police said the vandalism was not classified as "hate-motivated" but was carried out for "financial gain."

In other incidents, buses carrying members of the Orthodox Serb minority within Kosovo were targeted with stones. In one case, on November 7, 2007, police said young Kosovo Albanians blocked a road in Suchice village, Pristina, while Kosovo Serbs were celebrating a religious festival in the nearby church. No charges were brought against the three suspects in the case, reportedly because of their age.[43]

Amnesty International found that "fear of inter-ethnic attacks restricted the freedom of movement of Serbs and Roma in Kosovo," while the perpetrators of attacks were rarely brought to justice:

> Buses carrying Serb passengers were stoned by Albanian youths; grenades or other explosive devices were thrown at buses or houses. Orthodox churches continued to be looted or vandalized, including in an attack with a rocket-propelled grenade on the Orthodox monastery in Dečan.[44]

The Kosovo Police Service (KPS) spokesman in August 2007 said attacks on religious and cultural sites increased in 2007, with 52 attacks recorded as of that date, but that "the majority of these incidents have criminal activity, rather than ethnic intolerance, as motive and background." The KPS claimed to have solved 18 of the crimes.[45]

Turkey

The right to freedom of religion is provided by the Constitution and is "generally respected by the government."[46] While most religious groups in Turkey recognize that conditions for religious freedom have improved in the past decade, some Muslim and Christian religious minorities continue to experience restrictions on religious freedom. For many non-Muslim groups—particularly the Greek and Armenian Orthodox communities who have long existed in Turkey—these restrictions include "state policies and actions that effectively prevent [them] from sustaining themselves by denying them the right to own and maintain property, to train religious clergy, and to offer religious education above high school."[47]

Despite the legal safeguards, societal abuses and discrimination based on religious intolerance occur in Turkey, mainly affecting non-Muslim communities—who represent less than one percent of the Turkish population. Although all non-Muslim groups have been victims of bias-motivated violence in the past, in recent years, predominantly affected are those groups, such as the relatively new Protestant community, that are engaged in legally protected proselytizing activities, as well as Roman Catholics. Additionally, there have been reports of harassment by police of members of the Alevi Muslim minority community.[48]

In 2007 and in the first half of 2008, Roman Catholic and Protestant Christian religious leaders, members, and religious property were the subject of threats and sporadic violence, including murder. The Turkish government has generally responded adequately to the most serious attacks, conducting investigations and prosecuting perpetrators. For example, in October 2007 the Supreme Court upheld a sentence of 18 years and 10 months imprisonment imposed upon the accused murderer of Roman Catholic priest Andrea Santoro, who was killed in February 2006.[49]

Threats and violent attacks have taken place in the context of sometimes contradictory positions taken by government officials regarding certain aspects of religious freedom. To some extent, this reflects a society that is grappling with the growth in numbers of Protestant Christians who are ethnically Turkish, a relatively new phenomenon. (Virtually all other Christians in Turkey are members of a different ethnic

group.) For example, the Interior Ministry's Director General of Laws Niyazi Güney declared to Turkish parliamentarians that "missionary work is even more dangerous than terrorism and unfortunately is not considered a crime in Turkey."[50] In contrast, when asked by the media whether missionary work was in fact a danger to Turkey, Religious Affairs Director Ali Bardakoğlu responded by reaffirming the right to share one's beliefs: "It is their natural right. We must learn to respect even the personal choice of an atheist, let alone other religions."[51]

In the most serious incident of violence reported during 2007, a group of young men claiming to be defending Islam and Turkish nationalism murdered three employees of a Christian publishing house in Malatya on April 18. The killers bound and tortured the three Protestant Christians: Turkish citizens Necati Aydın and Uğur Yüksel, and a German colleague Tillman Geske.[52] Police promptly detained five suspects, students who shared a room in a hostel; each reportedly carried letters saying "We did this for our country. They are attacking our religion."[53] Prime Minister Recep Tayyip Erdoğan condemned the Malatya attack, and a small demonstration was held in central Istanbul to protest the murders.

In the months after the murders, Turkish authorities condemned violence against Christians and acted promptly to respond to new threats. On October 3, 2007, after a formal address to the Council of Europe Parliamentary Assembly in Strasbourg, France, Turkish President Abdullah Gül classified the attacks on Christians as political murders, adding that "there are no attacks targeting Christians in Turkey, but political crimes have occurred and one of them was against a Christian priest. The murderer was captured and is being tried by independent courts."[54]

However, representatives of Turkey's Protestant community continue to express concern about persistent violence. In an October 2007 statement, the Alliance of Protestant Churches in Turkey declared that violence had increased significantly in the wake of the April 2007 Malatya murders, noting that Turkish Protestants had already suffered "scores of threats or attacks" on congregations and church buildings during the previous year. In 2008, the organization reported 19 anti-Protestant incidents, including threats to church leaders and attempts to destroy church property, and urged authorities to take action to respond to these incidents. The head of the Alliance, Zekai Tanyar, stressed that Protestants continue to be intimidated by what is perceived as rising intolerance against their community, particularly in smaller cities and towns. As a consequence, many "are reluctant to go to the police when they receive anonymous threats or face what can only be described as discrimination in their dealings with public authorities: they fear they will only draw more attention to themselves and, in any case, will not succeed." Although state protection has sometimes been provided, this is only in a minority of cases, such as when there are "serious attacks on church buildings and serious threats to the lives of church leaders."[55]

On December 16, 2007, in Izmir, Turkey, a young man stabbed Roman Catholic priest Adriano Franchini after mass at St. Anthony's church. Another priest, belonging to the Syriac Christian community in southeast Turkey, was kidnapped on November 28, 2007 in Mardin, but released after two days.[56]

In other reported incidents, Protestant pastors have been threatened with murder and armed men have attempted to gain access to Protestant churches. In January 2008, a court in Samsun heard evidence that a 17-year-old had made repeated telephone death threats to Protestant pastor Orhan Pıçaklar of the Agape Church there, beginning on December 29, 2007. The suspect was detained on January 5, 2008, and sections of the police interrogation report were cited in evidence. The case was heard by Judge Sinan Sönmez of Samsun's First Minor Petty Offenses Court on January 6, who reportedly ordered the immediate release of the accused "because of his youth."[57] In December 2007,

the *Economist* cited threats against the Agape Church's pastor in an article on why some Christians currently feel under threat in Turkey:

> This has been a bad year for Orhan Pıçaklar. As a Protestant missionary in Samsun, on the Black Sea, he has had death threats and his church has been repeatedly stoned. Local newspapers called him a foreign agent. A group of youths tried to kidnap him as he was driving home. His pleas for police protection have gone unheeded.[58]

Other threats were reported in Ankara, Turkey's capital. On May 6, 2008, three men sought access to the locked Kurtulus Church. One man threatened the Church's Protestant pastor, and another threatened a church member with a gun.[59]

Ukraine

In Ukraine, where Orthodox Christianity is the dominant religion, property of Protestant churches and other minority religions were targeted in a range of incidents. The Armenian Apostolic Church, which has been in Ukraine since the fourteenth century, has also experienced attacks of vandalism. In April, vandals daubed a swastika on the Armenian Apostolic church in Kyiv, and the next day damaged the church's bell tower where construction work had just been completed.[60]

The Interior Ministry, according to press reports, said it had registered 873 instances of desecration of burial sites from January to mid-May, 2007 in Ukraine, but apparently did not indicate which targeted Jewish, Muslim, or other minorities.[61] The majority of reported desecrations targeted Jewish cemeteries (see additionally the Survey sections on *Antisemitic Violence* and *Ukraine*); although there were, however, several instances in which Christian churches and cemeteries were vandalized, particularly in the Donetsk and Odessa regions, and in the Crimea. On April 30, 2007, vandals destroyed more than 400 tombstones at the Old Crimea cemetery in Mariupol; police arrested the offenders and the trial was pending at the end of the year. In October, vandals desecrated some 30 tombstones in the form of a cross there, toppling them or daubing them with "satanic" symbols.[62]

Uzbekistan

In Uzbekistan, a longstanding government campaign targeting independent Muslims and alleged members of banned Islamic organizations has resulted in widely documented torture, arbitrary detention and imprisonment, as well as other human rights violations. Minority Christian groups have also suffered under increasing government restrictions on religious activities. In May 2008, members of minority religious congregations were reportedly "afraid to go out on the street where they live for fear of being persecuted" after the airing of a state-run television film that vilified Jehovah's Witnesses, Seventh-day Adventists, Presbyterians, and Methodists. The film used police footage taken during raids on places of worship and described minority Christian activities as "a global problem along with religious dogmatism, fundamentalism, terrorism and drug addiction."[63]

In June 2008, 26 Protestant congregations in Uzbekistan published an open letter protesting vilification in the media, which named individual religious leaders and churches. Public school and university administrators had been employed to promote these efforts by pressing students to watch a film attacking religious minorities. The letter said that "garbled facts, aggressive attacks, lies and slander" were used to encourage intolerance and hatred toward members of religious minorities.[64]

In December 2006, state television had screened a similar "prime-time national television attack on Protestant churches" over two consecutive nights. One Protestant commentator protested that "we were accused of everything, including turning people into zombies and driving them to psychiatric hospitals. Everyone points at us on the streets." The program cited officials of the government religious committee

condemning missionary activity, named some registered churches as "illegally operating," and alleged that the United States funded missionary activity through its Peace Corps program. A deacon of Uzbekistan's Russian Orthodox Church, who declared that "freedom of faith" was fully respected, told viewers "the spreading of sects can be compared to cancer. Members of such a system, whose mind has been poisoned by false religious ideas, try to lead other people to this wrong path."[65]

The climate of hostility toward minority religions was also encouraged by state action to fine or imprison Uzbek Protestant leaders for their religious activities. In one case in which monitors were asked to withhold certain details, a family was subjected to ongoing threats and violence:

> The daughter of a pastor was kidnapped in April [2007] by unknown young men before being freed in a traumatized state. ... The kidnapping is the latest in a series of attacks on the family, which has included telephoned threats, hostile visits from neighbors, and beatings, allegedly inspired by the mullahs at the local mosque angry that the pastor is a convert to Christianity who actively preaches his faith.[66]

Threats of prosecution for unregistered religious activity are combined with harassment and threats by local authorities and neighborhood structures, notably the local neighborhood committees (*mahallas*) to which local authorities summon residents to compulsory assemblies. In a September 2003 report, Human Rights Watch described the role of the mahalla system in implementing the government's policies to restrict all forms of religious expression outside official channels. Then, as now, a principal concern was to suppress "independent" Muslims who practice Islam outside of the government channels.

> For centuries, the mahalla was an autonomous institution organized around Islamic rituals and social events, but the current government transformed it into a national system for surveillance and control. Uzbekistan is divided up into approximately 12,000 mahallas, each containing between 150 and 1,500 households. The mahalla committees are

local government authorities with the power to administer a range of activities.

By keeping files on those considered "overly pious" in their religious expression, carrying out surveillance, and reporting people's "suspicious" religious activity to police, mahalla committees assist the government in its crackdown against peaceful, independent Muslims who practice Islam outside government-controlled religious institutions.

Mahallas also organize public rallies in which independent Muslims (and others) "are abused, threatened, and demonized." These are described as a modern version of public meetings organized in the Soviet era in order to denounce and discredit those acting contrary to the interests of the ruling party. Human Rights Watch, which called these "hate rallies" that target individuals to limit their religious freedom, described the procedure:

> They are carefully staged spectacles that function as a form of extrajudicial punishment, shaming and humiliating independent Muslims and their immediate relations. Speeches made by officials at the meetings serve as warnings, frightening people into abandoning religious practices the state finds objectionable or disavowing relatives or friends who have been branded "enemies." Officials discredit the meetings' subjects as worthless to society, and as bad mothers, fathers, and neighbors, thereby further isolating such people from the support networks that their community would otherwise provide.[67]

In June 2007, Bakhtier Tuichiev, the pastor of a Full Gospel Pentecostal Church in Andijan which was denied registration, declared that it had become "too dangerous" to continue, and said the church was to be closed. He referred to pressure "from the leaders of the local mahallas" and from the public prosecutor.[68]

Section Endnotes

[1] U.S. Department of State, Bureau of Democracy, Human Rights, and Labor, *International Religious Freedom Report 2007: Armenia*, September 14, 2007, http://www.state.gov/g/drl/rls/irf/2007/90162.htm.

[2] U.S. Department of State, Bureau of Democracy, Human Rights, and Labor, *International Religious Freedom Report 2007: Azerbaijan*, September 14, 2007, http://www.state.gov/g/drl/rls/irf/2007/90164.htm.

[3] Union of Councils for Jews in the Former Soviet Union, "Pastor's Son Beaten for Not Participating in Orthodox Prayer," *the Bigotry Monitor*, vol. 7, no. 35, September 14, 2007, http://www.fsumonitor.com/stories/091407BM.shtml, citing *Slavic Law and Justice Center*.

[4] Press Trust of India, "Hate crime: teenager escapes jail term,' *the Hindu*, June 8, 2008, http://www.hindu.com/2008/06/08/stories/2008060855200900.htm.

[5] Press Trust of India, "Sikh group seeks strict measures to curb hate crime in US," *the Hindu*, June 7, 2008, http://www.hinduonnet.com/holnus/001200806071102.htm.

[6] Jonathan Milne, "Anglican priest, Canon Michael Ainsworth, beaten up in 'faith hate' incident," *the Sunday Times*, March 15, 2008, http://www.timesonline.co.uk/tol/comment/faith/article3558715.ece.

[7] U.S. Department of State, Bureau of Democracy, Human Rights, and Labor, *International Religious Freedom Report 2007: Greece*, September 14, 2007, http://www.state.gov/g/drl/rls/irf/2007/90178.htm.

[8] "Militsiya goroda Chehova Moskovskoi Oblasti otkazyvaet obschine Svidetelej Iegovy v rassledovanii prichin pozhara v Zale Tsarstv," *Portal Credo.Ru*, August 13, 2008, http://portal-credo.ru/site/?act=news&id=64740&cf=/.

[9] Union of Councils for Jews in the Former Soviet Union, "Protestant Church in Moscow Torched," *the Bigotry Monitor*, vol. 7, no. 13, March 30, 2007, http://www.fsumonitor.com/stories/033007BM.shtml.

[10] Union of Councils for Jews in the Former Soviet Union, "Arsonist Targets Jehovah's Witness Building," *the Bigotry Monitor*, vol. 7, no. 6, February 9, 2007, http://www.fsumonitor.com/stories/020907BM.shtml, citing *RIA Novosti*.

[11] Interfax, "Na Kubani sovershen podzhog katolicheskoj chasovni," *Interfax-Religion*, December 24, 2007, http://www.interfax-religion.ru/?act=news&div=22067.

[12] "Vandalized Adventist Church Building Upsets Serbian President," *Adventist News*, January 2007, http://www.adventistreview.org/article.php?id=986.

[13] The Anti-Defamation League, "ADL Applauds Arrests in Virginia Church Vandalism Cases," Press Release, April 6, 2007, http://www.adl.org/PresRele/DiRaB_41/5020_41.htm.

[14] The Coordinating Forum for Countering Antisemitism, "Desecration of the Cemetery in Yekaterinburg," March 21, 2007, http://www.antisemitism.org.il/eng/events/23682/Russia%E2%80%93_Desecration_of_the_Cemetery_in_Yekaterinburg.

[15] Union of Councils for Jews in the Former Soviet Union, "Vandals Daub Swastikas on Armenian Gravestones," *the Bigotry Monitor*, vol. 7, no. 21, May 25, 2007, http://www.fsumonitor.com/stories/052507BM.shtml.

[16] Kosovo unilaterally declared independence in February 2008 and gained recognition by at least 40 governments; see the United Nations Security Council Resolution 1244.

[17] "Kosovo Serbs remember their dead in desecrated cemeteries," *B92*, March 2, 2008, http://www.b92.net/eng/news/society-article.php?yyyy=2008&mm=03&dd=02&nav_id=48099.

[18] Human Rights First correspondence with the OSCE Office for Democratic Institutions and Human Rights; draft of *Hate Crimes in the OSCE Region—Incidents and Responses: Annual Report for 2007*, May 2008.

[19] Union of Councils for Jews in the Former Soviet Union, "Governor Charges Missionaries with Spying," *the Bigotry Monitor*, vol. 7, no. 33, August 31, 2007, http://www.fsumonitor.com/stories/083107BM.shtml, citing *Novotulskij Metallurg*.

[20] U.S. Department of State, Bureau of Democracy, Human Rights and Labor, *Country Reports on Human Rights Practices 2007: Serbia*, March 11, 2008, http://www.state.gov/g/drl/rls/hrrpt/2007/100583.htm.

[21] European Commission Against Racism and Intolerance, *Report on Serbia*, CRI(2008)25, April 29, 2008, http://www.coe.int/t/e/human_rights/ecri/1-ecri/2-country-by-country_approach/serbia/Serbia_CBC_3.asp.

[22] U.S. Department of State, Bureau of Democracy, Human Rights, and Labor, *International Religious Freedom Report 2007: Armenia*, September 14, 2007, http://www.state.gov/g/drl/rls/irf/2007/90162.htm.

23 European Commission Against Racism and Intolerance, *Report on Serbia*, CRI(2008)25, April 29, 2008, http://www.coe.int/t/e/human_rights/ecri/1-ecri/2-country-by-country_approach/serbia/Serbia_CBC_3.asp.

24 U.S. Department of State, Bureau of Democracy, Human Rights, and Labor, *International Religious Freedom Report 2007: Kyrgyz Republic*, September 14, 2007, http://www.state.gov/g/drl/rls/irf/2007/90230.htm.

25 Mushfig Bayram, "Kyrgyzstan: Mob, police and administration chief obstruct Christian boy's burial," Forum 18, June 2, 2008, http://www.forum18.org/Archive.php?article_id=1138.

26 Mushfig Bayram, "Kyrgyzstan: Where Can the Dead be Buried," Forum 18, July 10, 2008, http://www.forum18.org/Archive.php?article_id=1156.

27 U.S. Department of State, Bureau of Democracy, Human Rights, and Labor, *International Religious Freedom Report 2007: Russia*, September 14, 2007, http://www.state.gov/g/drl/rls/irf/2007/90196.htm.

28 Galina Kozhevnikova, *Radical Nationalism and Efforts to Counteract it in 2007*, the SOVA Center for Information and Analysis, March 14, 2008, http://xeno.sova-center.ru/6BA2468/6BB4208/AC15D1E.

29 Alexander Verkhovsky and Olga Sibireva, *Restriction and Challenges in 2007 on Freedom of Conscience in Russia*, the SOVA Center for Information and Analysis, March 27, 2008, http://religion.sova-center.ru/publications/194EF5E/AD31F17.

30 Union of Councils for Jews in the Former Soviet Union, "Ultranationalists Storm Mormon Headquarters," *the Bigotry Monitor*, vol. 7, no. 6, February 9, 2007, http://www.fsumonitor.com/stories/020907BM.shtml.

31 Galina Kozhevnikova, *Radical Nationalism and Efforts to Counteract it in 2007*, the SOVA Center for Information and Analysis, March 14, 2008, http://xeno.sova-center.ru/6BA2468/6BB4208/AC15D1E.

32 Alexander Verkhovsky and Olga Sibireva, *Restriction and Challenges in 2007 on Freedom of Conscience in Russia*, the SOVA Center for Information and Analysis, March 27, 2008, http://religion.sova-center.ru/publications/194EF5E/AD31F17.

33 Alexander Verkhovsky and Olga Sibireva, *Restriction and Challenges in 2007 on Freedom of Conscience in Russia*, the SOVA Center for Information and Analysis, March 27, 2008, http://religion.sova-center.ru/publications/194EF5E/AD31F17.

34 Interfax, "Catholic chapel set on fire on Kuban," *Interfax-Religion*, November 27, 2007, http://www.interfax-religion.com/?act=news&div=4104; and Interfax, "Church rector's house set on fire for the fourth time," *Interfax-Religion*, August 28, 2008.

35 Alexander Verkhovsky and Olga Sibireva, *Restriction and Challenges in 2007 on Freedom of Conscience in Russia*, the SOVA Center for Information and Analysis, March 27, 2008, http://religion.sova-center.ru/publications/194EF5E/AD31F17.

36 Union of Councils for Jews in the Former Soviet Union, "Church Arsonist Convicted," *the Bigotry Monitor*, vol. 7, no. 9, March 2, 2007, http://www.fsumonitor.com/stories/030207BM.shtml, citing the SOVA Center.

37 U.S. Department of State, Bureau of Democracy, Human Rights, and Labor, *International Religious Freedom Report 2007: Serbia*, September 14, 2007, http://www.state.gov/g/drl/rls/irf/2007/90198.htm.

38 Drasko Djenovic, "Serbia: Violence continues against religious communities," Forum 18, October 9, 2007, http://www.forum18.org/Archive.php?article_id=1030.

39 Amnesty International, *The State of the World's Human Rights 2008: Serbia*, http://thereport.amnesty.org/eng/regions/europe-and-central-asia/serbia.

40 Drasko Djenovic, "Serbia: Violence continues against religious communities," Forum 18, October 9, 2007, http://www.forum18.org/Archive.php?article_id=1030.

41 U.S. Department of State, Bureau of Democracy, Human Rights and Labor, *Country Reports on Human Rights Practices 2007: Serbia*, March 11, 2008, http://www.state.gov/g/drl/rls/hrrpt/2007/100583.htm.

42 Kosovo unilaterally declared independence in February 2008 and gained recognition by many European states; see the United Nations Security Council Resolution 1244.

43 Human Rights First correspondence with the OSCE Office for Democratic Institutions and Human Rights; draft of *Hate Crimes in the OSCE Region—Incidents and Responses: Annual Report for 2007*, May 2008.

44 Amnesty International, *The State of the World's Human Rights 2008: Serbia*, http://thereport.amnesty.org/eng/regions/europe-and-central-asia/serbia.

45 "Kosovo attacks not ethnically motivated," *B92*, August 10, 2007, http://www.b92.net/eng/news/crimes-article.php?yyyy=2007&mm=08&dd=10&nav_id=42940, citing *Tanjug*.

46 U.S. Department of State, Bureau of Democracy, Human Rights, and Labor, *International Religious Freedom Report 2007: Serbia*, September 14, 2007, http://www.state.gov/g/drl/rls/irf/2007/90198.htm.

47 U.S. Commission on International Religious Freedom, *Annual Report 2008*, May 2008, http://www.uscirf.gov/images/AR2008/annual%20report%202008-final%20edition.pdf, p. 277.

[48] Izgi Güngör, "Police attack overshadows discrimination, say locals in Keçiören," *Turkish Daily News*, August 30, 2008, http://www.turkishdailynews.com.tr/article.php?enewsid=114072.

[49] "Top court upholds priest killer's sentence," *Turkish Daily News*, October 5, 2007, http://www.turkishdailynews.com.tr/article.php?enewsid=85195.

[50] Güzide Ceyhan, "Turkey: What causes intolerance and violence," Forum 18, November 29, 2007, available at http://www.forum18.org/Archive.php?article_id=1053 (accessed June 7, 2008); and "Turkey Jails Four Street Evangelists," *Compass Direct News*, April 27, 2007, citing *Milliyet*.

[51] Michael Gerson, "A Different Path in Turkey," *the Washigntor Post*, June 8, 2007, http://www.washingtonpost.com/wp-dyn/content/article/2007/06/07/AR2007060701867.html.

[52] "Top court upholds priest killer's sentence," *Turkish Daily News*, October 5, 2007, http://www.turkishdailynews.com.tr/article.php?enewsid=85195.

[53] "Turkey: Lawyers Demand Removal of Malatya Judges," *Compass Direct News*, February 28, 2008, http://www.compassdirect.org/en/display.php?idelement=5262&lang=en&length=long&page=news.

[54] Damaris Kremida, "Mixed feelings at Malatya massacre memorial," *Turkish Daily News*, April 22, 2007, http://www.turkishdailynews.com.tr/article.php?enewsid=102448.

[55] Güzide Ceyhan, "Turkey: One year after Malatya murders, time to address the causes," Forum 18, April 15, 2008, http://www.forum18.org/Archive.php?article_id=1115.

[56] "Turkish Christian Priest Abducted," *BBC News*, November 29, 2007, http://news.bbc.co.uk/2/hi/europe/7118475.stm.

[57] "Turkey: Judge Releases Minor who Threatened Pastor," *Compass Direct News*, January 8, 2008, http://www.compassdirect.org/en/display.php?page=news&idelement=5184&lang=en&length=short&backpage=index&critere=&countryname=&rowcur=225.

[58] "Turkey and its Christians: The cross and the crescent," *the Economist*, December 19, 2007, http://www.economist.com/world/europe/displaystory.cfm?story_id=10337900.

[59] "Turkey: Armed Men Threaten Church," *Compass Direct News*, May 7, 2008, http://www.compassdirect.org/en/display.php?page=news&idelement=5367&lang=en&length=short&backpage=index&critere=&countryname=&rowcur=225.

[60] Un on of Councils for Jews in the Former Soviet Union, "Armenian Church Vandalized," *the Bigotry Monitor*, Vol. 7, No. 17, 27 April 2007, http://www.fsumonitor.com/stories/042707BM.shtml.

[61] U.S. Department of State, Bureau of Democracy, Human Rights and Labor, *Country Reports on Human Rights Practices 2007: Ukraine*, March 11, 2008, http://www.state.gov/g/drl/rls/hrrpt/2007/100590.htm.

[62] "Satanists Vandalized Cemetery in Mariupol," Religious Information Service of Ukraine, October 15, 2007, http://www.risu.org.ua/eng/news/article;18341/.

[63] Mushfig Bayram, "Uzbekistan: More State Media Incitement of Intolerance," Forum 18, May 23, 2008, http://www.forum18.org/Archive.php?article_id=1133.

[64] Felix Corley, "Uzbekistan: Protestants Reject Government's Religious Hatred Encouragement," Forum 18, June 25, 2008, http://www.forum18.org/Archive.php?article_id=1148.

[65] Felix Corley, "Uzbekistan: Prime-time state TV incites intolerance of religious minorities and religious freedom," Forum 18, December 19, 2006, http://www.forum18.org/Archive.php?article_id=890.

[66] Felix Corley, "Uzbekistan: Protestants Face Prosecution, Fines, Raids, Kidnapping and Death Threats," Forum 18, April 20, 2007, http://www.forum18.org/Archive.php?article_id=945.

[67] Human Rights Watch, *From House to House: Abuses by Mahalla Committees*, September 23, 2003, http://www.hrw.org/reports/2003/uzbekistan0903/.

[68] Felix Corley, "Uzbekistan: Church Closes Because of Official Pressure," Forum 18, June 19, 2007, http://www.forum18.org/Archive.php?article_id=976.

Violence Against Roma

Table of Contents

Executive Summary

Roma, like members of other visible minorities, routinely suffer assaults in city streets and other public places as they travel to and from homes, workplaces, and markets. In a number of serious cases of violence against Roma, attackers have also sought out whole families in their homes, or whole communities in settlements predominantly housing Roma. These widespread patterns of violence are sometimes directed both at causing immediate harm to Roma—without distinction between adults, the elderly, and small children—and physically eradicating the presence of Roma in towns and cities in several European countries.

This report documents violence and other forms of intolerance against Roma in eleven countries during 2007 and 2008. The most widely reported incidents occurred in **Italy**, where efforts to vilify Roma involved high-ranking government officials. Thousands of Roma were driven from their homes in 2007 when mobs attacked, beating residents and burning Roma settlements to the ground, as police reportedly did not intervene in several cases to protect the victims. Some Italian political leaders encouraged a national clamor for Roma to be expelled from cities and deported. Violent incidents have also been reported in **Bulgaria**, the **Czech Republic**, the **Russian Federation**, **Serbia**, and **Slovakia**.

The bias-motivated violence against Roma often occurs in an environment in which local political leaders speak openly of their desire to expel Roma minorities. Even as police and local public authorities are in some cases complicit in driving Roma from their homes and seeking their relocation to other towns or cities—or even their deportation—others holding national public office, too, characterize Roma as outsiders who are less than citizens and are unwanted. The presence of Roma in new places of residence, including as a result of

migration within the newly expanded European Union, is often particularly precarious when anti-immigrant bias turns Roma into a scapegoat for broader societal ills, as is the case in several of the countries profiled in this report.

The discriminatory violence of private citizens and the inadequate responses of governments are manifestations of a broader framework of anti-Roma discrimination. This extends to the full range of civil, political, economic, social, and cultural rights. Even as public policy and private violence conspire to drive Roma from the shelter they can find in camps and abandoned buildings, pervasive discrimination denies them access to legal remedies for the loss of homes and property and the access to public housing or rental properties that would provide an alternative.

Indeed, the intensity of the recent anti-Roma violence in Italy should serve as a wake-up call to all of Europe. The multiple factors at work: the negative popular attitudes against Roma; the abuses that they experience at the hands of the police; the official and unofficial discrimination in employment, housing, health care, and other aspects of public life; the violent rhetoric of exclusion and expulsion used by public officials; the failure of many states to address the challenges of the marginalization of Roma—all combine to create a potentially explosive situation, with dire human consequences. As this report shows, this combustible mix of factors exists in several European countries. Yet, official monitoring of hate crimes that includes disaggregated public data on violence against Roma is practically nonexistent even among countries that have developed adequate monitoring systems on racist violence. Addressing hate violence against Roma, in the context of their unique situation, should be a matter of priority concern for policymakers and law enforcement officials.

I. The Context of Violence Against Roma

Violent hate crime is one issue among many other forms of discrimination—both public and private—that Roma and Sinti face throughout Europe.[1] The principal reports of harassment against Roma concern abusive treatment by agents of governments. Police ill-treatment is a priority concern of the Roma community that combines with other aspects of state-sponsored and state-tolerated discrimination to create a climate conducive to violence by ordinary citizens.[2] In situations where local government and police officials can act arbitrarily to violate the rights of Roma, others too expect to do so with impunity. International legal and political bodies have taken up and issued decisions in cases of police violence against Roma, including these recent ones:

■ On July 24, 2008, the United Nations Human Rights Committee found, in the case of *Andreas Kalamiotis v. Greece*, that the government of Greece violated Article 2 paragraph 3 (right to an effective remedy) together with Article 7 (prohibition of torture) of the International Covenant on Civil and Political Rights. The case concerned the lack of an effective investigation into allegations of police brutality against Andreas Kalamiotis, a Roma man, on June 14, 2001. The Committee ruled that Greece must provide the victim with an effective remedy and appropriate reparation, as well as take measures to prevent similar violations in the future.[3]

■ In July 2007, the European Court of Human Rights issued its judgment in the case of Belmondo Cobzaru, a Roma man beaten in custody by police officers in Mangalia, Romania, in 1997. The Court ruled that Romania was in breach of the prohibition of inhuman and degrading treatment, the right to an effective remedy, and the prohibition of discrimination.[4]

The racist violence against Roma that is reported publicly and does not involve state agents tends to concern only the most serious crimes, while even these crimes are generally reported only where nongovernmental organizations are active in protecting the rights of Roma and their communities.

The violence often occurs in an environment where local political leaders speak openly of their desire to expel Roma from their communities. Even as police and local public authorities are often complicit in driving Roma from their homes and seeking their relocation to other towns or cities—or even their deportation—others holding national public office, too, characterize Roma as outsiders who are less than citizens and are unwanted. Many Roma are in fact immigrants from within the newly expanded European Union or the nations of the former Yugoslavia. Their presence in new places of residence is often precarious—in particular when anti-immigrant bias turns to Roma as the scapegoat for broader societal ills.

The language of public discourse on Roma in Europe regularly refers to the *expulsion* of Roma, to *evictions*, to the *dismantling* of settlements, to the *destruction* of Roma homes and communities, to wholesale *incarceration*, or the *deportation* of Roma as a national objective. This is the kinetic language of exclusion that fuels police raids and mob action that place Roma under constant pressure to move on. In this climate, Roma people, reduced to living in camps and abandoned buildings, are attacked by mobs, burned out, their possessions destroyed or stolen by police, constantly uprooted to begin again.

Popular language concerning Roma is also rife with terms reflecting stereotypes portraying Roma as *untrustworthy, dishonest, dirty, lazy, violent,* and often as *criminals, thieves,* or *kidnappers.* Often when a Romani person is a suspect in a crime in Eastern,

Southern, and Central Europe, the media emphasize the ethnicity of the suspect as a reaffirmation of these stereotypes.

To the people of Europe's Roma communities in some countries, the newly virulent anti-gypsyism is an eerie reminder of the *Porrajmos*, the Romani Holocaust during the Second World War that killed more than half of Europe's Roma population. When senior European political leaders publicly discuss "solutions" to the "Roma problem," advocating the use of dynamite; electrified fences; mug shots; fingerprinting of men, women, and children; and deportations, historical parallels inadvertently come to mind.

Indeed, the intensity of the recent anti-Roma violence in Italy should serve as a wake-up call to all of Europe. The multiple factors at work: the negative popular attitudes against Roma; the abuses that they experience at the hands of the police; the official and unofficial discrimination in employment, housing, health care, and other aspects of public life; the violent rhetoric of exclusion and expulsion used by public officials; the failure of many European states to address the challenges of the marginalization of Roma—all combine to create a potentially explosive situation, with dire human consequences. As this report shows, this combustible mix of factors exists in several European countries. Addressing hate violence against Roma, in the context of their unique situation, should be a matter of priority concern for policymakers and law enforcement officials.

A. Racist Violence as an Obstacle to the Full Exercise of Rights

The discriminatory violence against Roma by private citizens and the state is a manifestation of a broader framework of anti-Roma discrimination. This extends to the full range of civil, political, economic, social, and cultural rights. The right to education, to housing, to health care, and to due process of law is often a dead letter. Even as public policy and private violence conspire to drive Roma from the shelter they can find in camps and abandoned buildings, pervasive discrimination denies them access to legal remedies for the loss of homes and property and the access to public housing or rental properties that would provide an alternative. Even as Roma are reviled in public discourse for being homeless, they are constantly under pressure to relocate.

This report focuses upon the violent manifestations of prejudice and hatred in which private persons are responsible for hate crimes. In addressing the issue of violence toward Roma, however, the intersections between popular prejudice and public policy, and between private violence and violence by state agents are part of the reality of violent hate crimes; as is the intersection of prejudice and violence with the systemic discrimination that excludes many Roma communities across Europe from the full enjoyment of their human rights. In many areas Roma are confined to segregated camps or ghettos, are denied access to basic education and prospects for formal employment, and may even be refused recognition as citizens in their own countries.

The denial of the full range of rights is enforced and exacerbated by the lawless resort to violence of local authorities and private citizens in what is often described as collective punishment against Roma communities. Whether taking the form of arbitrary police raids or officially sanctioned bulldozing of Roma property without financial compensation or judicial approval, discrimination and other rights violations take place in tandem with private racist attacks and mob violence. Consequently, stamped as "nomads," Roma are denied an opportunity to settle down.

Violations of other fundamental rights often derive from the denial of a permanent place of residence to Roma, even when Roma communities have been present in the area for hundreds of years. By denying Roma the personal documentation required to function freely in many societies (from birth certificates to housing permits), local authorities may effectively bar Roma children from attending public schools, exclude Roma families from receiving public housing, health care, and other social services, and make formal employment impossible.

In one example of international attention to this problem, in the February 2007 report on **Ukraine**, the U.N. Committee on the Elimination of Racial Discrimination (CERD) noted that "the lack of personal and other relevant identification documents effectively deprives many Roma of their right to equal access to the courts, legal aid, employment, housing, health care, social security and education." To overcome this reality, which can effectively bar many Roma from legal remedy to abuse, CERD recommended Ukraine to "take immediate steps, e.g. by removing administrative obstacles, to issue all Roma with personal and other relevant identification documents in order to enhance their access to the courts, employment, housing, health care, social security and education."[5]

The constant assertion that Roma "do not fit" in any society also extends to national frontiers. As the largest pan-European minority, Roma are present throughout the region, but have no single European homeland, although most have the citizenship of the European country of their birth or long residence—or the formal right to this. The breakup of the former Eastern Bloc countries and realignment of states initiated a process in which the new states—created out of Czechoslovakia,

Yugoslavia, and the Soviet Union—vied to exclude "their" Roma from the new landscapes of citizenship. In the new order of the expanded European Union, in turn, the lifting of restrictions on the movement of citizens within the E.U. brought with it concerns about the fact that tens of thousands of Roma were among those new E.U. citizens seeking employment outside of their own countries.

Some steps have been taken to address these problems. For example, in 2005, the heads of government of **Bulgaria**, **Croatia**, the **Czech Republic**, **Hungary**, **Macedonia**, **Montenegro**, **Romania**, **Serbia**, and **Slovakia** signed a joint declaration launching the Decade of Roma Inclusion: 2005-2015. In the declaration, they agreed to eliminate discrimination against Roma as well as to close existing gaps "between Roma and the rest of society," in accord with national action plans. As part of this commitment, the nine governments agreed to support the full participation and involvement of Roma communities in achieving the goals of the initiative—and in measuring progress. In order to facilitate this, Roma activists and researchers have joined forces in DecadeWatch, an organization supported by the Open Society Institute and the World Bank, aiming to produce periodic monitoring reports. In July 2008, **Albania** joined the initiative. **Ukraine** is an outstanding holdout from participation.

In March 2008, a group of eight nongovernmental organizations launched the European Roma Policy Coalition (ERPC) with a view to press the European Union to develop a coherent policy to counter social exclusion and discrimination against Roma. Goals include the E.U.'s adoption of a "Framework Strategy on Roma Inclusion, to be developed in full consultation with Roma communities," and to mesh with other European initiatives on Roma rights, and in particular the Decade of Roma Inclusion.[6]

II. Individual Country Overview

Hate violence against Roma has several particularly pernicious and disturbing aspects. Roma, like members of other visible minorities, routinely suffer assaults in city streets and other public places as they travel to and from homes, workplaces, and markets. But in many cases, including those involving very serious violence, attackers seek out whole families of Roma in their homes, or whole communities in settlements predominantly housing Roma. This pattern of violence is sometimes directed both at causing immediate harm to Roma—without distinction between adults, the elderly, and small children—and physically eradicating the presence of Roma in towns and communities in several parts of Europe.

The persistence of anti-Roma violence and discrimination by ordinary citizens occurs in the context of abusive patterns of treatment of Roma by police and public authorities. Private violence seeking the expulsion of Roma families and communities sometimes occurs in tandem with official efforts to achieve the same ends. The prevalence of racist anti-Roma rhetoric even by the highest public authorities in some countries further exacerbates the problem. Some of the principal developments in Europe regarding racist violence against Roma involve this combination of public and private prejudice and violence and are outlined in the country sections below.

Official monitoring of hate crimes in most countries in Europe is limited, and disaggregated public data on violence against Roma is practically nonexistent even among countries that have developed adequate monitoring systems on racist violence—like the **Czech Republic** and the **United Kingdom**. Moreover, official statistics on anti-Roma violence based on police data would likely capture only a small percentage of the overall number of incidents because of the particular

distrust of the police among many Roma. Media and NGO reports document primarily only the most egregious incidents of violence against Roma.

This section documents violent incidents in eleven countries during 2007 and 2008, with the most widely reported incidents occurring in **Italy**, where efforts to vilify Romanian immigrants and Roma involved members of the highest levels of government. Thousands of Roma were driven from their homes in 2007 and 2008 when mobs attacked, beating residents and burning Roma settlements to the ground, as police reportedly did not intervene in many cases to protect the victims. In Italy, the Roma became the object of a national clamor for expulsion from cities and deportation encouraged by political leaders.

Italy

In Italy, many national and local political leaders engaged in rhetoric during 2007 and 2008 that maintained that the recent extraordinary rise in crime was mainly a result of uncontrolled immigration. They often singled out a wave of immigration of people of Roma origin from new European Union member state Romania. The new anticrime rhetoric combined and exacerbated fear and hatred of immigrants with longstanding prejudices and stereotypes toward Roma. Italy's estimated 160,000 Roma, about half of which are Italian nationals, were all equally under threat (Roma have lived in Italy for some seven hundred years).[7]

The anti-Roma and anti-Romanian rhetoric became racist at times, even at the highest political levels. The prefect of Rome, Carlo Mosca, in declaring his intent to sign expulsion orders without hesitation, told the press that "the hard line is necessary" to deal with "these beasts."[8] National and local leaders declared their plans to expel Roma from settlements in and around major cities and to deport illegal immigrants. The mayors of Rome and Milan signed "Security Pacts" in May 2007 that "envisaged the forced eviction of up to 10,000 Romani people."[9] The clearance and destruction of Roma settlements without prior notice, compensation, or provision of alternative housing was reported throughout the year.

In October 2007, extraordinary anti-immigrant sentiment exploded into violence toward Romanian immigrants and Roma in general. The violence was triggered by the particularly heinous murder of 47-year-old Giovanna Reggiani, a naval captain's wife, which was attributed to a Romanian immigrant of Roma origin. Reggiani was raped, beaten, left in a ditch, and died the following week. The government responded with roundups of Romanian immigrants and summary expulsions of some two hundred, mostly Roma, disregarding E.U. immigration rules.[10]

On November 1, 2007, President Giorgio Napolitano signed a decree providing for the summary expulsion of E.U. citizens "for reasons of public safety," in direct response to what were described as "episodes of heavy violence and ferocious crime." The Decree Law, which was in violation of E.U. Directive 2004/38 /EC concerning the rights of E.U. internal migrants, appeared to be directed expressly at Roma. Within two weeks, 177 persons had been expelled under the new order.[11] Mayor of Rome Walter Veltroni blamed the increase in violent crime overall on the recent immigration of Romanian Roma, asserting that "before the entry of Romania into the European Union, Rome was the safest city in the world."[12]

Racist violence in the backlash to the murder of Giovanna Reggiani included a November 2, 2007 attack on Roma living in improvised shelters in a parking lot near the scene of the murder. Up to eight attackers seriously injured three Romanians with metal bars and knives; one of the injured had deep stab wounds in his back. Another squatter camp in the area in which the attack occurred, housing some 50 to 60 Roma, was bulldozed by city authorities on November 3, 2007.[13]

In other incidents, "a Romanian-owned shop was damaged by a crude bomb, a popular Romanian footballer playing for an Italian team heard anti-Roma chants of 'dirty Gypsy,' a Romanian actress visiting Italy was harassed by the Italian police, and messages like 'Romanians—Go Home' appeared on walls in the big Italian cities."[14]

In 2008, anti-Roma hate crimes continued, as Roma communities were targeted for arson attacks even as police seized Roma in random searches for illegal immigrants. In early May 2008, following claims that a Roma teenager had attempted to kidnap a child, mobs in several areas around Naples attacked Roma communities, setting homes alight, and forcing hundreds of Roma to flee. Others were escorted out of the camps by authorities, with no prospect of return. On May 11, 2008, newly appointed Interior Minister Roberto Maroni was widely reported declaring that "all Roma camps will have to be dismantled right away and the inhabitants will be either expelled or incarcerated."[15]

On May 11, 2008, attackers set fires with Molotov cocktails in a Roma camp in Via Novara, Milan. On May 13, a mob threw stones and Molotov cocktails at two Roma squatter camps in the Ponticelli district of northern Naples; many of the estimated eight hundred inhabitants fled. On May 14, attackers returned, including scores of young men on motor scooters, armed with iron bars and Molotov cocktails. They moved systematically through the area, burning the camp to the ground. According to press reports, local residents stood by applauding the arsonists, and the police presence did not stop the attackers.[16] Other arson attacks followed. On June 9, according to local monitors, "a settlement of approximately 100 Romanian

Roma in Catania, Sicily, was attacked and burned to the ground by unknown perpetrators."[17]

Although no arrests were reported for the arson attacks on Roma, a series of mass roundups of Roma and suspected illegal immigrants was carried out in the same period, with nearly four hundred detained.[18] In the aftermath of the violence, Interior Minister Maroni was quoted as declaring "that is what happens when gypsies steal babies, or when Romanians commit sexual violence."[19] Umberto Bossi, a cabinet member who also heads the extremist Northern League, was an apologist for the camp burnings, declaring that "people do what the state can't manage."[20]

In May 2008, on-site research on the situation in Italy was undertaken by a nongovernmental coalition including the Open Society Institute, the Center on Housing Rights and Evictions, the European Roma Rights Centre (ERRC), Romani Criss, and the Roma Civic Alliance in Romania. The resulting report, *Security a la Italiana*, found a dramatic rise in both the frequency and seriousness of attacks on Roma since the government of Silvio Berlusconi took office in April. The report found further that Italian authorities had "failed to condemn acts of violent aggression against Roma and not one person has yet to be held legally accountable for at least 8 incidents of anti-Romani pogroms leading to the razing of Romani camps with Molotov cocktails in Italy."[21]

The new government of Silvio Berlusconi, who described illegal immigrants as "an army of evil" in his election campaign, introduced a new "security package" on May 16, 2008, that provided for dismantling Roma camps; appointing "special commissioners for the Roma emergency" in Rome, Naples, and Milan; new border controls; and the summary deportation of immigrants "who cannot show they have a job or an 'adequate' income."[22] The security package provided for Roma encampments in the three cities to be placed under a "state of emergency," opening the way for prefects to exercise special powers to expel the residents and destroy the camps.

The Council of Europe Commissioner for Human Rights Thomas Hammarberg criticized Berlusconi's proposal, saying that "arrests should be used against criminals, which immigrants are not."[23] In another statement, Hammarberg declared that "the whole Roma community has been made a scapegoat for crimes committed by only a very few."[24]

On May 21, the government issued a decree declaring a state of emergency for one year "in relation to the settlements of the nomad community in the regions of Campania, Lazio and Lombardy."[25] The decree was based on 1992 legislation empowering the government to establish states of emergency in the event of "natural disasters, catastrophes or other events that, on account of their intensity and extent, have to be tackled using extraordinary powers and means." The premise of the decree was that the presence of Roma communities alone, because of their precarious conditions, was the cause of situations of "extreme critical nature" and "serious social alarm" that could have further serious repercussions for public order and security "for local populations."[26]

On May 30, Prime Minister Berlusconi issued further executive orders for the implementation of the special measures in the regions of Lazio (including Rome), Lombardia (Milan), and Campania (Naples). The wording of the decrees echoed the May 21 decree and referred expressly to measures of civil protection "in relation to settlements of the nomad community" in the three regions: the "nomads" in question were to be the object of police actions to protect others.

The Lazio ordinance, which employs language almost identical to the others, attributes the measures to the determination that the region, in particular Rome and its surroundings, was in an extremely critical situation, "because the presence of numerous irregular and nomadic citizens from outside the community is endangering stability." The "extreme precariousness" of the settlements had created a situation of "serious social alarm, with possible serious repercussions in terms of public order and security for the local populations."[27] The implication was that the "nomads" in question were both foreigners and criminals, whether housed in official camps or irregular settlements.

The ordinances designate the prefects of Rome, Milan and Naples as emergency commissioners with extraordinary powers to address the emergency. These include measures to identify camp residents, to include fingerprinting, and to facilitate the expulsion from settlements or deportation through administrative or judicial measures. The prefects were authorized to set aside legal provisions for the protection of the rights of those in question, "for instance the right to be informed when subject to an administrative procedure such as fingerprinting and the requirement that persons be dangerous or suspect or that they refuse to identify themselves before undergoing identity screening involving photographing, fingerprinting or the gathering of anthropometric data."[28]

In June 2008, the new mayor of Rome, Gianni Alemanno, expelled the first group from a settlement that had been present in the city for decades.[29] On June 8, Carlo Mosca, Rome's newly appointed Commissioner for Roma, reportedly declared that "Gypsies would be monitored, and a census would be carried out" and that "Gypsies would also be fingerprinted and photographed and this would allow the authorities to identify them."[30]

As part of the measures, the interior minister of the interior stated repeatedly that the purpose of taking fingerprints "is to carry out a census of the Roma population in Italy," and that to this end he intended to allow the fingerprinting of all Roma living in camps, including minors. The planned campaign was intended to register all Roma in Milan, Rome, and Naples by October 15, 2008. The European Parliament denounced these measures and called for an immediate halt to mass fingerprinting of Roma, noting in particular that with regard to children it was unacceptable "to violate their fundamental rights and to criminalize them" in the name of protecting them.[31]

The emergency measures were formalized even after a series of interventions by European and regional human rights authorities expressing concern over the government's proposals. On May 18, 2008, the Organization for Security and Cooperation's (OSCE) Office for Democratic Institutions and Human Rights (ODIHR) issued a press statement expressing concern at attacks on Roma communities in Italy, urging protection for vulnerable populations and an end to anti-Roma rhetoric by public officials and the media. Ambassador Christian Strohal, the director of the ODIHR, acknowledged frustrations about high crime levels, but said that "the current stigmatization of Roma and immigrant groups in Italy is dangerous as it contributes to fuelling tensions and increases the potential for violence." The head of the ODIHR's Contact Point for Roma and Sinti Issues, Andrzej Mirga, described a "worrying rise of anti-Roma and anti-immigrant rhetoric in recent months across Italy," and said there should be "no place for racial stereotyping and inciting hatred and violence in a tolerant democratic society."[32]

Similarly, European Union Social Affairs Commissioner Vladimir Spidla told the European Parliament that "the Roma people ... need to have the same liberties, the same rights as the others. They are not third country immigrants, they are citizens of the European Union and they should not be discriminated against."[33]

In a report of his findings from a visit to Rome on June 19 and 20, 2008, the Commissioner for Human Rights Hammarberg expressed "deep concern" at the "extremely violent" actions against Roma and Sinti in Italy, including the burning of Roma camps, "reportedly without effective protection by the police which has also carried out violent Roma camp raids." In addition, Hammarberg expressed concern at discriminatory statements by national leaders, and at legislation that conflated foreigners with criminals and identified the problem of security with "specific groups of population." The commissioner recommended a prompt reaction by authorities "to condemn strongly and publicly all statements, irrespective of their origin, that generalize and stigmatize certain ethnic or social groups, such as Roma and Sinti or migrants," while ensuring that government initiatives, including new security packages, "cannot be construed as facilitating or encouraging the objectionable stigmatization of the same groups."

A further recommendation was for the government to fulfill its obligations "to prevent and effectively protect Roma and Sinti populations from violent acts by private individuals that put, inter alia, their life and limb in real danger." To this end, the government must ensure that such incidents "always be subject to effective investigations, in accordance with the established case law of the European Court of Human Rights."[34]

At the end of July 2008, Interior Minister Maroni told Italian legislators he indignantly rejected Hammarberg's assertions that "violent acts were perpetrated against Roma encampments without effective protection by the police forces," and that police carried out violent raids on settlements. Maroni added that "these are outright lies, the police have never committed any act of violence of this nature." A ministry note issued at the same time declared that the Council of Europe had been provided "all the data that show how the worries about the lack of human rights are completely groundless."[35]

Attacks on individuals and families continued even as Roma camps faced continued raids and destruction. On June 17, 2008, two men, aged 35 to 40 attacked the Covaciu family in the Gianbellino area of Milan. Twelve-year-old Rebecca Covaciu, her 14-year-old brother Inoi, and their parents were beaten and pursued into a public park; bystanders offered no assistance.[36]

On June 13, 2008, a march protesting the 'scapegoating" and persecution of Roma in Italy was held in Rome, as the first evictions from longstanding Roma settlements were reported. In what was described as the first protest of its kind in Italy, participants included "Roma women dancing in traditional dress, Italian intellectuals and slow-marching Jewish survivors from Germany's death camps," wearing "the same black triangle bearing the letter Z as worn by Gypsy inmates at the camps."[37]

Bulgaria

On the night of August 12, 2007, a group of an estimated dozen skinheads assaulted six Roma—three men and three women—as they were returning to their homes in Fakulteta, a predominantly Roma neighborhood of Sofia. Four victims were injured and one of them required hospitalization. The victims were interviewed by the Romani Baht Foundation a Roma rights organization, which said the victims had telephoned for help to the district police but that police had refused to send a patrol car.[38]

This attack has been identified as the incident that triggered Roma protests and disturbances beginning the following day. In an initial incident on the night of August 13, Roma reportedly smashed up a café in the Krasna Polyana district and attacked four suspected skinheads. On August 14, three to four hundred Roma gathered in the same area, some reportedly armed with sticks and farm implements, in apparent response to rumors that skinhead mobs were going to attack the Roma community. The *Sofia Echo* cited one "elderly Roma" in the crowd who complained that his community "was constantly tortured by the skinheads." He said "skinheads were beating elderly Romani persons, children and pregnant women." The same source said the protest lasted about four hours.[39]

Members of the crowd reportedly clashed with police and caused some property damage, while acting in a threatening manner toward ethnic-Bulgarian observers.[40]

A representative of the Bulgarian Helsinki Committee said "there are many elements in it—ethnic tension, social problems, severe discrimination against the gypsy ghettos. ... The ghettos are like powder kegs which need just a small incident to explode."[41]

On August 20, Sofia Mayor Boyko Borissov, announced a proposal that Roma individuals accompany police patrols in the city, participating in security measures in parts of the city "where conflicts between the Roma and Bulgarians occur on a regular basis." He had also called for an enhanced police presence in these areas.[42]

On August 22, the Romani Baht Foundation hosted a meeting between Roma community leaders and the Interior Minister that aimed at both identifying the underlying causes of concern among the community and agreeing to concrete measures to address them. In addition to agreeing to hold monthly consultative meetings in the future, the Interior Ministry reportedly agreed to provide increased police protection aimed expressly at protecting the Roma community. This was to include a 24-hour police presence in the largely Roma-inhabited Krasna Polyana and Fakulteta districts, as well as attention "to 'vulnerable' spots—terminal stops of the public transportation system, catering shops and others," with special police centers to be created in those districts.[43]

While developments in the capital received national and international attention, attacks on Roma continued to occur elsewhere in the country. In Samokov, on August 21, 2007, a verbal encounter between a group of ethnic Bulgarian boys and Roma teenagers in the town square led to a fight and the beating to death of a 17-year-old Roma boy named Asparuh. A local Roma leader told the press that the boy had been with a group of Roma friends "when a group of Bulgarians approached them and beat them for no reason." Some one thousand Roma demonstrated in the square the next day to protest the killing.[44] According to the Bulgarian news agency *Mediapool*, psychologist Hristo Monov stated that the Bulgarian teenagers attacked the Romani youth because "they thought that Gypsies must not be let into the central part of the town."[45] Four ethnic Bulgarian teenagers were detained in relation to the incident, but local authorities rejected claims that the incident was founded on ethnic prejudice. The Roma community expressed concern with the possibility of further violence.[46]

The early August incidents, in which Roma took to the streets in Sofia, were taken as an opportunity by extreme nationalist groups and parties in Bulgaria, who cited the disturbances as evidence that Roma posed a threat to ordinary Bulgarians. On August 20, Vladimir Rasate, leader of the far-right Bulgarian National Union (BNU) announced the formation of a National Guard Party tied expressly to xenophobic fears of Roma. "We are witnessing how Bulgarians have been terrorized by Roma for the past 17 years and all governments are to blame for that because there is no punishment for the perpetrators," declared Rasate, as 12 prototype militiamen paraded in uniform. On August 21, however, Interior Minister Roumen Petkov declared that "there will be no such thing as a national guard," while threatening punishment for those who "disturb public order or cause ethnic tension."[47]

After meeting with Roma leaders, Sofia Mayor Boyko Borissov told the media that the BNU National Guard idea was "complete nonsense," and announced his plan to begin police patrols with Roma participation. The agreement reached by the Interior Ministry and Roma leaders on August 22 formalized a national commitment for a 24-hour-a-day police presence in crucial districts.[48]

Czech Republic

In Olomouc, on August 24, 2007, a group shouting anti-Roma epithets attacked two young Roma Czechs, aged 18 and 23, at an open air cinema. The younger victim received facial injuries while the other, who was knocked to the ground and kicked, suffered a broken nose and a concussion.

A few months earlier, in April, a criminal complaint was brought concerning a statement by Deputy Prime Minister and Christian Democrat leader Jiří Čunek. As mayor of Vsetín, Čunek was cited as declaring that "in order to be entitled to state subsidies like Roma, other people would need to get a suntan, behave in a disorderly way and light fires in town squares before politicians would regard them as badly off."[43]

Also in April, the Czech Senate declined to strip Senator Liana Janáčková of her parliamentary immunity in the context of an investigation under hate speech laws for racist statements concerning Roma. Janáčková, who is also mayor of Mariánské Hory and Hulváky district of Ostrava, was recorded as suggesting that problems in a Romany settlement could be resolved with "dynamite," that Roma had too many children, and that she believed they should be held behind an electric fence:

> Unfortunately, I'm a racist, I disagree with the integration of gypsies and their living across the district. Unfortunately, we've chosen Bedriska [locality], therefore they will be there, behind a tall fence with electricity.[50]

As in other new E.U. member states of Eastern Europe, 2007 saw the creation in the Czech Republic of a formal paramilitary structure expressly founded on anti-Roma and anti-immigrant foundations. In December 2007, the extreme nationalist National Party announced that it would begin recruiting members of a paramilitary National Guard in response to "the growing fear of the behavior of unadaptable minorities and immigrants," and the failings of the national police. The creation of the guard was announced at a demonstration on October 28, 2007. Interior Minister Ivan Langer said the group was "unacceptable" and would be under close police surveillance.[51]

In a March 2008 summary of submissions from nongovernmental organizations for the Universal Periodic Review of the Czech Republic, the Office of the United Nations High Commissioner for Human Rights (OHCHR) noted concerns over both "private individuals and State actors who have threatened the lives of Roma." Amnesty International, in particular, had stressed that "incidents of violence against Roma are reported to have been perpetrated by youths with extreme racist views;" even when involving repeat offenders, attackers received "only light or suspended sentences." Thomas Hammarberg, the Commissioner for Human Rights of the Council of Europe, in turn, was cited expressing his hope that increased awareness of racial motivations in crimes of violence by police and prosecutors would lead "to additional prosecutions and to the imposition of sanctions which are proportionate to the gravity of this type of crime and sufficiently dissuasive for the future."

The same OHCHR report cited submissions on the virulent "hate speech" that accompanied direct and indirect discrimination against Roma. According to NGO submissions, including those of the European Roma Rights Center:

> The regular and systemic human rights abuses against Roma in the Czech Republic are aggravated by the fact that anti-Romani hate speech is a regular part of public discourse in the country. Anti-Romani statements are a standard and often unquestioned part of public life in the Czech Republic, and officials as high-ranking as the Prime Minister, the President, Senators (including members of the Senate's Human Rights Committee), other members of the cabinet, and many local officials have either made anti-Romani statements or failed to counteract speeches denigrating the dignity of the Roma.[52]

Greece

In Greece, appalling housing for Roma and arbitrary actions expelling Roma from settlements were condemned by the Council of Europe's Commissioner for Human Rights, Thomas Hammarberg, after a December 2006 visit. The Commissioner had also condemned the apparent relation between government inaction and threatening behavior of ordinary citizens who rejected Roma presence near their communities. In a letter made public in 2007, to which Greek authorities made no response, Hammarberg described his visits to Roma settlements and the seeming indifference of police to the threatening behavior of people hostile to Roma:

> I saw Roma families living in very poor conditions. Also, I met with a family whose simple habitat had been bull-dozed away that same morning. It was obvious that the "procedures" for making them homeless were in total contradiction to human rights standards. ... I was also disturbed to notice that non-Roma people appeared on both sites during my visit and behaved in an aggressive, threatening manner to the extent that my interviews with some of the Roma families were disturbed. I had expected that the police would have offered more obvious protec-tion.[53]

Romania

The explosion of anti-Romanian and anti-Roma sentiment in Italy in November 2007 led to protests by European Union institutions and leaders, and consider-able tensions between Italy and Romania. Some Romanian political leaders who stood up for the plight of their conationals in Italy, however, qualified their stance with an echo of Italian anti-Roma sentiment, in some cases vilifying Romanian Roma in much the same terms as their Italian counterparts.

While demanding the respect and rights accorded all E.U. citizens for Romanians in Italy, the implication of the statements of Romanian leaders was that they distinguished their Roma citizens from other nationals. Some presented Roma as an embarrassment to Romania, while others questioned whether Roma who carried Romanian passports should really be considered Romanian.

Foreign Minister Adrian Cioroianu, for example, in a press conference shortly after the crisis broke, ex-pressed concern over "violent crimes committed by Romanians and 'so-called Romanians' of Roma origin who are labeled as Romanians only because they carry that country's passport."[54] On November 4, 2007, at the height of the crisis in Italy, Cioroianu told Antena 3 television that he was considering "buying a piece of land in the Egyptian desert to send there all the people who tarnish the country's image."[55]

President Traian Băsescu was widely quoted after an incident on May 19, 2007, in which he insulted journalist Andreea Pana, dismissing her by asking "don't you have anything to do today?" and commenting: "how aggressive that stinky gypsy was." (He subsequently apologized).[56]

On October 23, 2007, President Băsescu publicly apologized for the nation's role in the Roma Holocaust, the Porajmos, in the first statement of its kind by a Romanian leader. Speaking in part in the Romani language, he also called for the story of the Nazi genocide of Roma to be taught in schools. Băsescu awarded three survivors of the Porajmos with an Order for Faithful Services.

Russian Federation

Stereotyped as criminals, Roma have become a preferred scapegoat for criminality in parts of the the Russian Federation, as in Central and Eastern Europe. The public face of Russian internal security policy since the 1990s has associated particular national groups with the challenges of terrorism, corruption, and "the war on drugs." The European Roma Rights Center (ERRC) observed that "the 'war on drugs' gradually generated, during the 1990s, the image of the typical drug dealer, namely, the 'Gypsy.'" The result was that "the identification of the Roma with drug dealing has reached a point of near synonymous usage in the media."[57]

In the 2006 report on racial profiling in Russia, the Open Society Institute identified the stereotyping of Roma in the context of the larger pattern of racist stereotyping and discrimination against migrant workers:

Despite the labor shortage and the economic necessity of migration in Russia today, the media negatively depicts migrant workers as taking jobs from Russians. More odiously, the media stereotypes minority ethnic nationalities as criminals and drug dealers. Roma, in particular, have been singled out for unsubstantiated accusations of involvement in the drug trade.[58]

In practice, this disparaging public posture is echoed by the operational policies of public authorities and police. This includes persistent racial profiling in police stops and searches, sometimes extending to raids of entire Roma communities, during which homes are damaged or destroyed, property stolen, and individuals are subjected to police brutality and extortion. This occurs in the context of a general bias within the criminal justice system that translates into persistent police violence against Roma at the time of arrest and while in custody as well as a pattern of disproportionate arrests and prosecutions.

Victims of police abuse and official discrimination have little prospect of remedy for private violence as well. As a result, Roma victims are hesitant to file formal complaints of hate crimes against them, feeling a lack of confidence in public authorities and fearing further abuse. The European Roma Rights Center (ECCR) notes that racial discrimination against Roma "creates an environment in which both public officials and private actors feel confident that they will be absolved from responsibility for racially motivated violence and abuse and exposes the victims to further violence and abuse."[59]

In one particularly horrific incident of anti-Roma violence, on September 10, 2007, masked men broke into the home of the Lyalikov family in Ordzhonikidze, Ingushetia, and shot dead the father and two adult sons. Police told the media the crime was motivated by "ethnic hatred."[60]

Serbia

On the night of August 10, 2007, at least five young men went to a park in Novi Beograd, where they shouted insults at Roma living there, and set fire to a nylon sheet covering the hut of a Roma woman. Roma confronted the attackers, and the woman was reportedly seriously injured in the ensuing fight. Police had reportedly identified five of the attackers, including a minor, and were filing charges of "inflicting grievous bodily harm and inciting ethnic, racial and religious hatred and intolerance."

In Belgrade, on the night of August 16, 2007, three men armed with chains attacked Femija Bajrami, a 45-year-old Roma man, knocking him to the ground and beating him. Bajrami, a resident of the suburb Zemun, required medical attention. Roma community members in Zemun told the media that anti-Roma assaults were frequent, and radio station B92 said that Belgrade police had recorded five attacks on Roma in the first two weeks of August alone.[61]

In a statement on August 24, 2007, the head of the Organization for Security and Cooperation in Europe mission in Serbia, Ambassador Hans Ola Urstad, expressed serious concern over hate crimes against Roma in Serbia and called upon authorities to apprehend the suspects, prosecute the perpetrators, and prevent further such attacks. He said that "assaults on Roma, destruction of their homes and hate speech graffiti represent attacks on the integrity of the Roma and violate their basic human rights." He expressed concern regarding the situation of "several hundred Roma families living under the Gazela Bridge in Belgrade," in the face of city plans to destroy the settlement, and called on city authorities to ensure alternative housing.[62]

Slovakia

In May 2007, in Záhorská Ves, five masked men dressed to imitate policemen attacked the Sarközy family in a makeshift shelter at the site of the family compound that was destroyed in a similar attack in 2003. The attackers reportedly beat members of the family, including a mother and child, with wooden clubs and iron rods and destroyed all of their furniture.[63]

The Sarközy family had been under threat since September 29, 2003, when masked men attacked the compound of the Sarközy and Malik families in Záhorská Ves, beating members of the two extended families—then totaling 16 persons—with baseball bats and other weapons, causing serious injuries and destroying property.[64] These and subsequent incidents of violence were investigated by a special unit in Slovakia's Police Presidium only after "allegations arose regarding the possible involvement of local government officials and the failure of local police to accept testimony and evidence relating to the case. Roma activists also alleged that local officials attempted to relocate victims to another village."[65]

The U.S. Department of State's report on human rights in the Slovak Republic in 2007 concluded that "Roma were particularly singled out for violence," with "skinhead and neo-Nazi violence against Roma and other minorities continu[ing] to be a serious problem." While noting that police "detained numerous individuals for attacks against Roma motivated by racial hatred," there were also reports that police mistreated Roma. Incidents cited in the report included an assault on April 8, 2007, when three men broke into a Romani home in Trebišov and assaulted several family members; it said the three were arrested and charged. In another incident reported by the Department of State, on August 30, 2007 "a Romani man and his wife were attacked and seriously wounded in Detva." Although suspects were detained, no charges were brought, and human rights

groups "asserted that the police did not investigate the case properly."[66]

Slovenia

Nongovernmental organizations in January 2007 lodged a complaint with the official equality body, the Advocate of the Principle of Equality, concerning the forced expulsion through mob action of an extended Roma family from the village of Ambrus, near Ljubljana, in October 2006. The mob set fire to the compound of the Strohan family as police stood by and forced over 30 residents to flee. The Advocate had failed to produce an opinion on the matter by the end of 2007—the petition claimed the family was the object of direct discrimination by reason of its ethnic origin.[67]

Ukraine

The U.N. Committee on Economic, Social and Cultural Rights (CESCR), in the January 2008 concluding observations on the implementation by Ukraine of the International Covenant on Economic, Social, and Cultural Rights, identified as a matter of concern reports of the failure to provide effective protection against discrimination and violence against Roma, as well as anti-Roma police abuse. Moreover, it stressed "the reluctance of the police to investigate properly such incidents, and the tendency to prosecute and sentence perpetrators of such acts under lenient criminal law provisions on 'hooliganism.'"

In the *Third Report on Ukraine*, released in February 2008, the European Commission against Racism and Intolerance (ECRI), said it had continued to receive reports that police "illegally arrest and harass members of Roma communities," and that "Roma do not receive an adequate response from the police when they are the victims of crime." ECRI restated the recommendation of its previous report that Ukrainian authorities:

> Address manifestations of unlawful behavior on the part of law enforcement officials generally, and to take meas-

ures to ensure that the police react promptly and effectively to all crimes, including those committed against Roma and to ensure that the racist element of such offences is duly taken into account.[68]

In *Proceedings Discontinued: The Inertia of Roma Rights Change in Ukraine*, a report released in December 2006 and incorporating research conducted from 2004-2006, the European Roma Rights Centre (ERRC) described a pattern of mob violence that occurred in the face of the general indifference or acquiescence of local authorities. It said attacks can take the form of "random violence against individual homes or pogrom-like assaults against entire communities," their purposes including "to terrorize, to force a move out of a neighborhood, or vigilante acts of vengeance for crimes associated with Roma." Police, in turn, "rarely interfere," creating an environment of impunity in which violence against Roma is encouraged.[69]

United Kingdom

High levels of racist violence in the United Kingdom extend to the Roma community. Minority Rights Group International has reported that there have been racist attacks on campsites in the U.K., many of which are not reported to the police.[70]

Police in the United Kingdom have made considerable efforts to reach out to victim communities and have established some of the most comprehensive hate crime reporting systems in Europe, although still recognize high levels of underreporting. Police do not record separately violence targeting Roma.

Gay McDougall, the U.N. Independent Expert on Minority Issues, noted in connection with the United Kingdom's *Gypsy, Roma, and Traveler History Month* that the some 300,000 people who belong to these communities "face serious discrimination, exclusion, poverty and even violence. The equation is a simple one: ... the violations of the rights of members of these communities, in all walks of life, are due to the pervasive effects of racial discrimination and centuries of marginalization and exclusion that persist today. Negative and inaccurate reporting by certain sectors of the media has fuelled hostile attitudes towards Gypsies, Roma and Travelers."[71]

Section Endnotes

1 Sinti are considered to be either a different ethnic group or a major subcategory of Roma; they mainly reside in German-speaking areas of Central Europe.

2 Open Society Justice Initiative, *Ethnic Profiling in the Moscow Metro*, Open Society Institute, June 2006, http://www.soros.org/initiatives/osji/articles_publications/publications/profiling_20060613.

3 "UN body finds Greece did not provide effective remedy to Roma victim of police violence," Press Release, the World Organization Against Torture and the Greek Helsinki Monitor, August 13, 2008, http://cm.greekhelsinki.gr/uploads/2008_files/ghm1048_omct_ghm_unhrc_kalamiotis_english.doc.

4 Amnesty International, *The State of the World's Human Rights 2008: Romania*, POL 10/001/2008, June 2008, p. 246.

5 Committee on the Elimination of Racial Discrimination, *Consideration of Reports Submitted by States parties Under Article 9 of the Convention, Concluding observations of the Committee on the Elimination of Racial Discrimination*, CERD/C/UKR/CO/18, February 8, 2007, http://www.unhchr.ch/tbs/doc.nsf/898586b1dc7b4043c1256a450044f331/5a855cc45d65082dc1257214005d3c77/$FILE/G0740377.doc.

6 Decade for Roma Inclusion 2005-2015, "NGO Coalition Calls for EU Framework Strategy Against Roma Discrimination," Press Statement, March 07, 2008, http://www.romadecade.org/index.php?content=211.

7 Thomas Hammarberg, "Memorandum following the visit to Italy on 19-20 June 2008," the Council of Europe Commissioner for Human Rights, CommDH(2008)18, para. 26, July 28, 2008, https://wcd.coe.int/ViewDoc.jsp?Ref=CommDH(2008)18#P75_6880.

8 Liana Melella and Giovanna Vitale, "Romeni, scattano le espulsioni 'Via i primi cinquemila,'" *la Repubblica*, November 2, 2007, http://www.repubblica.it/2007/10/sezioni/cronaca/tor-di-quinto/scattano-espulsioni/scattano-espulsioni.html.

9 Amnesty International, *The State of the World's Human Rights 2008: Italy*, POL 10/001/2008, June 2008, pp. 171-172.

10 "Brutal Attack in Rome: Italy Cracks Down on Immigrant Crime Wave," *Spiegel Online*, November 2, 2007, http://www.spiegel.de/international/europe/0,1518,515008,00.html.

11 Amnesty International, *The State of the World's Human Rights 2008: Italy*, POL 10/001/2008, June 2008, p. 171.

12 "Sicurezza, Veltroni contro la Romania Per le espulsioni varato un decreto legge," *la Repubblica*, October 31, 2007, http://www.repubblica.it/2007/10/sezioni/cronaca/tor-di-quinto/reazioni-uccisa/reazioni-uccisa.html.

13 John Hooper, "Violence as Italy expels migrants," *the Observer*, November 4, 2007, http://www.guardian.co.uk/world/2007/nov/04/italy.johnhooper.

14 Cristina Bradatan, "Migration: The Italian Job," *Transitions Online*, January 8, 2008, http://www.icare.to/article.php?id=12899&lang=en.

15 Claude Cahn, "EU must act to stop Italy racism crisis," *EUobserver.com*, August 21, 2008, http://euobserver.com/9/26620.

16 Peter Popham, "Italian tolerance goes up in smoke as Gypsy camp is burnt to ground," *the Independent*, May 16, 2008, http://www.independent.co.uk/news/world/europe/italian-tolerance-goes-up-in-smoke-as-gypsy-camp-is-burnt-to-ground-829318.html; Richard Owen, "Gypsy shanty towns burn in Naples as Italian police swoop on illegal immigrants," *Times Online*, May 16, 2008, http://www.timesonline.co.uk/tol/news/world/europe/article3940192.ece; and Decade for Roma Inclusion 2005-2015, "ERIO Statement Concerning the Aggressive Racial Attacks against Roma people in Italy," May 20, 2008, http://www.romadecade.org/index.php?content=7.

17 Open Society Institute, *Security a la Italiana: Fingerprinting, Extreme Violence and Harassment of Roma in Italy*, OSI, July 15, 2008, http://www.soros.org/initiatives/brussels/articles_publications/publications/fingerprinting_20080715/fingerprinting_20080715.pdf.

18 Decade for Roma Inclusion 2005-2015, "ERIO Statement Concerning the Aggressive Racial Attacks against Roma people in Italy," May 20, 2008, http://www.romadecade.org/index.php?content=7; and the Associated Press, "Nearly 400 held in Italian crime crackdown," *USA Today*, May 15, 2008, http://www.usatoday.com/news/world/2008-05-15-italy-crime_N.htm.

19 Richard Owen, "Gypsy shanty towns burn in Naples as Italian police swoop on illegal immigrants," *Times Online*, May 16, 2008, http://www.timesonline.co.uk/tol/news/world/europe/article3940192.ece.

20 Tracy Wilkinson, "Italy's right targets Gypsies, migrants," *the Los Angeles Times*, May 24, 2008, http://articles.latimes.com/2008/may/24/world/fg-right24.

21 Open Society Institute, *Security a la Italiana: Fingerprinting, Extreme Violence and Harassment of Roma in Italy*, OSI, July 15, 2008, http://www.soros.org/initiatives/brussels/articles_publications/publications/fingerprinting_20080715/fingerprinting_20080715.pdf.

22 Sylvia Poggioli, "Italy Considers Special Body to Deal with Gypsies," *National Public Radio*, May 19, 2008, http://www.npr.org/templates/story/story.php?storyId=90584021.

23 Phil Stewart, "Berlusconi launches illegal immigrant clampdown," *Reuters*, May 21, 2008, http://www.reuters.com/article/latestCrisis/idUSL21884735.

[24] Thomas Hammarberg, "Hate crimes – the ugly face of racism, anti-Semitism, anti-Gypsyism, Islamophobia and homophobia," *Viewpoints*, the Council of Europe Commissioner for Human Rights, July 21, 2008, http://www.coe.int/t/commissioner/Viewpoints/080721_en.asp.

[25] Silvio Berlusconi, "Dichiarazione dello stato di emergenza in relazione agli insediamenti di comunita' nomadi nel territorio delle regioni Campania, Lazio e Lombardia," *Gazzetta Ufficiale*, no. 122, May 26, 2008, http://www.solidarietasociale.gov.it/NR/rdonlyres/9BF7E323-7BA8-4676-B167-554B73954D2B/0/Focus_N8_Allegato2_DPCMstatodiemergenzaROM.pdf.

[26] The European Parliament, "Census of the Roma on the basis of ethnicity in Italy," Resolution 2008/2614(RSP), July 10, 2008, http://www.europarl.europa.eu/sides/getDoc.do?pubRef=-//EP//TEXT+TA+P6-TA-2008-0361+0+DOC+XML+V0//EN&language=EN.

[27] Open Society Institute, *Security a la Italiana: Fingerprinting, Extreme Violence and Harassment of Roma in Italy*, OSI, July 15, 2008, http://www.soros.org/initiatives/brussels/articles_publications/publications/fingerprinting_20080715/fingerprinting_20080715.pdf.

[28] The European Parliament, "Census of the Roma on the basis of ethnicity in Italy," Resolution 2008/2614(RSP), July 10, 2008, http://www.europarl.europa.eu/sides/getDoc.do?pubRef=-//EP//TEXT+TA+P6-TA-2008-0361+0+DOC+XML+V0//EN&language=EN.

[29] "Immigrants New anti-immigrant measures introduced," *Wanted in Rome*, May 23, 2008, http://www.wantedinrome.com/news/news.php?id_n=4497.

[30] Open Society Institute, *Security a la Italiana: Fingerprinting, Extreme Violence and Harassment of Roma in Italy*, OSI, July 15, 2008, http://www.soros.org/initiatives/brussels/articles_publications/publications/fingerprinting_20080715/fingerprinting_20080715.pdf.

[31] The European Parliament, "Census of the Roma on the basis of ethnicity in Italy," Resolution 2008/2614(RSP), July 10, 2008, http://www.europarl.europa.eu/sides/getDoc.do?pubRef=-//EP//TEXT+TA+P6-TA-2008-0361+0+DOC+XML+V0//EN&language=EN.

[32] Organization for Security and Cooperation in Europe, "OSCE human rights body concerned about anti-Roma violence in Italy," Press Release, May 16, 2008, http://www.osce.org/item/31147.html.

[33] The Associated Press, "EU officials denounce attacks on Gypsies in Italy," *Romea.cz*, May 20, 2008, http://www.romea.cz/english/index.php?id=detail&detail=2007_912.

[34] Thomas Hammarberg, *Memorandum following the visit to Italy on 19-20 June 2008*, the Council of Europe Commissioner for Human Rights, CommDH(2008)18, para. 26, July 28, 2008, https://wcd.coe.int/ViewDoc.jsp?Ref=CommDH(2008)18#P75_6880.

[35] "Italy: Gov't rejects claims of police violence in Gypsy camps," *Adkronos International*, July 29, 2008, http://www.adnkronos.com/AKI/English/Security/?id=1.0.2375686317.

[36] "Rebecca Covaciu, 12-year-old Roma girl, winner of the 2008 Unicef Prize, assaulted in Milan," *Romea.cz*, June 23, 2008, http://www.romea.cz/english/index.php?id=detail&detail=2007_939.

[37] Tom Kington, "We won't be Berlusconi's scapegoats, say Gypsies," *the Observer*, June 15, 2008, http://www.guardian.co.uk/world/2008/jun/15/italy.race.

[38] European Roma Rights Centre, "Skinhead Attack of Roma Sparks Unrest," *Roma Rights Quarterly*, vol. 3, November 2007, http://www.errc.org/cikk.php?cikk=2869.

[39] Reuters, "Bulgaria Roma riots highlight discrimination-group," *AlertNet*, August 16, 2007, http://www.alertnet.org/thenews/newsdesk/L16241089.htm.

[40] "Bulgaria: Summary of riots in Sofia," *Romea.cz*, August 20, 2007, http://www.romea.cz/english/index.php?id=detail&detail=2007_487, citing *Sofia Echo*.

[41] Reuters, "Bulgaria Roma riots highlight discrimination-group," *AlertNet*, August 16, 2007, http://www.alertnet.org/thenews/newsdesk/L16241089.htm.

[42] "Sofia Mayor Proposes Roma to Join Police Patrols in Risky Districts," *Romea.cz*, August 21, 2007, http://www.romea.cz/english/index.php?id=detail&detail=2007_497, citing *Sofia News Agency*.

[43] "A meeting between representatives of the National Police Service and Romani Baht Foundation," *Romea.cz*, August 22, 2007, http://www.romea.cz/english/index.php?id=detail&detail=2007_498, citing *Romea*.

[44] "Roma Teenager Beaten to Death in Bularia's Somokov," *Romea.cz*, August 22, 2007, http://www.romea.cz/english/index.php?id=detail&detail=2007_500, citing *Sofia News Agency/Focus News Agency*.

[45] European Roma Rights Centre, "Romani Teenager Beaten to Death," *Roma Rights Quarterly*, vol. 3, November 2007, http://www.errc.org/cikk.php?cikk=2871.

[46] "Bulgaria Launches Investigation in Roma Boy Beaten to Death Case," *Romea.cz*, August 23, 2007, http://www.romea.cz/english/index.php?id=detail&detail=2007_505, citing *Sofia News Agency*.

[47] Union of Councils for Jews in the Former Soviet Union, "Bulgarian Leaders Nix Creation of Militia against Roma," *the Bigotry Monitor*, vol. 7, no. 33, August 31, 2007, http://www.fsumonitor.com/stories/083107BM.shtml.

[48] Union of Councils for Jews in the Former Soviet Union, "Bulgarian Roma Clash with Skinheads," the Bigotry Monitor, vol. 7, no. 32, August 24, 2007, http://www.fsumonitor.com/stories/082407BM.shtml.

[49] Amnesty International, The State of the World's Human Rights 2008: Czech Republic, POL 10/001/2008, June 2008, p. 109.

[50] "Janackova escapes racism charges," Prague Daily Monitor, April 24, 2008, http://www.praguemonitor.com/en/323/czech_politics/21902/.

[51] "Extremist National Guard Starts Recruitment Campaign," Prague Daily Monitor, December 8, 2007, http://www.praguemonitor.com/en/230/czech_national_news/15761/.

[52] United Nations Office of the High Commissioner for Human Rights, "Summary Prepared by the Office of The High Commissioner for Human Rights, Czech Republic," UN General Assembly, Human Rights Council, A/HRC/WG.6/1/CZE/3, March 6, 2008, http://daccess-ods.un.org/TMP/1196441.html.

[53] European Union Agency for Fundamental Rights, Annual Report, 2008, TK-AG-08-001-EN-C, http://fra.europa.eu/fra/material/pub/ar08/ar08_en.pdf, p. 61.

[54] Cristina Bradatan, "Migration: The Italian Job," Transitions Online, January 8, 2008, http://www.icare.to/article.php?id=12899&lang=en.

[55] Amnesty International, The State of the World's Human Rights 2008: Romania, POL 10/001/2008, June 2008, p. 246.; and "Romanian foreign minister criticised for saying citizens who commit crimes abroad should be sent to labor camps in the desert," Daily Mail, November 5, 2007, http://www.dailymail.co.uk/news/article-491886/Romanian-foreign-minister-criticised-saying-citizens-commit-crimes-abroad-sent-labour-camps-desert.html.

[56] Henry Scicluna, "Anti-Romani Speech in Europe's Public Space—The Mechanism of Hate Speech," European Roma Rights Centre, Roma Rights Quarterly, vol. 3, November 2007, http://www.errc.org/cikk.php?cikk=2921; and the Associated Press, "Romania president sorry for 'stinky Gypsy' slur; He lashed out at reporter; activists left him a bar of soap and Gypsy music," MSNBC, May 21, 2007, http://www.msnbc.msn.com/id/18789903/.

[57] European Roma Rights Center, In Search of Happy Gypsies: Persecution of Pariah Minorities in Russia, May 2005, http://www.errc.org/db/01/4A/m0000014A.pdf.

[58] Open Society Institute, "Ethnic Profiling in the Moscow Metro," OSI, June 2006, p. 47, http://www.soros.org/initiatives/osji/articles_publications/publications/profiling_20060613.

[59] European Roma Rights Center, In Search of Happy Gypsies: Persecution of Pariah Minorities in Russia, May 2005, http://www.errc.org/db/01/4A/m0000014A.pdf.

[60] Union of Councils for Jews in the Former Soviet Union, "Roma Family Shot Dead," the Bigotry Monitor, vol. 7, no. 35, September 14, 2007, http://www.fsumonitor.com/stories/091407BM.shtml; and Timofei Borisov, "V kogo strelyayut v Ingushetii," Rossijskaya Gazeta, September 12, 2007, http://www.rg.ru/2007/09/12/ingushetiya.html.

[61] European Roma Rights Centre, "Romani Man Beaten in Serbia," Roma Rights Quarterly, November, 2007, http://www.errc.org/cikk.php?cikk=2897.

[62] Organization for Security and Cooperation in Europe, "Head of OSCE Serbia Mission says perpetrators of Roma attacks should be prosecuted," Press Release, August 24, 2007, http://www.osce.org/item/26009.html.

[63] Zuzana Vilikovská, "Sarközy family suffers another attack at hands of masked assailants," the Slovak Spectator, May 31, 2007, http://www.spectator.sk/articles/view/27793.

[64] European Roma Rights Centre, "ERRC Letter to Slovak Prime Minister Mikuláš Dzurinda Concerning Events in Záhorská Ves," February 13, 2004, http://www.errc.org/cikk.php?cikk=350.

[65] U.S. Department of State, Bureau of Democracy, Human Rights and Labor, Country Reports on Human Rights Practices 2007: Slovak Republic, March 11, 2008, http://www.state.gov/g/drl/rls/hrrpt/2007/100584.htm.

[66] U.S. Department of State, Bureau of Democracy, Human Rights and Labor, Country Reports on Human Rights Practices 2007: Slovak Republic, March 11, 2008, http://www.state.gov/g/drl/rls/hrrpt/2007/100584.htm.

[67] European Union Agency for Fundamental Rights, Annual Report, 2008, TK-AG-08-001-EN-C, http://fra.europa.eu/fra/material/pub/ar08/ar08_en.pdf, p. 22.

[68] The Council of Europe, European Commission against Racism and Intolerance, Third Report on Ukraine, CRI(2008)4, February 12, 2008, http://www.coe.int/t/e/human_rights/ecri/1-ecri/2-country-by-country_approach/Ukraine/.

[69] European Roma Rights Centre, Proceedings Discontinued: The inertia of Roma rights change in Ukraine, Country Report Series, no. 16, December 2006, http://www.errc.org/db/01/F2/m000001F2.pdf, p. 39.

[70] Rachel Shields, "'No blacks, no dogs, no Gypsies,'" the Independent, July 6, 2008, http://www.independent.co.uk/news/uk/home-news/no-blacks-no-dogsno-gypsies-860873.html.

[71] Gay McDougall, "On UK National Gypsy, Roma and Traveller History Month," United Nations Independent Expert on Minority Issues, Statement, June 2008, http://www.grthm.co.uk/downloads/statement_from_IEMI.pdf.

Violence Based on Sexual Orientation and Gender Identity Bias

Table of Contents

Executive Summary

Continuing violence motivated by hatred and prejudice based on sexual orientation and gender identity, though still largely unseen, is an intimidating day-to-day reality for people across Europe and North America. The limited official statistics available suggest that these crimes represent a significant portion of violent hate crimes overall and are characterized by levels of serious physical violence that in some cases exceed those present in other types of hate crimes. None of the official reports suggest that incidents are decreasing; government data in some countries, as well as credible nongovernmental reports, suggest an increase. The victims include people who describe themselves as lesbian, gay, bisexual, or transgender (together, "LGBT"), as well as others who are targeted because they do not conform to stereotypes of gender identity. The victims of violence also include LGBT rights activists and organizations, openly gay commercial establishments, and those attending gay pride parades and other gay related public events. Bias crimes of this kind are often called "homophobic" crimes.

Nongovernmental monitoring, combined with incident reports available from the media, have reinforced official findings that homophobic violence is both frequent and of particular brutality. Annual reports by organizations in **France** and the **United States**, as well as new surveys and reports on **Germany**, **Turkey**, and the **United Kingdom** shed light onto the extent of harassment and violence in those countries, as well as the problem of underreporting to the police.

Few of the participating states of the Organization for Security and Cooperation in Europe (OSCE) track and provide official statistics on crimes motivated by sexual orientation bias. **Canada**, **Sweden**, the **United Kingdom**, and the **United States** are the countries where such monitoring is most developed. Other countries, like the **Netherlands** and **Norway**, have also recently undertaken to monitor homophobic hate crimes. Even in those countries where data is collected, however, the number of incidents is generally thought to be highly underreported. The lack of data on sexual orientation bias crimes for the vast majority of OSCE participating states makes it very difficult to assess the law enforcement response to violent incidents.

Only 12 of the 56 OSCE states have legislation that allows for bias based on sexual orientation to be treated as an aggravating circumstance in the commission of a crime. These are: **Andorra, Belgium, Canada, Croatia, Denmark, France, Portugal, Romania, Spain, Sweden**, the **United Kingdom**, and the **United States**. In the **United States**, although federal hate crime legislation does not make violence motivated by sexual orientation a crime, state legislation in 30 states and the District of Columbia provides enhanced penalties for offenses motivated by sexual orientation bias.

As in the past, the years 2007 and 2008 saw the greatest public visibility for LGBT persons in the form of gay pride parades, although that visibility triggered violence and other manifestations of intolerance in several countries. In a number of cases documented in this report, gay pride parades and events in Eastern Europe resulted in political diatribes attacking people of minority sexual orientations from political and other leaders, inadequate police protection, and acts of harassment and violence against the participants.

The way in which recent gay pride events transpired in some countries—including **Croatia, Estonia, Latvia, Poland**, and **Romania**—suggest that the authorities took additional precautions against violent disruption in comparison to previous years. In other countries—such as **Moldova** and the **Russian Federation**—the authorities themselves continued to contribute to the danger faced by the participants in gay pride parades. In another group of countries—notably **Bulgaria**, the **Czech Republic**, **Hungary** and **Slovenia**—incidents of violence occurred despite apparently significant police preparations to protect the marchers. In a number of cases, the police were able to identify the violent protestors as being affiliated with organized extremist groups.

The international response to hate crimes against people because of their sexual orientation or gender identity is hindered by the fact that these forms of discrimination are not well integrated into international human rights and antidiscrimination bodies and mechanisms. Indeed, there is no convention or treaty specifically focusing on the human rights of LGBT persons. Within the framework of the United Nations, the problem of bias-motivated violence against LGBT persons is only just beginning to gain recognition and has remained largely outside of the framework of the general human rights treaty bodies, as well as those special mechanisms that deal with related issues of discrimination and intolerance. The nonbinding Yogyakarta Principles, developed by human rights experts, offer a way forward by reflecting state obligations under international law to address human rights violations—including violent hate crimes—based on sexual orientation and gender identity.

Within Europe, several institutions of regional intergovernmental organizations and other bodies have incorporated the problem of homophobic hate crimes into their mandates and/or their activities, although challenges remain to a more integrated and comprehensive approach.

I. Violence Based on Sexual Orientation and Gender Identity Bias

Continuing violence motivated by hatred and prejudice based on sexual orientation and gender identity, though largely unseen, is an intimidating day-to-day reality for people across Europe and North America.

Although the full extent of the problem is not known because few governments collect and publish data on such incidents, violent hate crimes based on sexual orientation and gender identity occur in many parts of Europe and North America. Incident reports provide a basis to establish that homophobic violence is both frequent and particularly brutal. Indeed, as discussed below, the few official statistics available suggest that bias motivated violence against LGBT persons is a significant portion of violent hate crimes overall and is characterized by levels of physical violence that in many cases exceed those of other forms of reported hate crime. Although there is not enough data available to document trends in violence based on sexual orientation and gender identity bias, none of the official reports suggest that incidents are decreasing; reports in some countries suggest an increase.

The victims of violence include openly gay individuals and commercial establishments, gay rights activists and organizations, transsexuals and transgender individuals, and those attending gay pride parades and other gay related public events. Those targeted in what is often called homophobic violence include people who describe themselves as lesbian, gay, bisexual, or transgender (together, "LGBT"), as well as others who are victimized because they do not conform to stereotypes of gender identity, or are perceived to belong to the aforementioned groups.

A. Reporting from Nongovernmental Organizations

Credible studies by nongovernmental organizations report that homophobic violence is either on the increase or remains at historically high levels.

For example, in **France**, SOS Homophobie has been reporting on homophobia for more than a decade. In the annual report covering 2007, the organization documented 1,263 incidents of homophobia in France. Although this represents a 5 percent decrease over 2006, it is nonetheless the second highest figure in the history of reporting. The number of violent incidents (132) also decreased—by 14 percent over 2006 figures. The percentage of violent attacks in relation to overall incidents—11 percent in 2007—has remained steady at between 11 and 13 percent since 2003.[1]

In the **United States**, the National Coalition of Anti-Violence Programs (NCAVP) and more than thirty of its member organizations across the country released an annual report in May 2008, showing a 24 percent increase in incidents of violence against LGBT people in 2007, compared to 2006. They noted that 2007 also had the third-highest murder rate in the ten years that NCAVP has been compiling the report, with murders more than doubling from 10 in 2006 to 21 in 2007.

The report examines data based on incidents involving 2,430 LGBT persons who reported experiencing bias-motivated violence in major metropolitan areas, including Chicago, Columbus, Houston, Kansas City, Los Angeles, the New York City area, and the San Francisco Bay area; and in seven states in which monitoring was carried out: Colorado, Massachusetts, Michigan, Minnesota, Pennsylvania, Vermont, and Wisconsin.

NCAVP officials said their report was the most complete examination of antigay violence in the U.S., noting that the annual hate crime reports published by the Federal Bureau of Investigation (FBI) consistently contain information on far fewer cases than the NCAVP publication. The National Coalition noted that the FBI reports rely solely on law enforcement reports rather than victim service organization data.

In Michigan, for instance, hate crimes on the basis of sexual orientation more than doubled in 2007 from the previous year's total, according to NCAVP findings, which draw upon monitoring by Michigan's Triangle Foundation. The annual findings showed that Michigan led the nation in the increase of hate crime reports. 226 incidents were reported and documented in 2007, compared to 97 in 2006, constituting an increase of 133 percent.[2]

In other countries, NGO reports and surveys indicate that homophobic violence affects a substantial percentage of LGBT persons and is widely underreported to the police.

In **Germany**, a nationwide victim survey was conducted among gay and bisexual youths and adults on their experiences with violence. Almost twenty-four thousand people participated in the survey which was conducted between December 1, 2006, and January 31, 2007, by Maneo, a nongovernmental gay rights organization. The survey found that 35 percent of all respondents said they experienced bias-motivated violence in the past year, while almost two-thirds (63 percent) of young gay and bisexual men under the age of 18 reported being victims of such violence. Only 10 percent of the victims filed reports with the police.[3] A second survey was conducted one year later with 17,500 participants, and preliminary data showed that almost 40 percent reported having experienced bias-motivated violence.

Maneo expects to release more detailed results from the second survey in late 2008.[4]

With regard to **Turkey**, Human Rights Watch released a new report on May 22, 2008—*We Need a Law for Liberation: Gender, Sexuality, and Human Rights in a Changing Turkey*. The report highlighted the violence experienced by the LGBT community in Turkey, using victims' testimonies and case studies which spanned over a three year period.

The report found that "every transgender person and many of the gay men Human Rights Watch spoke to report having been a victim of a violent crime— sometimes multiple crimes—based on their sexual orientation or gender identity. Beatings in cruising areas, robberies by men or gangs who arranged to meet their victims over the internet and attempted murder were among the documented abuses." The vulnerable social position of gay men and transgender people was characterized as "living in fear" and "a social hell."

The interviewed lesbian and bisexual women "reported pressure, often extreme, from their families. Some were constrained to undergo psychological or psychiatric 'help' to 'change' their sexual orientation. Many faced physical violence." This situation has been referred to as a balance between "silence and violence."[5]

In the **United Kingdom**, on June 26, 2008, a UK-based NGO Stonewall published *Homophobic Hate Crime: The Gay British Crime Survey*. This report surveyed 1,721 members of the LGBT community across Great Britain. It exposed incidences of verbal abuse and violent hate crimes experienced by individuals who identify as LGBT throughout England, Scotland, and Wales. The report concluded that:

■ nearly 13 percent of lesbian, gay and bisexual people have experienced a homophobic hate crime or incident in the last year;

- 20 percent of lesbian and gay people have experienced a homophobic hate crime or incident in the last three years;

- 4 percent of the respondents reported a violent bias-motivated physical assault;

- 14 percent of victims of homophobic hate crimes or incidents did not report them to anyone because they happened too frequently to report;

- a third of lesbian and gay people alter their behavior so they are not perceived as being gay, specifically to prevent being a victim of hate crime.[6]

B. Violent Attacks on Individuals and Property

Incidents of bias-motivated violence include attacks on people who described themselves as openly gay, as well as incidents in which attackers wrongly identified the victims as gay. The fact that incidents listed below come from a limited number of countries does not necessarily mean that the problem of homophobic violence is more alarming there. More likely it reflects the fact that NGOs and media are more active in bringing exposure to such cases. Examples of violent attacks from among the incidents reported in the media and by NGOs in 2007 and early 2008 include the following:

In **Belarus**, on May 21, 2008, at about 11:00 p.m., Edward Tarletski, an openly gay Belarusian man and the founder of Lambda Belarus, the first gay rights organization in Belarus, was badly beaten upon arriving to his apartment building in Minsk. He was attacked by three young people between 20 and 25 years old. According to Tarletski: "I was approaching the entrance when I saw young people smoking nearby. ... One of them called me by my surname—to make it clear that it was me, I think. Another one unexpectedly hit me in the face, and I fell down. They kicked me many times, mostly in the head. Then they ran away. I lost con-

sciousness. A neighbor then helped me to reach my apartment. The attackers took nothing: in my bag I had money and a camera." Tarletski revealed that this was the third such assault on him. He added that he did not intend to report the incident to the police, as that "would be a waste of time."[7]

In **Croatia**, police investigated the 2006 attack by a dozen people on two gay British tourists in a bar, in which one of the tourists sustained a concussion, ear injury, and loss of teeth. Police also investigated a similar attack on two German gay tourists in Split, where they were attacked while walking on the waterfront holding hands; one of the victims sustained a nose fracture and the other a slight chest injury. No arrests were made in either case.[8]

In **France**, on February 24, 2008, six attackers, who ranged in ages of 17 to 28, tormented 19-year-old Mathieu Roumi in the Paris suburb of Bagneux, in what appeared to have begun as an argument over stolen goods. Prosecutors said the six held the victim for about nine and a half hours and "tortur[ed] him by punching him, sexually humiliating him and writing 'dirty Jew' and 'dirty faggot' on his forehead." They allegedly forced him to eat cigarette butts and forced a stick covered by a condom into his throat. The six alleged attackers were detained, and investigators filed preliminary charges against them. The charges included "group violence motivated by a person's real or supposed race, religion or sexual orientation, acts of torture, blackmail and theft." The Bagneux City Hall issued a statement, noting that officials were "shocked and outraged" by the attack.[9]

In **Germany**, five victims were hospitalized in June 2007 after eight right-wing extremists attacked a group of actors still costumed from their performance of *The Rocky Horror Picture Show* in Halberstadt (Saxony-Anhalt). Four previously convicted right-wing extremists went on trial for this attack on October 9, 2007, in Magdeburg. On December 5, the four men were released from custody on the basis of insufficient evidence. One suspect, who made a partial confession, was obliged to report his whereabouts periodically to the police.[10]

In **Hungary**, within a one week period, two different gay establishments in Budapest were attacked. On June 27, 2008 at 3 a.m., unknown perpetrators threw a petrol bomb at Action, a gay bar. The front room of this small bar burst into flames. The fire was extinguished, and no one was injured. It was reported that "shortly before the attack, someone called the bar and inquired if there were any guests and how long the bar would be open. Then the caller went on to threaten to attack the bar." The police department was reportedly investigating this incident as an act of vandalism. Several LBGT rights organizations, including the Patent Association, assert that the fire should be investigated as an act of attempted murder.[11]

On July 3, 2008, Magnum (a gay bath house, or sauna), was targeted in the early morning hours. As in the attack at Action, the perpetrators allegedly called Magnum prior to the attack. Then four petrol bombs were thrown into the sauna. The fire was promptly extinguished, although one person reported suffering from smoke inhalation.[12] Both attacks occurred in the run-up to Budapest's 2008 Gay Pride Week 2008.

In **Ireland**, on the night of June 4, 2008, 27-year-old Stephen Scott was walking home near Ballyduff Brae in Newtownabbey when he was attacked. Three youths, thought to be in their late teens, knocked him to the ground and continued kicking and punching him as they shouted homophobic insults. Scott was treated at a local hospital for a head injury, a leg injury and broken ribs. Scott stated that the attack was "enough to take a life—there were three of them on me and I was left for dead."[13]

In **Italy**, on May 24, 2008, openly gay Christian Floris, a radio personality for the popular radio station known for its LGBT-related content, *DeeGay*, was physically

attacked late at night outside his home in Rome. There were allegedly two attackers who awaited his return underneath his porch. They smashed his head against a wall and taunted him to stop advocating for the LGBT community. As a result of the injuries sustained, Floris spent seven days in the hospital.[14] In response to these and other incidents, Aurelio Mancuso, president of Arcigay, an LGBT rights organization, said Italy had been gripped by "a fit of homophobia."[15]

A Rome-based gay rights organization was also the subject of a violent attack. On April 17, 2008, a mob of youths burst into the Mario Mieli Homosexual Cultural Circle, ransacking the building while members of the center were still inside. The gang shouted antigay and antisemitic epithets when confronted by members of the center. Police were apparently investigating whether or not this group was linked to a neo-Nazi gang whose members had been arrested earlier that week.[16]

In **Kyrgyzstan**, on November 26, 2007, around 10 p.m., a transgender male was attacked in the streets of Bishkek. Kyrgyzstan's LGBT advocacy group, Labrys, reported on the incident, in which the victim recounted that two drunken men approached him and began to harass and threaten him. The victim went into a nearby supermarket to ask a security guard for assistance. The men followed him into the shop, and the guard refused to help. The assaulters continued to follow the victim through the streets, shouting obscenities and grabbing him. The victim was eventually able to escape. Labrys reported that "this situation is unfortunately very common for many LGBT people in Kyrgyzstan."[17]

In **Portugal**, in February 2008, a transgender woman was murdered in Lisbon. The victim, Luna, was 42 years old, partially deaf, and of Brazilian origin.

According to the Panteras Rosa, an organization combating hatred against LGBT persons, "Luna was a woman who fought against many obstacles and died the victim of great violence, possibly fed by hatred, prejudice and ignorance. Her body was left in a dumpster, hidden by rubble and dust, as if it was garbage, as if her life had not been worth living."[18]

In the **Russian Federation**, on June 17, 2007, several right-wing groups organized "antigay patrolling" of the Ilyinsky square in Moscow. One of the participants in the patrol, a member of the neo-Nazi Slavic Union, was seen hitting a man in the face and declaring that such people should be beaten. The victim ran away.[19]

Also in the Russian Federation, on February 14, 2008, a group of LGBT activists in collaboration with young antifascist activists organized a manifestation on the occasion of St. Valentine's Day. The peaceful event was targeted by a large group of neo-Nazis. Several people were attacked and one was severely wounded and hospitalized.[20]

In **Sweden,** on July 27, 2008, two gay men, aged 25 and 30, were attacked by three men at a park in Stockholm. Allegedly, the couple was stopped after the attackers saw them kissing. The attackers asked for directions, then asked about the couple's sexuality. The three offenders drew knives and robbed them of mobile phones and money. They stabbed one man in the stomach, resulting in a serious injury. Police have investigated this attack as a hate crime due to hostile slurs and the unprovoked stabbing of one of the gay men. No arrests had been made as of the end of July 2008.[21]

In **Turkey**, on July 2008, 26-year-old Ahmet Yıldız was shot while leaving a cafe in Istanbul. The victim nonetheless managed to reach his car and attempted to escape the attackers. But he lost control of the car and crashed it on the side of the road. He died shortly after being brought to a local hospital. Friends of Yıldız believe that he was shot because of his sexual orientation. Yıldız had previously received death threats because of his sexuality and had on an earlier occasion filed a complaint with the police. Sedef Çakmak, an activist for Lambda Istanbul and a friend of the victim, commented: "I feel helpless: we are trying to raise awareness of gay rights in this country, but the more visible we become, the more we open ourselves up to this sort of attack."[22]

In the **United Kingdom**, Stonewall's *Homophobic Hate Crime: The Gay British Crime Survey* included some of the following testimonies of harassment and violence:

- "My son was constantly teased and bullied because his mum likes girls... It is the kids in the area where you live that are the problem and if it is out of school hours the schools cannot do anything. One time my son was chased up a tree and four kids stood at the bottom throwing rocks and even an open pen knife at him yelling things like 'gay lord' and 'faggot.'"

- "My partner was attacked before Christmas receiving a cut to the top of his head and a broken wrist. He told the nurse at the hospital he was drunk and fell over the night before. He was in truth struck twice with a cricket bat, once from behind on his head and the second hit his arm."

- "He was not drunk! We had just left a gay club, he was on call so could not drink. The attacker called him a fag and queer. He was chased off by a taxi driver. My partner will not report it and most of us don't!"

- "Unfortunately I think that when it is known that someone is gay/lesbian this does put them at a higher risk. I have experienced this myself when I lived in a different area and I was seeing a girl at the time and some louts saw us walking home together. This was not in terms of very serious crimes but shouting, harassment and throwing stones, apples, etc. at us or any visitors to my house."[23]

In the **United States**, a number of cases were marked by particular brutality and lead to death.

On February 13, 2007, in Detroit, Michigan, 72-year-old Andrew Anthos was riding a bus home, and a stranger asked Anthos if he was gay, followed him off a bus, and beat him with a pipe. Anthos spent the next ten days in a coma, paralyzed from the neck down, before dying on February 23. Witnesses say the assailant, who has not been apprehended as of mid-July 2008, spewed antigay expletives in the process of attacking the senior citizen victim.[24]

On March 14, 2007, in Wahneta, Florida, 25-year-old Ryan Keith Skipper was brutally murdered. Skipper's body—with 20 stab wounds and a slit throat—was found on a dark, rural road in Wahneta less than 2 miles from his home. William David Brown, Jr., 20, and Joseph Eli Bearden, 21, were later indicted on robbery and first degree murder charges. Their trial, originally set for August 2008 was pushed to February 2009. The accused killers allegedly drove Ryan's blood-soaked car around the county and bragged of killing him. According to a sheriff's department affidavit, Ryan's murder should be considered a hate crime since one of the men stated that Ryan was targeted because "he was a faggot."[25]

On February 12, 2008, in Oxnard, California, 15-year-old Lawrence King was shot twice in the head while sitting in his classroom at E.O. Green Junior High School. He was pronounced brain-dead the following afternoon and was subsequently taken off life support.[26] According to his classmates, King was considered a social outcast and often wore makeup, jewelry and high heels to school, making him the subject of ridicule among other boys. Brandon McInerney, 14, was charged with the premeditated murder of King.[27]

II. The Response of Governments to Violence on the Basis of Sexual Orientation and Gender Identity Bias

A. Official Statistics

Although essential to an effective strategy to combat hate crime, very few of the 56 European and North American governments that constitute the Organization for Security and Cooperation in Europe (OSCE) collect and publish data on crimes motivated by bias based on sexual orientation and gender identity. **Canada**, **Sweden**, the **United Kingdom**, and the **United States** are the countries where such monitoring is most developed. Other countries, like the **Netherlands** and **Norway**, have also undertaken more recently to monitor homophobic hate crimes. As discussed earlier, even in those countries where data is collected, the number of incidents is generally thought to be highly underreported.

In **Canada**, on June 9, 2008, the government released national hate crime statistics for the first time. This report is based upon data on 892 hate-motivated cases from 2006. Police-reported data found that approximately eighty incidents (10 percent) represented hate crimes motivated by sexual orientation. Homophobic hate crimes were the third most frequent hate crime after race/ethnicity (61 percent) and religion (27 percent). Incidents motivated by sexual orientation were primarily of a violent nature, thereby standing out from other hate crimes. The report showed that 56 percent of the documented homophobic hate crimes were of a violent nature. In comparison, 38 percent of all racially motivated offenses were of a violent nature.[28]

In addition to these national figures, a number of Canadian police agencies in metropolitan areas report on hate crimes, including those motivated by sexual orientation. In Toronto, the police's 2006 report showed an increase of sexual orientation-based hate crimes over 2005. 18 cases of LGBT victimization represented 11 percent of the 162 reported hate crimes. In 2007, even though there was a sharply reduced number of recorded hate crimes (130), the number of those motivated by sexual orientation bias was similar (17), representing a higher percentage (13 percent) of the overall number.[29]

In **Sweden**, the Swedish Security Service began publishing statistics on hate crimes with xenophobic, antisemitic, or homophobic motives in 1997; in 2006, the National Council for Crime Prevention was commissioned to produce hate crime statistics. Data from this source revealed that 3,536 hate crimes were reported in 2007. 723 cases had a homophobic motive (20.4 percent of total reported hate crimes).[30] The Swedish Federation for Lesbian, Gay, Bisexual and Transgender Rights (RFSL) expressed deep concern that 'the report clearly indicates an increase of 21 percent in hate crimes with homophobic motives compared with 2005. In addition, the statistics show that an alarmingly large number of perpetrators are under the age of 20 (53 percent).'[31]

There are national hate crime figures in the **United Kingdom**, but these do not track crimes motivated by bias based on sexual orientation and gender identity. Within the country, London's Metropolitan Police produces the most consistent and comprehensive monitoring and reporting on sexual orientation bias crimes. Although hate crimes overall in London have been on the decline over the past two years, the number of crimes motivated by sexual orientation has remained steady, with 1,294 in 2005/2006 (representing 8.3 percent of overall hate crime), and 1,260 from 2006/2007 (representing 10.1 percent).[32]

The Police Services of Northern Ireland, in statistical reporting for the period of April 1, 2007, through March 31, 2008, reported details on 160 "homophobic" incidents and 7 "transphobic" incidents.[33] 68.4 percent of those incidents were reported to be violent crimes against persons (as opposed to property crimes), significantly higher than for any other bias category. By contrast, as concerns racially motivated crimes, the percentage of violent crimes (37.4 percent) is much lower. Compared with the previous year, there were 5 more homophobic incidents reported (+3.2 percent) and a decrease by 25 transphobic incidents (-78.1 percent).[34]

In the **United States**, the Uniform Crime Reporting Program of the Federal Bureau of Investigation reported that in 2006 there were 9,076 hate crime offenses. Of those, 1,415 hate crime offenses (15.5 percent) were motivated by sexual orientation bias.[35] This constitutes an increase of 17.2 percent over the 1,171 incidents reported to the FBI from state and local law enforcement jurisdictions in 2005. As in previous years, FBI hate crime data shows that attacks founded on sexual orientation continue to be characterized by a high level of violence, with a higher proportion of personal assaults than in other categories of hate crime.[36]

In two other countries, police have also recently begun to record and report on violence motivated by animus based on sexual orientation. In the **Netherlands**, the Amsterdam police for the first time in 2007 registered antigay incidents separately, recording 234 such incidents. Most of them involved verbal abuse, but in 79 cases violence was used.[37] Moreover, the Amsterdam

City Council asked the University of Amsterdam to do a study on perpetrators of antigay violence. The main aim of the study is to get more insight into the motives behind homophobic hate crimes. In-depth interviews with about thirty perpetrators will provide the core data for analysis. Results are expected in autumn 2008.

In **Norway**, according to the Equality and Antidiscrimination Ombudsman, the government took new steps in March 2007 to combat hate crime, with a decision by the Department of Justice and Police that all incidents of hate crime are henceforth to be registered by the police. The Ombudsman's Office further informed Human Rights First that it has been cooperating with the police in this matter, that registration of hate crimes has been discussed, and that police will begin recording bias motivations based on ethnic origin, sexual orientation, and religion.[38] In September 2007, Justice Minister Knut Storberget told the press that "Norwegian police have begun registering all episodes of so-called 'hate crimes,' involving violence against certain groups of people," and cited findings of a recent survey conducted by the ministry indicating a rise in violence of this kind. This survey identified people targeted because of racial differences, gay men, and the elderly as particularly vulnerable to bias attacks.[39]

In 2007, the Norwegian police, together with the National Association for Lesbian and Homosexual Emancipation (LLH), introduced a hate crime campaign on violence against lesbians and gay men. The goal is to prevent homophobic violence, increase reporting, and make sure that crimes are registered correctly.[40]

B. Law Enforcement and the Framework of Criminal Law

The lack of data on sexual orientation bias crimes for the vast majority of OSCE participating states makes it very difficult to assess the law enforcement response to violent incidents. Even where such statistics are recorded, underreporting is a major problem with regard to the LGBT community.

Victims of hate crimes driven by homophobia often face cultural or social obstacles to reporting attacks and threats. Attacks on LGBT people sometimes go unreported because to do so would bring into light an individual's sexual orientation, possibly resulting in further abuse. LGBT persons may fear additional victimization and have little confidence that the criminal justice system will act appropriately in response to criminal complaints.

Compounding the problems of underreporting and police intolerance is the reality that homosexuality remains socially unacceptable in broad social sectors in many countries of the OSCE. Antigay rhetoric of some political and community leaders have strongly reinforced that message, as have failures of the police to protect participants in gay pride parades (discussed below).

In addition, legislation on bias as an aggravating circumstance extends to sexual orientation in only 12 of the 56 OSCE participating countries. These are: **Andorra, Belgium, Canada, Croatia, Denmark, France, Portugal, Romania, Spain, Sweden,** the **United Kingdom,** and the **United States** (in some of the states, but not the national law). Bias based on gender identity is explicitly mentioned in criminal law only in the **United States**—and even there only at the state level in eleven states and the District of Columbia.[41]

In the absence of national legislation expressly identifying sexual orientation bias as an aggravating factor, at least one country has sentencing instructions or guidelines acknowledging these bias elements as aggravating circumstances. In the **Netherlands**, a Discrimination Directive, issued every four years by the Board of Procurators General, while falling short of a legislative act, instructs prosecutors to request a 25 percent penalty enhancement in the sentencing of common crimes motivated by discrimination, including on the grounds of sexual orientation.

In the **United States**, although federal hate crime legislation does not make violence motivated by sexual orientation a crime, state legislation in thirty states and the District of Columbia provides enhanced penalties for offenses motivated by sexual orientation bias.[42] Efforts in 2007 to expand federal hate crime legislation through the adoption of the Local Law Enforcement Hate Crime Prevention Act of 2007 (LLEHCPA) were unsuccessful. The LLEHCPA was passed by the House of Representatives on May 3, 2007, and the Senate on September 27, 2007, but was not finally enacted into law. The proposed legislation sought to eliminate the requirement that prosecutors must demonstrate that a victim was targeted expressly because of that person's participation in one of the six federally protected categories, one of the current requirements for application of the federal law.[43] The bill also would have extended the bias categories under federal protection to include gender identity, sexual orientation, and disability. On December 10, 2007, the bill was detached from the Department of Defense Authorization Bill (FY2009). President George W. Bush indicated he would veto the bill if it was sent to his desk as a stand-alone bill, and Congressional leadership decided to suspend any further action until 2008 at the earliest.

In the **United Kingdom**, where bias based on sexual orientation is an aggravating factor in the criminal law in England, Wales, and Northern Ireland, efforts have been made by the Crown Prosecution Service to enhance the prosecution of homophobic hate crimes. In November 2007, the CPS released a report to provide guidance on the prosecution of hate crimes motivated by bias based on sexual orientation. The report—*Guidance on Prosecuting Cases of Homophobic and Transphobic Crime*—reiterates the importance of thorough investigation and prosecution of such cases, stating that

> prejudice, discrimination or hatred of members of any part of our community based on their sexual orientation or gender identity have no place in a civilized society; any such prejudice, discrimination or hate that shows itself in the commission of crime must be thoroughly and properly

investigated and firmly and rigorously prosecuted in the courts. A clear message must be sent so that those who commit such crimes realize that they will be dealt with firmly under the criminal law: the CPS has a vital role to play in delivering this aim, not only in terms of its own role but also in terms of advising its partners in the criminal justice system—the police, the courts, magistrates, judges and those in the voluntary sector—that this sort of crime must no longer be tolerated.[44]

C. Assaults on Gay Pride Parades and Events and the Response of Police

As in the past, the year 2007 and early 2008 saw the greatest public visibility for the LGBT community in the form of gay pride parades, although that visibility triggered incidents of intolerance and violence in several countries. In some cases, gay pride parades and events in Eastern Europe resulted in homophobic diatribes from political and other leaders, poor police protection, and acts of harassment and violence against the participants. The way in which recent events transpired in some countries—including **Croatia**, **Estonia**, **Latvia**, **Poland**, and **Romania**—suggest that the authorities took additional precautions to prevent violence in comparison to previous years. In other countries—particularly **Moldova** and the **Russian Federation**—the authorities themselves continued to contribute to the danger faced by the participants in gay pride parades. In another group of countries—notably **Bulgaria**, the **Czech Republic**, **Hungary**, and **Slovenia**—incidents of violence occurred despite apparently significant police preparations to protect the marchers. In a number of cases, police authorities were able to identify the violent protestors as being affiliated with an organized neofascist or other extremist groups operating within that particular country.

Both legal guidance and political concern have been expressed in the last two years by several European institutions regarding the duty of the state to protect people in their exercise of freedom of assembly.

In a May 3, 2007, decision in *Baczkowski and Others v. Poland*—a case brought in response to the decision of the Polish authorities to ban a gay pride march in Warsaw in June 2005—the European Court of Human Rights held that "a genuine and effective respect for freedom of association and assembly cannot be reduced to a mere duty on the part of the State not to interfere; a purely negative conception would not be compatible with the purpose of Article 11 nor with that of the Convention in general. There may thus be positive obligations to secure the effective enjoyment of these freedoms." This could be interpreted as a duty on the government to protect the participants of gay pride marches from hate motivated acts committed against them while enjoying freedom of assembly.[45]

On April 26, 2007, the European Parliament adopted a resolution on *Homophobia in Europe*, addressing many concerns related to the discrimination and violence experienced by the LGBT community in Europe. The resolution was prompted by a "series of worrying events, such as the prohibition imposed by local authorities on holding equality and gay pride marches, the use by leading politicians and religious leaders of inflammatory or threatening language or hate speech, the failure by the police to provide adequate protection against violent demonstrations by homophobic groups, even while breaking up peaceful demonstrations."[46]

What follows is a chronicle of some of the incidents of violence that occurred in a wide range of countries—largely in Eastern and Southeastern Europe—since 2007.

Bulgaria

On June 28, 2008, in the country's first gay pride parade in Sofia, protestors threw Molotov cocktails, stones, bottles, and gasoline bombs at 150 participants. The police—present in numbers that nearly equaled the number of participants—were largely able to provide protection to the marchers, arresting 88 people for their involvement in attacks against the parade.

Various extremist groups were identified as contributing to the attacks. Among those arrested was Boyan Rasate, head of the Bulgarian National Union, an extreme right party. The group organized a "week of intolerance" right before the gay pride march with the motto "Be normal, Be intolerant." The group held seminars on restricting "homosexual ideas" from spreading in Bulgaria.[47]

Croatia

On July 7, 2007, violence broke out during the Zagreb Pride march. Skinheads threw eggs, ashtrays, and glass bottles, disrupting the parade. Some five hundred police officers provided a barrier, shielding participants from much of the harassment and violence. Roughly twenty participants were targeted individually in the parade, and ten people were harmed, two of whom required medical treatment.[48]

The Zagreb Pride march ended in Cvijetni Trg (Flowers Square), where a group of young people began throwing petrol bombs and tear gas canisters at the participants. Two women and one man were held for questioning in connection with those acts.

Josip Šitum, one of the protestors against the march, was held accountable for the petrol bombs and charged with a misdemeanor. The prosecutor's office subsequently initiated a criminal procedure.[49] On February 25, 2008, Šitum, 25, was found guilty of a hate crime endangering lives, and property. He was sentenced to 14 months in jail and mandatory psychiatric treatment. He is the first person convicted of a hate crime in the country since hate crimes became an offence under the country's Penal Code in 2006.[50]

On June 28, 2008, Zagreb celebrated the seventh annual gay pride parade. Unlike the prior year, there were no reported incidences of violence. The only

disruption reported came from one protester who yelled into the crowd of marchers: "This is Croatia! Remember Vukovar! Shame on you! Remember the generals!" The protester was ultimately removed from the area by the police. There were reports of some parade participants being targets of harassment and violence after the conclusion of the parade.[51]

Czech Republic

On June 28, 2008, in Brno, about five hundred people participated in the country's first gay pride parade. Several hundred police officials were present at the parade to provide protection to the marchers from an aggressive group of right-wing extremists. The protestors shouted insults and assaulted the marchers with rocks, eggs, fireworks, and tear gas. At least twenty marchers were injured. The tear gas sent two civilian victims to the hospital for emergency care, and one police officer collapsed and was subsequently hospitalized. According to *Agence France-Presse*, fifteen antigay demonstrators were jailed and two were charged with public disturbance.[52]

Estonia

In 2007, while the gay pride parade in Tallinn was officially sanctioned, authorities attempted to place restrictions on the event by initially forbidding the activists from marching through the Old Town. However, gay rights activists prevailed, and on August 11, 2007, some three hundred people walked through the historic Old Town, in an event that culminated a week-long gay culture festival with the first-ever official Gay Pride Parade in Old Town Tallinn. Thousands of people watched the parade, which was well protected by police and private security. The only challenge came from a small alternative procession that followed the demonstrators and chanted "No Pride!"[53]

The year before, on August 13, 2006, during Estonia's Gay Pride, a group of twenty antigay protesters armed with sticks and stones attacked some of the estimated five hundred gay rights supporters moving through the streets of Tallinn carrying rainbow-colored flags. Parade spokeswoman Lisette Kampus said twelve people were injured; she also criticized the police, noting that "there were too few police present so they could not really handle the violent attack."[54]

Hungary

On July 7, 2007, despite a police escort, approximately two thousand participants in the annual gay pride march in Budapest encountered a crowd of several hundred antigay protestors who hurled smoke bombs, beer bottles, eggs, and nylon bags filled with sand at them. Later in the evening, after police had departed after observing the dispersal of the antigay demonstrators, witnesses reported a number of physical assaults on persons entering and leaving a nightclub that marked the terminus of the march. Several NGOs criticized police for inaction and for charging the seventeen persons arrested in connection with the parade with "group disorderly conduct," instead of the more serious charge of incitement against a community or violation of the freedom of assembly.[55]

On July 5, 2008, hundreds of marchers participated in the Budapest Dignity March. Participants and police forces had prepared for potential attacks after two different LGBT-affiliated businesses were victims of violence earlier in the week. As hundreds of far-right demonstrators gathered near the square where the march was taking place, police officials erected high metal barriers on both sides of the road in an effort to restrict access to the march route and protect the participants. In response, the rioters threw petrol bombs and stones at the police. One police van was set on fire and two police officers reported injuries from the event. Other protestors shouted antisemitic slogans while throwing eggs, firecrackers, and Molotov cocktails at the people in the parade. Ambulance personnel reported at least eight marchers were injured in the attacks.[56] Police spokeswoman Eva Tafferner stated that riot police

detained forty-five people. Observers called this event "the worst violence during the dozen years the Gay Pride Parade has taken place in Budapest."[57]

Latvia

On June 3, 2007, Latvia's LGBT community held the first officially sanctioned gay pride celebrations. The parade took place in a park surrounded by two rows of officers cordoning the area.[58] A small number of protesters shouted verbal abuse and made obscene gestures. Two homemade bombs were set off in the park during the march.[59] There were no reported injuries. Two people were detained and charged with hooliganism in connection with the bombings.[60]

Overall, police were credited with having made a serious effort to protect the marchers, although activists stated that improvements still needed to be made in order to guarantee the right to freedom of assembly of LGBT persons.[61] In contrast, the 2006 gay pride event was marred by intolerance, as antigay protesters hurled feces and eggs at gay rights activists and supporters leaving a church service in the Latvian capital. Police reportedly did little to stop the attacks in 2006.[62]

In January 2008, the Vidzeme District Court in Riga found 32-year-old Jānis Dzelme guilty of throwing a bag of excrement at a car during the 2006 Riga Gay Pride Parade. He was sentenced to 100 hours of "compulsory labor" due to his actions of "gross public disorderliness as manifested in an obvious lack of respect toward the public by ignoring universally accepted norms of behavior."[63] In appreciation of the district court's successful prosecution, Kristīne Garina, the chairman of Latvian LGBT organization Mozaīka, was quoted as saying "This is an enormously important precedent which will send very strong signals to those people in Latvia who believe that freedom of assembly and freedom of speech should be limited with violence. Let them understand that such behavior will have serious consequences. ... Today we can feel safer and more equal than we did in the summer of 2006."[64]

Moldova

On April 27, 2007, the LGBT rights organization GenderDoc-M organized the sixth gay pride march in Chisinau, although the event was marred by threats from authorities and protesters. The proposed march had been banned by the authorities, although a small gathering of about twenty LGBT activists did take place. A group of protestors, double their size, encircled them, yelling homophobic slurs and pelting eggs at the group. The activists nonetheless made their way to the Monument to the Victims of Repression, where they intended to lay flowers. A large group of police prevented this from happening on the pretext that they needed permission from the Chisinau City Hall.[65]

On May 11, 2008, GenderDoc-M attempted to organize the seventh gay pride parade in the capital. However, the bus which carried approximately 60 pride participants was met with opposition from extremist neofascist and other groups. Hundreds of protestors surrounded the bus for over an hour. The large mob shouted violent slurs at the bus: "let's get them out and beat them up," and "beat them to death, don't let them escape."[66] Eventually, the bus doors were forced open by two men from the angry crowd, who demanded that if the participants wished to leave the bus without being physically harmed, they must destroy the pride parade materials. The overwhelmed and outnumbered LGBT advocates complied and the planned pride march was called off. Moldovan police was reportedly present at the event; however they stood passively about one hundred meters away and made no attempt to help the trapped participants. GenderDoc-M claims that nine calls were made to the police from inside the bus, but the LGBT activists received no assistance from the law enforcers.[67]

Poland

On June 7, 2008, over one thousand participants took part in Warsaw's annual Equality Parade under the "Live, Love, Be" slogan. More than a hundred protestors from a variety of extremist right-wing groups attended the parade.[68] Despite the vocal disturbances, there were no incidents of physical violence. Hundreds of Warsaw police officials were present at the parade, successfully blocking the protestors from entering parade route from downtown Warsaw to the prime minister's office.

The 2008 parade was largely a continuation of the peaceful atmosphere in which the parade transpired the previous year. On May 19, 2007, the second official LGBT Equality March took place in Warsaw. Over five thousand participants took part in the march. An audience watched the parade through a heavy police presence in what was described by observers as a generally peaceful environment.[69]

In 2006, the first officially sanctioned parade brought together several thousand activists, who were countered by a group of egg-throwing protestors. The police responded affirmatively to prevent an escalation of violence. The parade took place in what some gay rights activists called "an atmosphere of hate," fueled in part by homophobic statements and policies of the country's leadership. In 2004 and 2005, the parade had been banned, even though it went ahead both years.[70]

Romania

Following an outbreak of violence during the 2006 gay pride march in Bucharest, police reportedly made an effort to upgrade the protection to the 2007 march.[71] On June 9, 2007, the day began with a counter march of approximately three hundred right-wing extremists. Later, there were two separate gay activist marches. The first was a demonstration against discrimination, specifically demanding marriage equality. Some five hundred activists, guarded by seven hundred police officers, marched through the city as antigay demonstrators threw stones into the crowd. Police sprayed tear gas into the group of protesters, and made some arrests.[72]

The second demonstration was a parade with some four hundred participants. Police trucks and over four hundred officers formed a barricade between the parade and the protestors.[73] These barricades, however, did not protect the parade participants from cobblestones, eggs, tomatoes, and garbage thrown by the protestors. By the end of the day, over one hundred protestors were arrested. According to a report by the International Lesbian and Gay Association of Europe (ILGA-Europe), the police response was encouraging, as they were able to provide forceful protection throughout the day. After the parade, police secured many metro stations to protect the parade participants, thus learning from the previous year's mistake, when most attacks were committed in the aftermath of the march.[74] Following the 2007 march, five young men were charged with violent actions and 50 persons received fines for misconduct.[75]

On May 24, 2008, the fifth annual gay pride festival was held in Bucharest without incident. Despite protests from two extreme-right groups, hundreds of people peacefully marched through the streets of their capital. The participants were under the protection of approximately twelve hundred police officers. Michael Cashman, president of the Intergroup on Gay and Lesbian Rights at the European Parliament, was quoted saying "I want to thank the police here today ... but we should be able to march and be ourselves without the police marching along."[76]

Russian Federation

Efforts to organize a gay pride parade in Moscow have been marred since 2006 by hostility from the city authorities, denunciations by community leaders, violent protests, and poor police protection. Most recently, in 2008, a march originally scheduled for May 31 was banned by the authorities. As a result, the official demonstration planned in front of the city hall was

cancelled due to security concerns. Nevertheless, on June 1, a group of about thirty demonstrators gathered in another location—in front of a monument to Tchaikovsky—where they held a brief picket for LGBT rights before quickly dispersing."[77]

Similarly, in 2007, LGBT activists in Moscow were also denied the right to assemble for a peaceful demonstration. Days before the intended date of the 2007 gathering, organizers had submitted march plans for the Moscow Pride march to Mayor Yury Luzhkov, who banned the march repeatedly over the past years, calling it "satanic."[78] Participants made plans instead to assemble in front of City Hall to deliver a petition challenging the right of assembly and freedom of expression.

On May 27, 2007, police secured Tverskaya Square around city hall. Skinheads and nationalist extremists had begun occupying the square, yelling "Moscow is not Sodom! No to pederasts!" as thirty participants slowly gathered. The pride organizers were immediately arrested as they entered the square. Even as the organizers were being arrested, protesters attacked other participants while the police reportedly stood by.

At least eleven women and two men among the march participants were arrested and held for several hours in police vehicles before being taken to a police station. They were left in the heat, denied medical attention, and verbally harassed by police officers. One officer said: "No one needs lesbians, no one will ever get you out of here." When a group of the participants were released from police custody after several hours, protesters pelted eggs and shouted hateful epithets at them.[79]

Slovenia

On June 30, 2007, the seventh annual gay pride parade in Ljubljana took place with the support of local government officials, although there were reports that bystanders shouted homophobic slurs at participants, and antigay graffiti and stickers were seen in various locations around the city. Organizers reported a satisfactory police presence during the parade. However, at a gay pride event that evening, four persons attacked a gay man who subsequently required hospitalization. Police responded immediately and reported the assault as a homophobic attack, but were unable to locate the attacker.[80]

Similarly, on June 21, 2008, the participants of the Ljubljana gay pride parade were attacked. Five marchers reported being physically assaulted at sites of parade events. In all cases, the attackers allegedly punched their victims in the face or kicked them in the head, while shouting antigay slurs. One of the victims claimed that the attackers kicked him to the point where he began to bleed.[81]

III. The Work of Intergovernmental Organizations

The international response to hate crimes against people because of their sexual orientation or gender identity is hindered by the fact that these forms of discrimination are not well integrated into the international human rights and antidiscrimination bodies and mechanisms. Indeed, there is no convention or treaty specifically focusing on the rights of LGBT persons. Within the framework of the United Nations, the problem of bias-motivated violence against LGBT persons is only just beginning to gain recognition and has remained largely outside of the framework of the general human rights treaty bodies as well as those special mechanisms that deal with related issues of discrimination and intolerance. Positive exceptions have included the activities of the United Nations Special Rapporteur for Human Rights Defenders, and some aspects of the work of the Human Rights Committee.

The Yogyakarta Principles, developed by human rights experts in November 2006, offer a way forward, reflecting state obligations under international law to address human rights violations based on sexual orientation and gender identity. The Principles include a recommendation that the UN treaty bodies "vigorously integrate these principles into the implementation of their mandates, including ... general comments or other interpretive texts on the application of human rights law to persons of diverse sexual orientations and gender identities."[82] However, the Yogyakarta Principles are a nonbinding document.

Nevertheless, at the time of their launch in November 2007, the High Commissioner for Human Rights Louise Arbour issued the following statement:

> Just as it would be unthinkable to deny anyone their human rights because of their race, religion or social status, we must also reject any attempt to do so on the basis of sexual orientation or gender identity. The Princi-

ples are a timely reminder of these basic tenets. States have a legal obligation to investigate and prosecute all instances of violence and abuse with respect to every person under their jurisdiction. Respect for cultural diversity is insufficient to justify the existence of laws that violate the fundamental right to life, security and privacy by criminalizing harmless private relations between consenting adults.[83]

The Yogyakarta Principles include important provisions related to violence, particularly Principle 5 on the "Right of the Security of the Person," which reads as follows:

Everyone, regardless of sexual orientation or gender identity, has the right to security of the person and to protection by the State against violence or bodily harm, whether inflicted by government officials or by any individual or group.

States shall:

a) Take all necessary policing and other measures to prevent and provide protection from all forms of violence and harassment related to sexual orientation and gender identity;

b) Take all necessary legislative measures to impose appropriate criminal penalties for violence, threats of violence, incitement to violence and related harassment, based on the sexual orientation or gender identity of any person or group of persons, in all spheres of life, including the family;

c) Take all necessary legislative, administrative and other measures to ensure that the sexual orientation or gender identity of the victim may not be advanced to justify, excuse or mitigate such violence;

d) Ensure that perpetration of such violence is vigorously investigated, and that, where appropriate evidence is found, those responsible are prosecuted, tried and duly punished, and that victims are provided with appropriate remedies and redress, including compensation;

e) Undertake campaigns of awareness-raising, directed to the general public as well as to actual and potential perpetrators of violence, in order to combat the prejudices that underlie violence related to sexual orientation and gender identity.[84]

Within Europe, a number of regional intergovernmental organizations have addressed the problem of homophobic hate crimes, although this type of violence has been left outside of the official mandates of many European regional antidiscrimination bodies. Thus, challenges remain to apply a more integrated approach to combating discrimination that addresses violence on the basis of sexual orientation along with other forms of violent discrimination.

The OSCE's Office for Democratic Institutions and Human Rights (ODIHR) has been credited with a number of efforts to address the problem of homophobic violence. The ODIHR regularly reports on homophobic violence in the context of its annual reporting on hate crime in the OSCE region. In the 2006 annual report, the ODIHR listed numerous attacks and government responses, noting that "homophobic and transphobic incidents and crimes targeting LGBT people are believed to be among the most underreported and under-documented."[85] The ODIHR has developed a working definition of hate crimes that includes sexual orientation among the grounds of discrimination. The ODIHR also conducts a number of programs that aim to strengthen the response of law enforcement bodies and civil society organizations to hate crimes, including those motivated by homophobia. Nevertheless, the OSCE as a whole has yet to adopt any commitments or ministerial decisions in which discrimination and intolerance—including cases of violence—on the basis of sexual orientation are explicitly mentioned as an area of concern for the organization to address.

The mandate of the Council of Europe's main antidiscrimination body, the European Commission against Racism and Intolerance (ECRI) does not expressly encompass discrimination on the basis of sexual

orientation or gender identity, despite the space that the term "intolerance" creates to include this type of discrimination. Thus, bias-motivated violence against LGBT persons is largely outside of the framework of ECRI's extensive reporting and recommendations on individual countries, as well as general recommendations.

Another body of the Council of Europe—the Office of the Human Rights Commissioner—has defined LGBT issues, including violence against LGBT persons, as a core priority. Commissioner Thomas Hammarberg has taken up the issue of hate crimes against LGBT persons in his reports and country visits and has criticized political leaders in many countries for failing to rise to the challenge posed by discrimination and harassment based on sexual orientation. In a June 2008 article on hate crimes, the Commissioner highlighted a number of recent cases of homophobic violence, calling them "the tip of the iceberg."[86] He has recommended that "hate crimes against LGBT persons should be seen as serious crimes."[87]

As concerns the European Union's Fundamental Rights Agency (FRA), the problem of homophobic hate crimes is not expressly mentioned in the agency's mandate. The regulation establishing the FRA states that: "the work of the Agency should continue to cover the phenomena of racism, xenophobia and antisemitism, the protection of rights of persons belonging to minorities, as well as gender equality, as essential elements for the protection of fundamental rights."[88] The FRA's regular activities related to hate crimes have to date focused on "racist violence and crime," while addressing homophobic hate crime only through a recent study of discrimination on the grounds of sexual orientation.

In June 2008, the FRA released a study on *Homophobia and Discrimination on Grounds of Sexual Orientation in the EU Member States*. The study examined, among other things, the legal basis for European Union States to address bias based on sexual orientation as an aggravating circumstance in the commission of violent crimes. A second report detailing social aspects of the problem is planned for release in autumn 2008.[89]

Section Endnotes

[1] SOS Homophobie, *Rapport sur l'homophobie 2008*, May 16, 2008, http://www.sos-homophobie.org/index.php?menu=1&menu_option=12&news=75#chap75.

[2] While not purporting to provide comprehensive or country-wide coverage, NCAVP draws upon monitors in major cities including San Francisco, Chicago, Columbus, Ohio, Houston, Kansas City, Los Angeles, Milwaukee, and New York, and the states of Colorado, Massachusetts, Michigan, Minnesota, Pennsylvania, and Vermont. The National Coalition of Anti-Violence Programs, *Anti-Lesbian, Gay, Bisexual and Transgender Violence in 2007*, NCAVP, New York: 2008, http://www.ncavp.org/common/document_files/Reports/2007HVReportFINAL.pdf.

[3] Maneo, *Maneo Survey 2006/2007*, Berlin: 2007; Human Rights First correspondence with Bastian Finke, Maneo Project Director, on August 7, 2008.

[4] Maneo, *Homophobia and Violence Against Gays in Public Space. How can light be shed on unreported cases – can gays be better protected against attacks?*; and Human Rights First correspondence with Bastian Finke, Maneo Project Director, August 7, 2008.

[5] Human Rights Watch, *We Need a Law for Liberation: Gender, Sexuality, and Human Rights in a Changing Turkey*, May 2008, http://hrw.org/reports/2008/turkey0508/turkey0508webwcover.pdf.

[6] Stonewall, *Homophobic Hate Crime: The Gay British Crime Survey*, June 26, 2008, http://www.stonewall.org.uk.

[7] Svyatoslav Sementsov, "Increase in Assaults on Gay Men in Belarus," *Gaywired.Com*, July 5, 2007, http://www.gaywired.com/Article.cfm?ID=19455.

[8] U.S. Department of State, Bureau of Democracy, Human Rights and Labor, *Country Reports on Human Rights Practices 2007: Croatia*, March 11, 2008, http://www.state.gov/g/drl/rls/hrrpt/2007/index.htm.

[9] "Jewish teenager leaves city where he was attacked," *European Jewish Press*, March 5, 2008, http://www.ejpress.org/article/24944.

[10] U.S. Department of State, Bureau of Democracy, Human Rights and Labor, *Country Reports on Human Rights Practices 2007: Germany*, March 11, 2008, http://www.state.gov/g/drl/rls/hrrpt/2007/index.htm.

[11] "Police Criticised After Budapest Gay Bar Set on Fire," *UK Gay News*, June 28, 2008, http://www.ukgaynews.org.uk/Archive/08/Jun/2801.htm.

[12] "Another Gay Business Torched in Budapest: One injured in Sauna Attack," *UK Gay News*, July 3, 2008, http://www.ukgaynews.org.uk/Archive/08/Jul/0303.htm.

[13] "Man's horror at homophobic attack," *BBC News*, June 6, 2008, http://news.bbc.co.uk/2/hi/uk_news/northern_ireland/7439296.stm.

[14] "La sporca guerra dell'omofobia," *Arcigay*, May 28, 2008, http://www.puta.it/blog/2008/05/28/queer/la-sporca-guerra-dellomofobia/.

[15] "Italian Government lobbied for gay hate crime law," *Topix Gay News*, May 27, 2008, http://www.topix.com/news/gay/2008/05/italian-government-lobbied-for-gay-hate-crime-law.

[16] "Mob Ransacks Rome Gay Center," *365Gay.Com*, April 18, 2008, http://www.365gay.com/Newscon08/04/041808rome.htm.

[17] Labrys Kyrgyzstan, "FtM Transsexual attacked by two drunk men in Bishkek city center," November 27, 2007, http://kyrgyzlabrys.wordpress.com/2007/11/27/ftm-transsexual-attacked-by-two-drunk-men-in-bishkek-city-center/.

[18] Doug Ireland, "Transphobia kills again: international call for action!" *Panteras Rosa*, March 14, 2008, http://gayswithoutborders.wordpress.com/2008/03/14/portugal-transphobia-kills-again-international-call-for-action/.

[19] Vassily Parovozov and Andrei Lavrikov, "Bitva za 'Plevnu,'" *Komsomolskaya Pravda*, June 19, 2007, http://www.kp.ru/daily/23919/68319/.

[20] "Stolknoveniya natsi-skinhedov i antifashistov na gej-parade," the SOVA Center for Information and Analysis, February 15, 2008, http://xeno.sova-center.ru/45A29F2/A9D172D, citing *Gazeta.Ru*.

[21] "Gay Couple in Hate Crime," *News24*, July 28, 2008, http://www.news24.com/News24/World/News/0,,2-10-1462_2365561,00.html.

[22] Nicholas Birch, "Was Ahmet Yildiz the victim of Turkey's first gay honor killing," *the Independent, July 19, 2008*, http://www.independent.co.uk/news/world/europe/was-ahmet-yildiz-the-victim-of-turkeys-first-gay-honour-killing-871822.html.

[23] Stonewall, *Homophobic Hate Crime: The Gay British Crime Survey*, June 26, 2008, http://www.stonewall.org.uk.

[24] "Gay Senior Citizen Brutally Beaten in Detroit Hate Attack Dies," *Towleroad*, February 24, 2007, http://www.towleroad.com/2007/02/gay_senior_citi_1.html.

[25] Viki Nantz, "In Florida, hate crimes against gays and lesbians are among the most violent," *RyanSkipperDocumentary.com*, 2008, http://www.ryanskipperdocumentary.com/.

[26] Jessica Carreras, "Murder of California teen being charged as a hate crime Victim was taken off ventilator and pronounced dead last night," *Pride Source*, February 13, 2008, http://www.pridesource.com/article.shtml?article=29271.

[27] Ann Turner, "Teen Killer of Gay Classmate Lawrence King Will Be Tried as an Adult," *Gaywired.Com*, July 25, 2008, http://www.gaywired.com/Article.cfm?ID=19738.

[28] Mia Dauvergne, Katie Scrim and Shannon Brennan, *Hate Crime in Canada 2006*, Canadian Centre for Justice Statistics, 2006, http://www.statcan.ca/english/research/85F0033MIE/85F0033MIE2008017.pdf.

[29] Toronto Police Service, Hate Crime Unit, *2007 Annual Hate/Bias Crime Statistical Report*, http://www.torontopolice.on.ca/publications/files/reports/2007hatecrimereport.pdf.

[30] The Swedish National Council for Crime Prevention (*Brottsförebyggande rådet—Brå*), *Hate crime 2007*, 2008, http://www.bra.se/extra/measurepoint/?module_instance=4&name=Hatbrott_2007_webb.pdf&url=/dynamaster/file_archive/080627/4a35a31f178add58672ff57f0fcdb92c/Hatbrott%255f2007%255fwebb.pdf.

[31] The Swedish Federation for Lesbian, Gay, Bisexual and Transgender Rights, "RFSL Comments on Hate Crimes Statistics; No One Is Born a Homophobe," June 29, 2007, http://www.rfsl.se/public/070629_hatecrimesstats.pdf.

[32] Metropolitan Police, Violent Crimes Directorate, United Kingdom.

[33] "Homophobic" is defined by the Crown Prosecution Service as follows: a fear of or a dislike directed towards lesbian, gay or bisexual people, or a fear of or dislike directed towards their perceived lifestyle, culture or characteristics, whether or not any specific lesbian, gay or bisexual person has that lifestyle or characteristic. The dislike does not have to be as severe as hatred. It is enough that people do something or abstains from doing something because they do not like lesbian, gay, or bisexual people. "Transphobic" is defined as follows: a fear of or a dislike directed towards transpeople, or a fear of or dislike directed towards their perceived lifestyle, culture or characteristics, whether or not any specific transperson has that lifestyle or characteristic. The dislike does not have to be as severe as hatred. It is enough that people do something or abstains from doing something because they do not like transgender people. Crown Prosecution Services, *Policy for Prosecuting Cases of Homophobic and Transphobic Hate Crime*, November 2007, http://www.cps.gov.uk/publications/docs/htc_policy.pdf.

[34] Northern Ireland Central Statistics Branch, Operational Support Department, *Hate Incidents and Crimes 1st April 2007 – 31st March 2008*, 2008, http://www.psni.police.uk/3._hate_incidents_and_crimes-4.pdf.

[35] U.S. Department of Justice, Federal Bureau of Investigation, Criminal Justice Information Services Division, *Hate Crime Statistics, 2006*, Fall 2007, http://www.fbi.gov/ucr/hc2006/incidents.html.

[36] The FBI does not collect statistics on hate crime offenses based on gender identity bias. U.S. Department of Justice, Federal Bureau of Investigation, *Uniform Crime Reports*, http://www.fbi.gov/ucr/ucr.htm.

[37] U.S. Department of State, Bureau of Democracy, Human Rights and Labor, *Country Reports on Human Rights Practices 2007: the Netherlands*, March 11, 2008, http://www.state.gov/g/drl/rls/hrrpt/2007/index.htm.

[38] Response of the Equality and Antidiscrimination Ombudsman to a Human Rights First questionnaire, October 2, 2007.

[39] "Justice Ministry urges crackdown on hate crimes," *Aftenposten*, September 17, 2007, http://www.aftenposten.no/english/local/article1998761.ece.

[40] National Association for Lesbian and Homosexual Emancipation, *Hatvold*, http://www.llh.no/hatvold.

[41] The 11 states include: California, Colorado, Connecticut, Hawaii, Maryland, Minnesota, Montana, New Jersey, New Mexico, Oregon, and Vermont.

[42] Regarding data collection, the Hate Crimes Statistics Act of 1990 – a federal law – includes provisions for the collection of statistics on sexual orientation bias crimes.

[43] The 1968 "Federal Hate Crime Statute," 18 USC 245, outlines the six federally protected activities as follows: " (1) A student at or applicant for admission to a public school or public college; (2) A participant in a benefit, service, privilege, program, facility or activity provided or administered by a state or local government; (3) An applicant for private or state employment; a private or state employee; a member or applicant for membership in a labor organization or hiring hall; or an applicant for employment through an employment agency, labor organization or hiring hall; (4) A juror or prospective juror in state court; (5) A traveler or user of a facility of interstate commerce or common carrier; (6) A patron of a public accommodation or place of exhibition or entertainment, including hotels, motels, restaurants, lunchrooms, bars, gas stations, theaters, concert halls, sports arenas or stadiums."

[44] Crown Prosecution Service, *Guidance on Prosecuting Cases of Homophobic and Transphobic Crime*, November 2007, http://www.cps.gov.uk/publications/doc/htc_guidance.pdf.

[45] The European Court of Human Rights, *Baczkowski and Others v. Poland*, para. 64, Strasbourg, May 3, 2007.

[46] European Parliament, *Homophobia in Europe*, P6_TA(2007)0167, April 26, 2007, http://www.europarl.europa.eu/sides/getDoc.do?pubRef=-//EP//NONSGML+TA+P6-TA-2007-0167+0+DOC+PDF+V0//EN.

[47] Claudia Ciobanu, "Hate Wave Threatens Bulgaria's New Gay Pride," *OneWorld.net*, July 3, 2008, http://us.oneworld.net/article/hate-wave-threatens-bulgarias-new-gay-pride.

[48] Agence France-Presse, "Violence at Croatian Gay Pride march," Internet Centre Anti Racism Europe, July 7, 2007, http://www.icare.to/news.php?en#GAY%20PRIDE%20%20POLITICAL%20WILL%20NEED%20TO%20CHANGE%20ATTITUDES%20.

[49] "Hate crime charge over petrol bombs at Pride," Pink News, July 16, 2007, http://www.pinknews.co.uk/news/articles/2005-4945.html.

[50] Tony Grew, "Pride petrol bomber jailed for attempted attack " Pink News, February 26, 2008, http://www.pinknews.co.uk/news/articles/2005-6961.html.

[51] "Gay Pride Parade Marches through Zagreb," Zagreb-Pride, June 28, 2008, http://www.zagreb-pride.net/j/.

[52] Jan Richter and Michal Záboj, "Country's first-ever gay parade clashes with extremists," Radio Praha, June 30, 2008, http://www.radio.cz/en/article/105648.

[53] "Tallinn Pride attracts tourists not violence," Pink News, August 13, 2007, http://www.pinknews.co.uk/news/articles/2005-5167.html.

[54] "12 Injured as Gay Pride Marchers Attacked in Estonia," Mosnews.com, August 13, 2006, http://www.mosnews.com/news/2006/08/13/gaypride.shtml.

[55] U.S. Department of State, Bureau of Democracy, Human Rights and Labor, Country Reports on Human Rights Practices 2007: Hungary, March 11, 2008, http://www.state.gov/g/drl/rls/hrrpt/2007/index.htm.

[56] Sandor Peto and Krisztina Than, "Anti-gay violence mars Hungarian parade," the Star Online, July 6, 2008, http://thestar.com.my/news/story.asp?file=/2008/7/6/worldupdates/2008-07-06T094921Z_01_NOOTR_RTRMDNC_0_-343906-1&sec=Worldupdates.

[57] Stefan Bos, "Violent Protests Disrupt Hungary's Gay Rights Parade," VOA News, July 6, 2008, http://voanews.com/english/2008-07-06-voa1.cfm.

[58] "Gay rights groups protest in Riga," BBC News, June 3, 2007, http://news.bbc.co.uk/2/hi/europe/6716287.stm.

[59] Amnesty International, "Latvia: Riga Pride 2007: championing equal rights," AI News Service, EUR 52/004/2007, June 14, 2007 http://www.amnestyusa.org/document.php?lang=e&id=ENGEUR520042007.

[60] Ilvija Pūce, Legal Study on Homophobia and Discrimination on Grounds of Sexual orientation, Latvia, the European Union Agency for Fundamental Rights, Riga: February 2008, http://fra.europa.eu/fra/material/pub/comparativestudy/FRA-hdgso-NR_LV.pdf.

[61] "Peaceful Gay Pride Staged in Riga Amid Tight Security," UK Gay News, June 3, 2007 http://ukgaynews.org.uk/Archive/07/June/0305.htm.

[62] Reuters, "Latvian Gay Priders Hit With Eggs and Excrement," Internet Centre Anti Racism Europe, July 22, 2006, http://www.icare.to/news.php?en/2006-07.

[63] "Lawmaker's Assistant Convicted of Throwing Faeces at Riga Gay Pride," UK Gay News, January 15, 2008, http://ukgaynews.org.uk/Archive/08/Jan/1502.htm.

[64] "Aide to Latvian MP convicted of Pride attack," Pink News, January 16, 2008, http://www.pinknews.co.uk/news/articles/2005-6567.html.

[65] Karen Ryan, "No pride in Moldova; gay event attacked by homophobic mob," the Tiraspol Times, May 4, 2007, http://www.tiraspoltimes.com/news/gays_no_pride_in_moldova.html.

[66] Christian Taylor, "Gay Pride Parade Trapped on Bus," SameSame.com.ua, May 12, 2008, http://www.samesame.com.au/news/international/2413/Gay-Pride-Parade-Trapped-On-Bus.htm.

[67] GenderDoc-M, "Moldovan Gay Pride Threatened, Cops Refuse Protection for Marchers," May 11, 2008, http://mpetreis.blogspot.com/2008/05/moldovan-gay-pride-threatened-cops.html.

[68] Deutsche Presse-Agentur, "Polish gay pride marchers under police guard (Roundup)," M&C, June 7, 2008, http://www.monstersandcritics.com/news/europe/news/article_1409857.php/Polish_gay_pride_marchers_under_police_guard__Roundup_.

[69] "Thousands Celebrate Warsaw's First Legal Pride," 365Gay.Com, May 19, 2007, http://www.365gay.com/Newscon07/05/051907warsaw.htm.

[70] Agence France-Presse, "Thousands Rally For Gay March in Warsaw," Deutsche Welle, June 10, 2006, http://www.dw-world.de/dw/article/0,2144,2051002,00.html.

[71] ILGA-Europe, "Various news items and reports from Bucharest Pride 2007," June 10, 2007 http://www.ilga-europe.org/europe/news/bucharest_pride_2007.

[72] Reuters, "Protesters clash with police at Romania gay parade," AlertNet, June 9, 2007 http://www.alertnet.org/thenews/newsdesk/L09656251.htm.

[73] "Roundup: Bucharest gay-rights marchers attacked, police intervene," EUX.TV, June 9, 2007 http://www.eux.tv/article.aspx?articleId=9659.

[74] ILGA-Europe, "Various news items and reports from Bucharest Pride 2007," June 10, 2007 http://www.ilga-europe.org/europe/news/bucharest_pride_2007.

[75] U.S. Department of State, Bureau of Democracy, Human Rights and Labor, Country Reports on Human Rights Practices 2007: Romania, March 11, 2008, http://www.state.gov/g/drl/rls/hrrpt/2007/index.htm.

[76] Reuters, "Gay activists march in Romania despite opposition," *Reuters UK,* May 24, 2008, http://uk.reuters.com/article/worldNews/idUSL245959720080524.

[77] "From Russia with Gay Love–Blogging from Moscow Pride," *UK Gay News,* June 3, 2008, http://www.ukgaynews.org.uk/Archive/08/May/3107.htm.

[78] Doug Ireland, "Moscow Pride Banned Again," *UK Gay News,* May 17, 2007, http://www.ukgaynews.org.uk/Archive/08/May/3107.htm.

[79] Human Rights Watch and ILGA-Europe, *We Have the Upper Hand: Freedom of assembly in Russia and the human rights of lesbian, gay, bisexual, and transgender people,* June 2007, http://www.ilga-europe.org/europe/guide/country_by_country/russia/report_on_moscow_pride_2007_in_english.

[80] U.S. Department of State, Bureau of Democracy, Human Rights and Labor, *Country Reports on Human Rights Practices 2007: Slovenia,* March 11, 2008, http://www.state.gov/g/drl/rls/hrrpt/2007/index.htm.

[81] ILGA-Europe, "Ljubljana Pride ends in Violence," June 24, 2008, http://www.ilga-europe.org/europe/guide/country_by_country/slovenia/ljubljana_pride_2008_ends_in_violence.

[82] *Yogyakarta Principles on the Application of International Human Rights Law in relation to Sexual Orientation and Gender Identity: Additional Recommendations,* March 26, 2007, http://www.yogyakartaprinciples.org/principles_en.htm.

[83] Douglas Sanders, "The Role of the Yogyakarta Principles," International Gay and Lesbian Human Rights Commission, August 4, 2008, http://www.iglhrc.org/site/iglhrc/section.php?id=5&detail=868.

[84] *Yogyakarta Principles on the Application of International Human Rights Law in relation to Sexual Orientation and Gender Identity: Right of the Security of the Person,* March 26, 2007, http://www.yogyakartaprinciples.org/principles_en.htm.

[85] OSCE Office for Democratic Institutions and Human Rights, *Hate Crimes in the OSCE Region: Incidents and Responses - Annual Report for 2006,* September 18, 2007, OSCE http://www.osce.org/odihr/item_11_26296.html.

[86] Thomas Hammarberg, "Hate crimes – the ugly face of racism, anti-Semitism, anti-Gypsyism, Islamophobia and homophobia," *Viewpoints,* the Council of Europe Commissioner for Human Rights, July 21, 2008, http://www.coe.int/t/commissioner/Viewpoints/080721_en.asp.

[87] Thomas Hammarberg, "Homophobic policies are slow to disappear," *Viewpoints,* the Council of Europe Commissioner for Human Rights, May 16, 2007, http://www.coe.int/t/commissioner/Viewpoints/070516_en.asp.

[88] The European Union, "Council Regulation (EC) No 168/2007 of 15 February 2007 establishing a European Union Agency for Fundamental Rights," *Official Journal of the European Union,* L 53/1, February 22, 2007, http://fra.europa.eu/fra/material/pub/FRA/reg_168-2007_en.pdf.

[89] The European Union Agency for Fundamental Rights, *Homophobia and Discrimination on Grounds of Sexual Orientation in the EU Member States Part I – Legal Analysis,* June 2008, http://fra.europa.eu/fra/material/pub/comparativestudy/FRA_hdgso_part1_en.pdf.

Government Responses to Hate Crime

Systems of Monitoring and Reporting

Table of Contents

Executive Summary

An effective government response to violent hate crimes is difficult, if not impossible, without a clear picture of the extent of the problem, the types of offenses being committed, and the characteristics of the victims. Without adequate monitoring, it is impossible to identify emerging trends or hate crime hotspots, develop strategies for prevention and protection, and determine which groups are most susceptible to violent hate crimes. Without public reporting on the criminal justice response to hate crimes, it is difficult to ensure that adequate legal tools and resources are in place to investigate and prosecute such crimes and to reassure the public that efforts are being made to provide protection from violent forms of discrimination. OSCE states have committed to "collect and maintain reliable data and statistics on hate crimes and incidents."

Efforts to introduce or enhance already existing monitoring systems are especially important in light of the increasing availability of crime victimization surveys, NGO monitoring, and media reports that suggest that hate crimes are occurring at a significant rate throughout the OSCE region and are seriously underreported to and underrecorded by the authorities.

Within the European Union, the Fundamental Rights Agency (FRA), the E.U.'s antiracism and human rights body, has determined that only 11 of the 27 member states have criminal justice data collection systems that can be considered "good" or "comprehensive" in their coverage of hate crimes. Outside of the E.U., only Canada and the United States have well-developed reporting systems. Thus, only 13 of the 56 participating states of the OSCE are fulfilling their basic commitments to monitor hate crimes: **Austria**, **Canada**, the **Czech Republic**, **Denmark**, **Germany**, **Finland**, **France**, **Ireland**, **Poland**, **Slovakia**, **Sweden**, the **United Kingdom**, and the **United States.**

Over 40 states collect and publish either limited or no information specifically on the incidence of violent hate crimes. Those states include: **Albania, Andorra, Armenia, Azerbaijan, Belarus, Belgium, Bosnia and Herzegovina, Bulgaria, Croatia, Cyprus, Estonia, Georgia, Greece, Holy See, Hungary, Iceland, Italy, Kazakhstan, Kyrgyzstan, Latvia, Liechtenstein, Lithuania, Luxembourg, Macedonia, Malta, Moldova, Monaco, Montenegro,** the **Netherlands, Norway, Portugal, Romania,** the **Russian Federation, San Marino, Serbia, Slovenia, Spain, Switzerland, Tajikistan, Turkey, Turkmenistan, Ukraine,** and **Uzbekistan.** Several countries that publish limited information do so more frequently on nonviolent violations of hate speech laws than on violent hate crimes.

Over the past year, a number of countries have introduced improvements in their monitoring and reporting systems. Steps have been taken in at least eleven countries to improve the registration of hate crimes. Three countries have also enhanced the way in which they publicly report on hate crimes, with **Canada** releasing national data for the first time.

In the absence of government data on all or certain types of hate crimes, NGOs can paint a more accurate picture of the problem and the government response. Yet there are larger gaps in the information than NGOs currently have the capacity to fill. Indeed, increased support and training is sorely needed for NGOs to enhance their monitoring capacity. Nevertheless, in 2008, NGOs in **Germany** and the **United Kingdom** conducted surveys that revealed high levels of homophobic violence—a phenomenon that official reporting systems in both countries have largely overlooked.

I. Assessment of Monitoring Systems

To confront the menace of any form of violent crime it is essential to know what happened, where, when, and to whom, with a view to punishment, deterrence, and protection. The same holds for hate crimes—acts of violence motivated by bias based on race, religion, ethnicity, national origin, sexual orientation, gender, disability, or other similar attributes, or a combination thereof. If such crimes are to be deterred and future victims protected there is also a need to develop a system of data collection and public reporting that distinguish the elements of discrimination that drive these crimes and the particular populations under threat.

Transparent systems of monitoring and reporting are also essential to determine whether the law is in fact being enforced, and enforced equitably. The most effective monitoring systems not only register incidents and offences, but also track them through the criminal justice system, from the moment charges are filed to the outcome of cases before juries or judges.

International human rights standards provide a strong framework for the protection of all people against discrimination. Additionally, there are a series of opinions, standards, and directives that provide authoritative guidance and sometimes binding norms on the way in which international guarantees against discrimination should be implemented. Among these, E.U., Council of Europe, and OSCE norms provide detailed special attention to the fight against violence motivated by racism and related intolerance through effective monitoring and reporting, among other things. Most recently, in December 2007, OSCE states committed to "collect and maintain reliable data and statistics on hate crimes and incidents."[1] Human Rights First discussed these norms in more detail in its December 2007 *Hate Crime Report Card*.

The quality of the data provided by government agencies on violent hate crimes varies widely throughout the OSCE region. In our *Hate Crime Report Card*, Human Rights First looked across the 56 countries of the OSCE to assess the type of data that is collected, which government bodies are collecting that data, as well as what the data says about the characteristics of the victims and the bias motivations. In light of the fact that few governments collect comprehensive data, we also discussed the various obstacles hindering better data collection and public reporting.

This report aims to update our findings by looking at developments—both positive and negative—in the ways in which states are meeting their commitments to develop systems of monitoring and public reporting on violent hate crimes.

In the European Union, the Fundamental Rights Agency (FRA) regularly assesses the quality of data collection mechanisms for the registration of racist crimes in E.U. countries using a four-tier system. In its latest assessment, FRA determined that only 11 countries—down from 12 in its previous assessment—have data collections systems that are either "comprehensive" or "good." Those countries include:

- Tier 1—Comprehensive (Extensive data collection, with detail about victim and offender characteristics): **Finland**, **Sweden**, and the **United Kingdom**.

- Tier 2—Good (A system exists to register incidents/crimes, and/or the system focuses on right-wing extremism): **Austria**, **Czech Republic**, **Denmark**, **France**, **Germany**, **Ireland**, **Poland**, and **Slovakia**.

Since its previous assessment, FRA re-evaluated the quality of reporting and made an adjustment to two countries within these two tiers. **Sweden** was upgraded from "good" to "comprehensive" as a result of improvements introduced by the Swedish National Council for Crime Prevention to the categorization of hate crimes. On the contrary, **Belgium**, previously a Tier 2 country, was downgraded to a Tier 3 country due to the fact that information from criminal justice sources about racist crime is not transparent and only available upon request.

Countries with limited or no official data include the following:

- Tier 3—Limited (Limited reporting on investigations and court cases or focus on general discrimination): **Belgium, Bulgaria, Estonia, Hungary, Italy, Latvia, Lithuania, Luxembourg, Malta**, the **Netherlands, Portugal**, and **Slovenia**.

- Tier 4—No official data available (No official data collected or readily available in the public domain): **Cyprus, Greece, Romania**, and **Spain**. There have been reports of bias-motivated violence in all of these countries.

FRA similarly re-evaluated several countries' positions with regard to these tiers. **Italy** shifted from Tier 4 to Tier 3 after the government provided hate crime data upon a request from the FRA's National Focal Point. **Portugal** was similarly upgraded from Tier 4 to Tier 3 because "limited data is sporadically available from year to year." **Romania**, on the contrary, moved from to Tier 4 from Tier 3 because it failed to provide information on the relevant legal articles.[2]

Outside of the E.U., only **Canada** and the **United States** have well-developed reporting systems. There are no countries in southeastern Europe or the former Soviet Union with such systems of monitoring and regular public reporting expressly on violent hate crimes.

Thus, only 13 of the 56 participating states of the OSCE are fulfilling their basic commitments to monitor hate crimes, with countries in the European Union and North America leading the way. These countries include: **Austria, Canada**, the **Czech Republic, Denmark, Germany, Finland, France, Ireland, Poland, Slovakia, Sweden**, the **United Kingdom**, and the **United States.**

While a number of other governments provide some limited statistics—although more frequently on nonviolent violations of hate speech laws than on violent hate crimes—over 40 states provide only limited or no public reporting specifically on the incidence of violent hate crimes. Those states include: **Albania, Andorra, Armenia, Azerbaijan, Belarus, Belgium, Bosnia and Herzegovina, Bulgaria, Croatia, Cyprus, Estonia, Georgia, Greece, Holy See, Hungary, Iceland, Italy, Kazakhstan, Kyrgyzstan, Latvia, Liechtenstein, Lithuania, Luxembourg, Macedonia, Malta, Moldova, Monaco, Montenegro**, the **Netherlands, Norway, Portugal, Romania**, the **Russian Federation, San Marino, Serbia, Slovenia, Spain, Switzerland, Tajikistan, Turkey, Turkmenistan, Ukraine**, and **Uzbekistan.**

II. Updates: Systems of Monitoring and Reporting

A. Measures to Improve the Collection of Data

The proper registration of hate crimes by police and other state authorities is essential to accurate data. Measures were taken in a number of countries to enhance registration and thus to improve the effectiveness of data collection. In some cases, the measures came in the form of instructions from senior law enforcement and criminal justice officials.

In **Denmark**, the Justice Minister instructed the State Advocate to collect information and material as of January 1, 2007, on cases of hate crimes that have gone to court.[3]

In **Lithuania**, in 2007 the Interior Ministry instructed territorial police institutions to collect and provide information on crimes against foreigners because of their ethnicity, nationality or race.[4]

In the **Netherlands**, in line with the requirements set forth by the Discrimination Directive, a directive issued every four years (most recently in December 2007) by the Board of Procurators General, regional consultations must take place between police, prosecutors, and antidiscrimination bodies concerning cases of discrimination. Focal points from the police and prosecution service are to meet with representatives from the antidiscrimination bureaus to consult on cases of discrimination, including hate crimes. A case tracking system has been developed, which will allow representatives of these three bodies to track hate crimes from the time a complaint is filed either with the police or the local antidiscrimination bureau, through court processing.[5] As of September 2008, 22 of the 25 police jurisdictions throughout the country were working with the tracking system.[6]

In **Norway**, the Equality and Antidiscrimination Ombudsman reported that a decision by the Justice Department in March 2007 requires that all incidents of hate crime be registered by the police. The Ombudsman's Office is cooperating with the police, which have begun recording bias motivations based on ethnic origin, sexual orientation, and religion.[7]

In several countries, measures to enhance registration were taken in the form of seminars, training workshops, and other projects and studies.

In **Belgium**, on November 27, 2007, the Center for Equal Opportunities and Opposition to Racism (CEOOR), Belgium's national antidiscrimination body, organized a seminar on racist violence with various representatives from the police and courts to review the progress made in the registration of hate crimes. Since 2006, a system has been in place whereby police have been able to register bias motivations in a separate context section on crime reporting forms. The number of registered hate crimes remains small, which the CEOOR attributes to the fact that registration as such is not a priority. The police and court system apparently register hate crimes, but this information is incomplete and is not made public. The seminar was a part of efforts by the CEOOR to press the police and criminal justice authorities to systematically collect and publish such data.[8]

In **Canada**, on July 18, 2008, according to news reports, the Ontario Province leadership introduced a program to train Ontario Provincial Police on the subject of hate crimes. The training aims to prepare frontline officers to identify and sensitively handle violent cases motivated by bias.[9]

In **Finland**, where the police have produced annual reports on racist crimes since 1998, information on judicial responses has been lacking. Accordingly, the authorities are conducting a study on the way in which racist crimes are treated in the judicial system. The results of the study are expected to be released at the end of 2008.[10]

In **Germany**, the initiative to facilitate a conference on data collection was taken by an NGO. On May 16-17, 2008, the gay rights organization Maneo organized its third European conference with representatives of police forces, government authorities, and organizations from numerous German federal states, as well as France, Poland, Spain, the Netherlands, Belgium, Ireland, and Israel. The conference focused on how light could be shed on homophobic violence and how gay and bisexual men could be better protected against attacks. Participants examined problems surrounding reporting, registration and police response to homophobic violence.[11]

In the **Netherlands**, on March 20, 2008, the Dutch police launched a hate crime pilot project in two police regions. The purpose of this project was to conduct targeted outreach to members of the LGBT community with the aim of increasing hate crime reporting among the LGBT community. The project allows victims to file a confidential report and offers the victim limited anonymity. Additionally, the police are undertaking related efforts to enhance reporting by making it possible for victims to file an online report. Police are also receiving training and developing protocols that aim to systematize the line of questioning in cases of racist or homophobic violence.[12]

In **Sweden**, law enforcement authorities took a number of measures in 2007 and 2008 to increase the reporting and registration of hate crimes.

- Personnel answering the police emergency phone lines were trained to identify possible hate crimes and to register the victims' characteristics.

- As of January 2008, an additional box is available on the crime report form allowing for the registration of a suspected hate crime.

- The Swedish police have made it possible to report crimes—including hate crimes—using a form accessible through the Internet.

- Police have been given special training aimed at increasing their ability to identify and investigate hate crimes as well as to develop methods to combat them.[13]

- Additionally, within local police departments, either all officers are being trained to recognize and respond to hate crimes, or special focal points with expertise on hate crimes are appointed.[14]

Also in **Sweden**, the National Council for Crime Prevention (Brå), the body responsible for monitoring hate crimes, undertook to examine the problem of the serious data deficit as concerns violence against people with disabilities. In a report released at the end of 2007, Brå concluded that, in order to collect systematic data, it was necessary to enhance the use of the existing crime registration process by improving the level of knowledge among those working in disability care as well as those within the criminal justice system. Brå further recommended that the justice system focus on developing methods that will "increase the opportunities available to people with disabilities to make their voices heard and to be understood" in cases of violence.[15]

In the **United Kingdom**, the Home Office's data collection requirements oblige all police forces to submit certain data on bias-motivated crimes to the Home Office for national aggregation. To date, and with respect to hate crimes, forces are only required to submit data on racially and religiously aggravated offences established under the Public Order Act (covering England and Wales). In reporting, no distinction is made between racially and religiously aggravated offences, nor is it possible to further disaggregate hate crimes by race or religion.

As part of a report providing the government's response to the 2006 All-Party Parliamentary Inquiry into Antisemitism, the government described a number of measures to enhance hate crime reporting, including the following:

- Pilot changes were introduced to the data collection practices, including the establishment as of April 2008 of a Home Office Data Hub. The Data Hub is to enable the analysis of data at a greater level of detail and allow officials to aggregate and disaggregate data on many levels.

- The reintroduction of online reporting facilities that allow victims and witnesses to report directly to the police. This includes the production of a checklist for information that should be included in a third party reporting form.

- The commitment to ensure that all forces will record antisemitic crimes by April 1, 2009.[16]

While most efforts to improve data collection focus on law enforcement and criminal justice bodies, efforts have also been made to enhance the reporting of other state bodies. In the **United States**, efforts have long been undertaken to produce hate crime data in educational institutions, and those requirements have recently been upgraded to make the resulting data correspond more closely to data produced by the Federal Bureau of Investigation (FBI). The Higher Education Act of 1965 requires colleges and universities to report campus incidents, including violent, bias-motivated crimes, to the Office of Postsecondary Education (OPE). Reporting requirements have until recently been less rigorous than those of the FBI and have resulted in inconsistencies between FBI and OPE hate crime statistics. With the passage of a new bill on July 31, 2008, amending the Higher Education Act of 1965, the U.S. Congress has mandated that the hate crime data reported by campus security personnel must be uniform to that reported by state and local authorities to the FBI.[17]

B. Measures to Improve Public Reporting

A few countries have introduced improvements or refinements in their public reporting of hate crimes over the past year. Most significantly, **Canada** released national statistics for the first time in 2008. In **Denmark**, hate crime statistics reported by the security police include a range of new categories. In **Austria**, public hate crime statistics for 2007 have been expanded to include disaggregated statistics on hate crime against Muslims.

In **Canada**, on June 9, 2008, the Canadian Centre for Justice Statistics released the first report on national hate crime data; the report covered 87 percent of the population. Data from the Hate Crime Supplemental Survey and the Uniform Crime Reporting Survey—which contributed to the report—indicate that 892 hate crimes occurred in 2006. This number includes violent crimes, property crimes, as well as offenses such as disturbing the peace, threatening phone calls, and weapon violations. The data are disaggregated into race/ethnicity, religion, and sexual orientation biases, including sub-groups of these categories.[18] The Canadian Centre for Justice Statistics anticipates publishing hate crime statistics on an annual basis with 2007 hate crime statistics to be published in early 2009.[19]

In **Denmark**, PET, the Danish Security Service, released a report which provided data for 2007 and a new and more detailed analysis of hate crimes reported by the organization in 2005 and 2006. PET now provides a breakdown of data that distinguishes crimes that are directed (among other categories):

- toward people of other ethnic backgrounds than Danish;

- toward ethnic Danish;

■ between people of different ethnic backgrounds than Danish;

■ between ethnic Danish.

The largest proportion of hate crimes (29 of the 35 hate crimes in 2007) are motivated by xenophobia and directed against people of another ethnic background.[20] In fact, xenophobic bias has accounted for the majority of such crimes registered over the last three years: 65 (74.7 percent) in 2005; 200 (88.1 percent) in 2006; 29 (82.9 percent) in 2007. Hate crime data is further disaggregated into the following crime categories: murder, arson, violence/physical attacks, threats, propaganda, vandalism, and written or personal harassment.

In 2007, there were 35 hate crime cases recorded, of which 5 were violent hate crimes. This represents a decrease in violent hate crimes in comparison to the 13 violent hate crimes reported in 2006. According to PET, the low number of cases recorded in 2007 is a result of a serious decline in reporting of hate crime incidents, and does not necessarily reflect an actual decline in this type of crime. Going forward, PET plans to gain more access to police reports in order to better collect, adjust, and analyze the relevant information directly in the police electronic case processing system. This will allow the organization to gain a fuller, more accurate picture of the developments in this field.[21]

In **Austria**, police in 2007 introduced the category of violence against Muslims, extracting the data from the general category of xenophobic/racist violence. Two such cases were registered in 2007.[22]

III. The Contribution of NGOs to Monitoring and Reporting

While it is ultimately the responsibility of governments to monitor and report on the incidence of and response to hate crimes in a transparent way, information from nongovernmental organizations (NGOs) can begin to fill in some of the gaps of incomplete or nonexistent official reporting. Such information can likewise help to flesh out the hate crime picture in the face of popular media reports that may misrepresent the nature of hate crimes, severely understate their scope, or report only the most extreme bias violence.

NGO monitoring in some parts of the OSCE region has expanded in recent years – in the **Russian Federation**, for example, the SOVA Center for Information and Analysis has been monitoring and reporting on hate crime incidents and prosecutions since 2004 and has been a particularly useful source of information in the absence of government reporting on hate crime (For more discussion, see the separate section of the *2008 Hate Crime Survey* on **The Russian Federation**). Yet systematic data that allows for an analysis of trends still only exists in a few countries, and often only relates to specific types of hate crime. Furthermore, NGO monitoring is generally limited to incident reports—most NGOs are unable to track the government response to those incidents in any systematic way. In several regions of the OSCE, regular NGO monitoring of hate crimes is largely absent. Thus, there is a need for greater resources, capacity, and training for NGOs to undertake monitoring hate crimes and advocacy for a vigorous government response. Intergovernmental organizations have an important role to play and the OSCE has developed a civil society training program—the first training took place in May 2008—that seeks to enhance the capacity of NGOs working in this field. Yet more support needs to be provided to NGO monitoring and advocacy efforts as part of overall efforts to document and address hate crimes.

In 2007 and 2008, new reports from NGOs in **Germany** and the **United Kingdom**—both countries with established official monitoring systems—help to fill in the data deficit as concerns violence against LGBT persons and people with disabilities.

In **Germany**, for the first time, a nationwide victim survey was conducted among gay and bisexual youths and adults on their experiences with violence. Almost 24,000 people participated in the survey, which was conducted between December 1, 2006 and January 31, 2007 by the nongovernmental organization Maneo.[23] The survey found that 35 percent of all the respondents experienced bias-motivated violence in the past year and almost two-thirds (63 percent) of the young gay and bisexual men under the age of 18 were victims of such violence in the past year. Only 10 percent of the victims filed reports with the police.[24] A second survey was conducted one year later with 17,500 participants, and preliminary data shows that almost 40 percent reported having experienced bias-motivated violence. Maneo expects to release more detailed results from this second survey in Fall 2008.[25]

In the **United Kingdom**, on June 26, 2008, the U.K.-based NGO Stonewall published *Homophobic Hate Crime: The Gay British Crime Survey*. This report surveyed approximately 1,721 members of the LGBT community across the United Kingdom. It exposed incidences of verbal abuse and violent hate crimes experienced by individuals who identify as LGBT throughout England, Scotland, and Wales. *The report found that 12.5 percent of the respondents had been the victim of a hate crime or incident within the past* year (20 percent in the past three years). Four percent of the respondents reported a violent physical assault. Three quarters of the victims of hate crimes and incidents did not report the incident to the police believing that the complaint would not be investigated.[26]

Similarly, surveys of hate crime against the disabled conducted by NGOs in the **United Kingdom** have shown that disabled people also frequently become victims of hate crime but often fail to report the incident to the police. In those cases in which the incident is reported, in turn, police often failed to register it properly. According to the mental health charity Mind, a recent study showed that three quarters of people with mental health problems have been the victim of crime within the past two years, including "alarming levels of disability hate crime."[27]

Section Endnotes

1 Organization for Security and Cooperation in Europe, "Tolerance and Non-Discrimination: Promoting Mutual Respect and Understanding," OSCE Ministerial Council Decision, no. 10/07, MC.DEC/10/07, November 30, 2007, http://www.osce.org/documents/mcs/2007/12/28629_en.pdf.

2 European Union Agency for Fundamental Rights, *Annual Report*, 2008, TK-AG-08-001-EN-C, http://fra.europa.eu/fra/material/pub/ar08/ar08_en.pdf, pp. 30-31.

3 Bashy Quraishy, *ENAR Shadow Report 2006: Racism in Denmark*, European Network Against Racism, http://cms.horus.be/files/99935/MediaArchive/pdf/Denmark_2006.pdf, p.30.

4 European Union Agency for Fundamental Rights, *Annual Report*, 2008, TK-AG-08-001-EN-C, http://fra.europa.eu/fra/material/pub/ar08/ar08_en.pdf, pp. 30-31.

5 Human Rights First correspondence with the Dutch National Police, a program folder *"Start Project Hate Crimes en Expertmeeting Regionaal Discriminatie Overleg,"* September 14, 2008.

6 Human Rights First correspondence with Tas Floris, Discrimination focal point in the Dutch National Police, September 14, 2008.

7 Response of the Equality and Antidiscrimination Ombudsman to a Human Rights First questionnaire, October 2, 2007.

8 Centre for Equal Opportunities and Opposition to Racism, *Discriminatie, Diversiteit, Jaarverslag 2007*, http://www.diversiteit.be/?action=publicatie_detail&id=32&thema=2.

9 Marcus McCann, "Ontario earmarks cash to respond to hate crimes," *Capital Xtra*, July 19, 2008, http://www.xtra.ca/public/Ottawa/Ontario_earmarks_cash_to_respond_to_hate_crimes-5157.aspx.

10 Response of the Finnish Ministry of Foreign Affairs to a Human Rights First questionnaire, August 28, 2008.

11 Maneo, *Summary Report on Maneo Workshop 3: Homophobia and Violence Against Gays in Public Space, Berlin*, May 16-17, 2008.

12 Human Rights First interview with Floris Tas, Discrimination focal point in the Dutch National Police, and Jan Snyder, Hate Crimes Project Officer, June 24, 2008.

13 Training amounts to the equivalent of five weeks of full-time study. *Rikspolisstyrelsen, "Polisens årsredovisning 2007,"* CO-902-6546/06, 2008, http://www.polisen.se/mediaarchive/4347/3474/3928/Polisens_AR_2007.pdf.

14 *Rikspolisstyrelsen, "Polisens årsredovisning 2007,"* CO-902-6546/06, 2008, http://www.polisen.se/mediaarchive/4347/3474/3928/Polisens_AR_2007.pdf.

15 The Swedish National Council for Crime Prevention, *Violence Against People with Disbilities*, Stockholm, 2007, http://www.bra.se/extra/measurepoint/?module_instance=4&name=2007_26_Violence_against_people_with_disabilities.pdf&url=/dynamaster/file_archive/080722/3d8defdab490764cf782192089268ee6/2007 percent255f26 percent255fViolence percent255fagainst percent255fpeople percent255fwith percent255fdisabilities.pdf.

16 The Minister of State for Communities and Local Government, *All-Party Inquiry into Antisemitism: Government Response One year on Progress Report*, May 12, 2008, http://www.official-documents.gov.uk/document/cm73/7381/7381.pdf.

17 Chris Johnson, "Campus and FBI hate crime reporting to be uniform," *Human Rights Campaign*, August 1, 2008, http://www.hrcbackstory.org/2008/08/campus-and-fbi.html.

18 Mia Dauvergne, Katie Scrim and Shannon Brennan, *Hate Crime in Canada 2006*, Canadian Centre for Justice Statistics, 2006, http://www.statcan.ca/english/research/85F0033MIE/85F0033MIE2008017.pdf.

19 Human Rights First correspondence with a senior analyst at the Policing Services Program, Canadian Centre for Justice Statistics, Statistics Canada, August 18, 2008.

20 The report covers only crimes with a possible racial or religious motivation: homophobic hate crimes are not included.

21 The Danish Security Intelligence Service, *RACI-report 2007*, http://www.pet.dk/upload/raci2007.pdf.

22 Human Rights First correspondence with Dieter Stelzer, German Ministry of the Interior, Federal Agency for State Protection and Counter Terrorism, July 22, 2008.

23 Maneo provides a gay emergency hotline and victim support services homosexual and bisexual men and youths in Berlin. For more information, see Maneo at http://www.maneo.de/highres/english/e_hindex.html.

24 Maneo, *Maneo Survey 2006/2007*, Berlin: 2007. Human Rights First correspondence with Bastian Finke, Maneo Project Director, on August 7, 2008.

[25] Maneo, *Summary Report on Maneo Workshop 3: Homophobia and Violence Against Gays in Public Space, Berlin*, May 16-17, 2008.

[26] Stonewall, *Homophobic Hate Crime: The Gay British Crime Survey*, June 26, 2008, http://www.stonewall.org.uk.

[27] Mind, "Mind reveals alarming levels of disability hate crime," November 29, 2007, http://www.mind.org.uk/News+policy+and+campaigns/Press/2007_11_29_AA.htm.

Framework of Criminal Law

Table of Contents

Executive Summary

While governments have an obligation to combat all crime, the hate crime concept is a simple acknow - edgement of the greater seriousness of crimes motivated by racial, religious, or other prejudice and hatred that harm whole communities. Hate crime legislation signals a society's commitment to combat violent discrimination and gives force to this by providing for more severe penalties. In the last two years, the European Union has required and the Council of Europe has recommended that member states consider racist and xenophobic motives as an aggravating factor in violent criminal offenses, while the European Court of Human Rights has deplored "treating racially induced violence and brutality on an equal footing with cases that have no racist overtones."

A growing number of the 56 countries in the OSCE are adopting criminal laws to expressly address violent hate crimes, largely in the form of penalty enhancement provisions. At present, there are over 30 countries in which legislation treats at least some bias-motivated violent crime as a separate crime or in which one or more forms of bias is regarded as an aggravating circumstance that can result in enhanced penalties.

However, 23 OSCE countries still have no express provisions defining bias as an aggravating circumstance in the commission of a range of violent crimes against persons. They are: **Albania, Bosnia and Herzegovina, Bulgaria, Cyprus, Estonia, Germany, Greece, Holy See, Hungary, Iceland, Ireland, Luxembourg, Lithuania, Macedonia, Monaco, Montenegro,** the **Netherlands, Poland, San Marino, Serbia, Slovenia, Switzerland,** and **Turkey.**

Data from government bodies, NGOs and media in several of these countries indicate that violent hate crimes are occurring, but criminal justice authorities are unable to treat them as the more serious crimes that they are due to the lack of a legislative basis to do so.

Of the 39 countries where legislation addresses bias-motivated violence as a separate crime or as an aggravating circumstance, those provisions all cover bias founded on race, ethnicity, and/or national origin, while 32 also cover religious bias. However, hate crime legislation extends to bias motivated by animus based on sexual orientation in only twelve countries and disability in only seven.

In 2007 and in the first half of 2008, there were legislative developments in several countries. In **Latvia,** new aggravating circumstances provisions addressing racist motivations entered into force. In **Portugal,** following criminal code amendments, bias based on sexual orientation can now be considered an aggravating factor in cases of homicide and assault. In the **Russian Federation,** also following amendments to its criminal code, aggravating circumstance provisions were extended to a range of new crimes. The biases were also expanded from "racial, national and religious hatred" to include "political" and "ideological" bias as well as bias against "a social group." Observers have expressed concern that this latter development could be misused to punish political dissent.

In the **United States,** the latest effort to adopt amendments that would expand the scope of federal hate crime legislation, including to cover sexual orientation, gender identity and disability bias was unsuccessful, but new legislative initiatives are pending. In three other countries—**Germany, Norway,** and the **United Kingdom** (Scotland), draft criminal law amendments are at various stages of the legislative process.

Determining the extent to which the law is enforced in response to incidents of violent hate crime remains a challenge for all OSCE member states. Most states without laws on violent hate crime do not keep statistics on the law enforcement response to bias-motivated incidents of violence. Moreover, there is little official data from anywhere in the region with which to asses the effectiveness of the implementation of the laws that do exist on violent hate crimes. There is also a dearth of monitoring or other information on the implementation of these laws by specialized antidiscrimination bodies or NGOs. Nonetheless, NGO monitors in a few countries, including the **Russian Federation** and **Ukraine**, have reported on an ad hoc basis on prosecutions, and specialized agencies in **Belgium** and **Sweden** have also engaged in some monitoring of hate crime cases. New measures have been undertaken in the **United Kingdom** to enhance the criminal justice response to hate crime as well as to track hate crime cases from incident to prosecution. The **Netherlands** has also announced that a pilot project to track hate crime cases through the courts will be extended throughout the country.

I. International Standards and Commitments

A number of political and legal guidelines for the adoption and implementation of hate crime laws have been established by European multilateral institutions within the last two years. The European Union has required and the Council of Europe has recommended that member states consider racist and xenophobic motives as an aggravating factor in violent criminal offenses, while the European Court of Human Rights has deplored "treating racially induced violence and brutality on an equal footing with cases that have no racist overtones."[1]

The European Union Framework Decision on Combating Racism and Xenophobia, adopted on April 20, 2007, is a binding political agreement that E.U. Member States must now implement in their national law. The Decision provides that racist and xenophobic motives are to be considered an aggravating factor in criminal offenses and that such motives may be taken into consideration by the courts in fixing the penalty.[2]

Similarly, the European Commission against Racism and Intolerance (ECRI)—the antiracism body within the Council of Europe (CoE)—has since 2002, with the adoption of its Policy Recommendation No. 7 on "national legislation to combat racism and racial discrimination," encouraged the 47 CoE member states to adopt criminal laws under which racist motivation is treated as an aggravating circumstance. Most recently, in its newly adopted Policy Recommendation No. 11 on combating racism and racial discrimination in policing, adopted on June 29, 2007, ECRI reiterates this recommendation, while focusing on the role of the police in encouraging better reporting of such incidents. The recommendation includes the following points:

■ To ensure that the police thoroughly investigate racist offences, including by fully taking the racist motivation of ordinary offences into account.

■ To establish and operate a system for recording and monitoring racist incidents, and the extent to which these incidents are brought before the prosecutors and are eventually qualified as racist offences.

■ To encourage victims and witnesses of racist incidents to report such incidents.[3]

Decisions of the European Court of Human Rights have articulated a duty on state authorities to investigate potential racial motives behind violent incidents and to bring perpetrators to trial. The court first made this reference in its 2005 *Nachova and Others vs. Bulgaria* decision, in which it noted that states "have the additional duty to take all reasonable steps to unmask any racial motive and to establish whether or not ethnic hatred and prejudice may have played a role in the events."[4]

Two other subsequent decisions in 2007—*Angelova and Iliev vs. Bulgaria* and *Secic vs. Croatia*—made similar points in cases of racially motivated violence. Both cases involved violence committed by private individuals, unlike the Nachova case, in which the police were the perpetrators.

■ On May 31, 2007, in the case of *Secic vs. Croatia*, the court delivered a judgment regarding the lack of proper investigation carried out by the Croatian authorities into a racially motivated attack on a Romani man. The Court reiterated its position in the Nachova case "that when investigating violent incidents, State authorities have the additional duty to take all reasonable steps to unmask any racist motive and to establish whether or not ethnic hatred or prejudice may have played a role in the events." The decision further stated that "treating racially induced violence and brutality on an equal footing with cases that have no racist overtones would be turning a blind eye to the specific nature of acts that are particularly destructive of fundamental rights.[5]

■ On July 26, 2007, the court issued a judgment in the case of *Angelova and Iliev vs. Bulgaria*, which involved the murder of two Romani men by a group of teenagers in 1996. In this case, there was ample evidence indicating that the murders were racially motivated, yet for the next nine years, the investigating authorities failed to bring the perpetrators to justice.[6] In its decision, the court found that it was "completely unacceptable that, while aware that the attack was incited by racial hatred, the authorities did not expeditiously complete the preliminary investigation against the assailants and bring them to trial." It notes in this respect the widespread prejudices and violence against Roma during the relevant period and the need to reassert continuously society's condemnation of racism and to maintain the confidence of minorities in the authorities' ability to protect them from the threat of racist violence.[7]

The participating states of the OSCE have not established a specific obligation to enact hate crime offenses or aggravating circumstance provisions into their criminal law. They have, however, committed to consider increasing their efforts to ensure that national legislation provides equal and effective protection of the law to all persons and prohibits acts of intolerance and discrimination.[8] The OSCE's Office for Democratic Institutions and Human Rights is also preparing a set of practical guidelines on various aspects of developing, adopting and, implementing hate crime laws. The guidelines, which have been prepared during the course of 2007 and 2008 with input from human rights advocates, hate crime experts, and law enforcement and criminal justice professionals are expected to be released in late 2008.[9]

II. Updates: Hate Crime Provisions

As Human Rights First discussed in more detail in its *2007 Hate Crime Report Card*, while governments have an obligation to combat all crime, the hate crime concept is a simple acknowledgement of the greater seriousness of crimes motivated by racial, religious, or other prejudice and hatred that harms whole communities. Hate crime legislation signals a society's commitment to combat violent discrimination and gives force to this by providing for more severe penalties.[10]

A growing number of the 56 countries in the OSCE are adopting criminal legislation to expressly address violent hate crimes. At present, there are over 30 countries in which legislation treats at least some bias-motivated violent crime as a separate crime or in which one or more forms of bias is regarded as an aggravating circumstance that can result in enhanced penalties.

However, 23 OSCE countries still have no express provisions in their criminal law defining bias as an aggravating circumstance in the commission of violent crimes against persons. These countries include: **Albania, Bosnia and Herzegovina, Bulgaria, Cyprus, Estonia, Germany, Greece, Holy See, Hungary, Iceland, Ireland, Luxembourg, Lithuania, Macedonia, Monaco, Montenegro, the Netherlands, Poland, San Marino, Serbia, Slovenia, Switzerland**, and **Turkey**.

Data from government bodies, NGOs, and the media in a number of these countries, such as **Estonia, Germany, Greece, Hungary Ireland, Lithuania, the Netherlands, Poland, Serbia, Slovenia, Switzerland**, and **Turkey** indicate that hate crimes are occurring, but criminal justice authorities lack a legislative basis to treat bias as an aggravating circumstance in the commission of these crimes.

Of the 39 countries where legislation addresses bias-motivated violence as a separate crime or as an aggravating circumstance, those provisions all cover bias founded on race, ethnicity, and/or national origin, while 32 also cover religious bias. However, hate crime legislation extends to bias motivated by animus based on sexual orientation in only twelve countries and disability in only seven.[11] Bias based on gender identity is explicitly mentioned in criminal law only in the United States—and even there only at the state level in 11 states and the District of Columbia.[12] Legislation that extends to all forms of bias is both a better guarantee of the commitment to provide equal protection of the law to all as well as a practical incentive for criminal justice officials to track incidents, assess public policy, and develop preventative measures for all forms of bias-motivated violence.

A. Newly Adopted Criminal Law Provisions

There have been changes since 2006 in national legislation in three countries. **Latvia** adopted new provisions defining racist and other bias motivations as an aggravating circumstance. In **Portugal**, bias based on sexual orientation is now considered an aggravating circumstance in some violent crimes. In the **Russian Federation**, new legislation has expanded the range of bias motivation and crimes to which preexisting aggravating circumstances provisions could be applied.

In **Latvia**, on October 12, 2006, the Latvian Parliament amended section 48 of the criminal code dealing with aggravating circumstances in the commission of a crime. According to the newly amended part 14 of that section, a "racist motivation" now constitutes an aggravating circumstance. The amendment entered into force in July 2007.

In **Portugal**, the criminal code before the recent amendments provided that incidents of homicide, severe assault, and assault can be considered "aggravated" and subject to more severe punishments when those crimes are motivated by racial, religious, or political hatred.[13] As a result of amendments in September 2007, bias based on sexual orientation can now similarly be considered an aggravating factor in those same crimes.[14]

In the **Russian Federation**, several parallel legislative initiatives in 2007 resulted in the adoption of new and amended criminal law provisions that address violent hate crimes. On May 10, 2007, bias motivations were added to article 214 of the criminal code dealing with vandalism. This article was amended to include an enhanced punishment when the act of vandalism is committed "with a motive of ideological, political, racial, national, or religious hatred." Whereas bias motives based on "racial, national, or religious hatred" had already been taken into account in criminal law, this amendment introduced for the first time the notions of "ideological" and "political" hatred as aggravating circumstances in the commission of a criminal offense. Article 244 was also amended so that an act of desecration motivated by bias can be punished by a maximum sentence of five years (up from three years previously).

On August 10, 2007, amendments to antiextremist legislation were also passed, resulting in a number of changes to provisions addressing bias-motivated violence. These amendments expanded the concept of bias motivations in terms similar to those of the amended article 214. Whereas Russian law previously addressed bias motivations based on "national, racial and religious hatred," the amendments expanded this definition to include motivations based on "*ideological, political*, racial, national, and religious hatred and enmity or *hatred and enmity toward some social group.*"

Similar changes regarding bias motivations were introduced to article 63 on general aggravating circumstances for all crimes, as well as to six other articles of the criminal code dealing with specific offenses where bias motivations provided for sentence enhancement.[15] Bias motivations as aggravating circumstances in the same terms were also extended to five new articles of the criminal code.[16]

Some observers have argued that these provisions will now allow prosecutors to seek enhanced penalties in cases of neo-Nazi violence against antifascists and other youth subcultures (which might now be prosecuted as "ideological" hate crimes). Others have raised concerns, however, that the new range of "hatred" is too broad, not clearly defined, and opens the way to arbitrary application of the law in order to punish political dissent.[17]

B. Efforts to Adopt New Hate Crime Provisions

In **Germany**, while the courts have the right under paragraph 2 of section 46 (Principles for determining punishment) of the Criminal Code to consider the motives of the perpetrator in determining the sentence, there is no express mention of racist or other bias motivations. Lower courts, particularly in the eastern German states, often appear to be reluctant to consider the bias motivations in assaults and other acts of violence by right-wing extremists.[18]

Two eastern German states, Brandenburg and Saxony-Anhalt, which have been experiencing a steady rise in the number of crimes with an obvious right-wing extremist background, submitted new draft legislation to the Parliament's upper chamber, the *Bundesrat*, at the end of 2007.[19] The current draft seeks to amend, among other provisions, section 46 paragraph 2 such that crimes motivated by "the political attitude, nationality, ethnicity, race, color of skin, religion, philosophical conviction, origin, personal appearance, disability or sexual orientation of the victim" would lead to enhanced penalties.[20]

In **Norway**, provisions on aggravating circumstances already exist under Section 232 of the Criminal Code and extend to felonies against another person's life, body, and health in which the offence has been committed with a racist motive.[21] Proposed amendments to the Criminal Code would introduce general aggravating circumstance provisions that would allow for enhanced penalties in all crimes at the sentencing stage. The provisions would also broaden the forms of bias to be taken into account by allowing for penalty enhancements in cases in which the crime was motivated by bias based on one's "religion or philosophy, skin color, national or ethnic origin, sexual orientation, disability."[22] Some observers have reported that the new provisions could be adopted in 2010.[23]

In the **United Kingdom**, in Scotland, a bill was introduced on May 19, 2008 that would extend hate crime legislation to cover crimes motivated by malice or ill-will based on the victim's actual or presumed sexual orientation, transgender identity, or disability. The Policy Memorandum that accompanied the bill—which was introduced on the basis of recommendations from a Working Group on Hate Crimes established several years earlier by the government—noted that the Cabinet Secretary for Justice has indicated the Scottish government's support for legislation in this area.

Hate crime legislation in Scotland currently applies to offenses motivated only by racial or religious prejudice. On the contrary, in England and Wales and in Northern Ireland, the legislation already extends to sexual orientation and disability.

The bill in Scotland also aims to enhance the system of data collection in hate crime cases. The supporting memorandum states that:

> The provisions will also allow the existence of the aggravations to be recorded at all levels in the criminal justice system from the initial recording of a crime through to the charging stage, prosecution, conviction and eventual sentence. Upon conviction, where the sentence is different as a result of the aggravation, the court will be required to state and record the extent of, and reasons for, that difference. This will enable Government and practitioners to build up an accurate picture of the extent of these particular hate crimes in Scotland and inform policy accordingly.[24]

In the **United States**, efforts to adopt the Local Law Enforcement Hate Crime Prevention Act of 2007 (LLEHCPA) were unsuccessful. The LLEHCPA, a federal measure that would have expanded the scope of national hate crime legislation, was passed by both houses of Congress, but was ultimately withdrawn in the face of a promised veto by President George W. Bush. The proposed law would have eliminated the requirement that prosecutors must demonstrate that a victim was targeted expressly because of that person's participation in one of the six federally protected categories, one of the current requirements for application of federal law to a violent hate crime.[25] The bill would also have extended the bias categories under federal protection to include gender identity, sexual orientation, and disability.

III. Implementation of Criminal Law Provisions

Determining the extent to which the law is enforced in response to violent hate crime requires data collection. The most effective monitoring systems would not only register incidents and offences, but would also track them through the criminal justice system. However, few, if any, official data collection systems on violent hate crimes are coordinated with systems that track cases through the criminal courts. This deficit in tracking data poses obstacles to the assessment of the enforcement of hate crime laws, which must accordingly be undertaken using incomplete information and the review of particular cases.

Statistics on the use of bias crime sentencing norms, including those convictions resulting in enhanced sentences, are also largely unavailable. The absence of statistical evidence on sentence enhancement in violent hate crimes leaves an enormous gap as to how these most serious crimes are dealt with in the justice system. Were those charged convicted? Were the sentences enhanced on the grounds of bias motivation? There is little public data to answer these questions.[26]

Notwithstanding these general deficiencies in official data collection, some government agencies responsible for law enforcement, as well as some specialized antidiscrimination bodies, have begun to take initial steps to track the implementation of hate crime laws. In **Canada**, for example, the government generally does not collect statistics on the use of article 718.2 (a)(i)—a penalty enhancement provision that includes bias motivations—although the Research and Statistics Division of the Department of Justice Canada is reportedly undertaking a study that will examine the use of these provisions. In a response to a questionnaire from Human Rights First, the Canadian government reported that "a preliminary review of published case law indicates that between 1996 and 2006 at least 48

cases have applied hate as an aggravating factor at sentencing."[27]

In the **Netherlands**, a case tracking system has been developed to allow representatives of the police, prosecution services, and antidiscrimination bodies to track hate crimes from the time a complaint is filed with either the police or the local antidiscrimination bureau, through court processing. Such a tracking system was initially employed on a pilot basis in several regions around the country, and as of September 2008, 22 of the 25 police jurisdictions throughout the country were working with the tracking system.[28]

In the **United Kingdom**, the Crown Prosecution Service (CPS) in the past year took a number of important steps to enhance prosecution of hate crime cases. With regard to combating antisemitic hate crime, the CPS reported on its follow-up to the 2006 All-Party Parliamentary Inquiry into Antisemitism. That report highlighted a number of shortcomings, including the low number of hate crime prosecutions, and set out recommendations for action. The CPS reported in particular on several measures that it had taken, including the following:

> Data was obtained from the Metropolitan Police Service and the Greater Manchester Police on antisemitic incidents reported in 2006/7. The progress of each incident was then tracked from initial report to the conclusion of the case in order to establish, wherever possible, the reasons behind the final outcome.

The CPS also reported on its intention to develop an action plan for combating antisemitic hate crime to be developed in cooperation with the police and other criminal justice partners, as well as with representatives from the Jewish community.[29]

Moreover, the CPS sought to enhance its response to homophobic crime. In November 2007, it issued a report on *Guidance on Prosecuting Cases of Homopho-*

bic and Transphobic Crime. The report reiterates the importance of a thorough investigation and prosecution of such cases, stating that:

> Prejudice, discrimination or hatred of members of any part of our community based on their sexual orientation or gender identity have no place in a civilized society; any such prejudice, discrimination or hate that shows itself in the commission of crime must be thoroughly and properly investigated and firmly and rigorously prosecuted in the courts. A clear message must be sent so that those who commit such crimes realize that they will be dealt with firmly under the criminal law: the CPS has a vital role to play in delivering this aim, not only in terms of its own role but also in terms of advising its partners in the criminal justice system—the police, the courts, magistrates, judges and those in the voluntary sector—that this sort of crime must no longer be tolerated."[30]

In **Belgium**, the Center for Equal Opportunities and Opposition to Racism (CEOOR), which is one of the few antidiscrimination bodies with a strong legal mandate to pursue individual hate crime cases through the courts, tracks such cases and their prosecutions. In its latest annual report, the CEOOR reported that 18 hate crime cases (up from 14 cases in 2006) involving manslaughter or bodily injury—were registered in the court system in 2007.[31]

In **Sweden**, the Office of the Ombudsman against Discrimination on the grounds of sexual orientation has monitored cases in which enhanced penalties have been handed down on the basis of chapter 29, section 2(7) of the Criminal Code for crimes committed with a homophobic motive. The office posts examples on its web site of such cases when it comes across relevent judgments through its own research or when a court sends them a copy of the judgment. All courts are obliged to send the ombudsman all judgments in which a bias motive has been considered or applied as an aggravating circumstance. In practice, however, courts rarely follow through on this obligation.[32] In 2007, the Ombudsman reported on one case in which it raised questions as to the proper application of aggravating circumstances.

In a very briefly reasoned judgment, a district court of southern Sweden convicted a woman of assaulting another woman. She was charged with hitting her victim twice in the face with her open hand, pulling her hair and forcefully grabbing her left wrist causing her pain. The defendant was sentenced to pay a fine. The court found the assault to be a minor offence, referring to "the circumstances of the crime" and to "the material presented to the court," however without revealing either what those circumstances were nor what that material consisted of.

The Ombudsman's comment: Both the sentence and the reasoning are intriguing. The case had received some media coverage, according to which the defendant was the mother of the female victim, the reason for the assault being that she did not approve of the fact that her daughter was a lesbian. When her daughter refused to leave the home of her girlfriend to go back home with her mother, the mother beat her daughter up. According to Chapter 29 Section 2(7) of the Swedish Penal Code, when a motive for a crime has been the victim's sexual orientation that is an aggravating circumstance, which should lead to a more severe sentence. In this case the reverse seems to have been the case.[33]

Although nongovernmental organizations in several countries play an important role in documenting and publicly reporting on hate crime cases, there are no systematic studies by NGOs on the disposition of such cases by police investigators, prosecutors, and the courts in any of the 56 OSCE countries. One group that attempts to track hate crime convictions is the SOVA Center for Information and Analysis. This leading nongovernmental monitor of hate crimes in the **Russian Federation** reported that the use of hate crime laws had decreased in 2007, following a steady increase from 2004 through 2006. The SOVA Center reported that there were nine guilty verdicts in hate crime charges in 2004, 17 in 2005, and 33 guilty verdicts (involving 109 defendants) in 2006. In 2007 however, there were only 24 guilty verdicts (involving 68 defendants) even though the number of incidents had increased dramatically.[34]

In the absence of more readily available data, monitoring of individual cases provides some insight into the circumstances under which these provisions are used in practice.

In **Croatia**, for example, where hate crime provisions were adopted in October 2006, a court on February 25, 2008, found Josip Situm guilty of a hate crime for his role in throwing petrol bombs at the participants of a gay pride parade in Croatia's capital Zagreb in July 2007. He was sentenced to 14 months in jail and to mandatory psychiatric treatment. He is the first person convicted of a hate crime in the country since such crimes became offences under the country's Penal Code in 2006.[35]

In **Ukraine**, the criminal code contains general provisions that permit a racist or other bias motive of the offender to be taken into account by the courts as an aggravating circumstance when sentencing. Article 67 of the criminal code is a general sentencing provision that identifies aggravating circumstances that give rise to more serious penalties, including "a motive of racial, national, or religious hatred" in the commission of crimes. A judge is not obliged however to consider these motivations in the sentencing and there are no reported cases in which a judge has considered such motivations in the sentencing.

Article 161 criminalizes incitement to hatred, insults or discrimination based on nationality, race, or religion. Although this provision is more applicable to cases of hate speech and discrimination, it has also been applied in some cases involving violent hate crimes, and has served in those cases as a means for the state to recognize the bias motivations inherent in the crimes. In early 2008, there were three guilty verdicts handed down in hate crime cases in which violations under article 161 were among the charges. These were the first cases reported to apply Article 161 since the early 1990s.

- On April 17, 2008, the Darnitsky district court of Kyiv convicted four suspects in the murder of Kunon Mievi Godi in October 2006. Alexandr Shepitko was found guilty of first degree murder and incitement of ethnic hatred (article 115, part 2, and article 161) and was sentenced to eleven years in prison, while Yana Komlyuk was convicted solely of incitement of ethnic hatred, receiving a four and a half year sentence. The other two defendants avoided prosecution: one of them was a minor, and the other testified as a witness.[36]

- On April 17, 2008, the Podolsky district court of Kyiv sentenced 18-year-old skinhead Vyacheslav Dmitruk to three years in prison for attacking a Japanese tourist on October 27, 2007. Dmitruk was also found guilty of incitement of ethnic hatred (article 161, part 2).[37]

- On May 16, 2008, four youths were convicted in the April 2007 premeditated murder of a 31-year-old Korean citizen. The murder was described as exceptionally cruel in the police report, as the attackers beat the victim while screaming racial slurs and profanities at him. Each defendant was sentenced to thirteen years of imprisonment, as well as fines totaling one million *hryvnias* ($220,000) to be paid to the victim's family.[38]

Section Endnotes

[1] European Court of Human Rights, *Secic v. Croatia*, para. 67, Strasbourg, July 5, 2005.

[2] European Union, "EU: Common Criminal Provisions Against Racism and Xenophobia," Press Release, April 20, 2007, http://www.eu2007.de/en/News/Press_Releases/April/0420BMJRassismus.html.

[3] European Commission Against Racism and Intolerance, "ECRI general policy recommendation no.11 on combating racism and racial discrimination in policing," CRI(2007)35, July 6, 2007, http://www.coe.int/t/e/ egal_affairs/legal_co-operation/fight_against_terrorism/2_Adopted_Texts/ECRI%20GP%20Rec%2011%20racism%20and%20policing%20E.pdf.

[4] European Court of Human Rights, *Nachova and Others v. Bulgaria*, para. 161, Strasbourg, July 5, 2005.

[5] European Court of Human Rights, *Secic v. Croatia*, paras. 66-67, Strasbourg, July 5, 2005.

[6] European Roma Rights Center, "Strasbourg Court Sanctions Bulgaria for Failure to Bring Perpetrators of racist Killing to Justice," Press Release, August 6, 2007, http://www.errc.org/cikk.php?cikk=2854.

[7] European Court of Human Rights, *Angelova and Iliev v. Bulgaria*, para. 116, Strasbourg, July 26, 2007.

[8] Organization for Security and Cooperation in Europe, "Tolerance and Non-Discrimination: Promoting Mutual Respect and Understanding," OSCE Ministerial Council Decision, no. 10/05, MC.DEC/10/05, December 6, 2005, http://www.osce.org/documents/mcs/2005/12/17441_en.pdf.

[9] OSCE Office for Democratic Institutions and Human Rights, "ODIHR helps states to tackle hate crimes with new guidelines," April 11, 2008, http://www.osce.org/odihr/item_2_30631.html.

[10] Human Rights First, *Overview: Hate Crime Report Card*, December 2007, http://www.humanrightsfirst.info/pdf/071217-discrim-hc-report-card-overview-2007.pdf, p. 33.

[11] Bias based on sexual orientation is an aggravating circumstance in Andorra, Belgium, Canada, Croatia, Denmark, France, Portugal, Romania, Spain, Sweden, the United Kingdom, and the United States. In the United States, although federal hate crime legislation does not extend to sexual orientation, state legislation in 30 states and the District of Columbia does. Bias based on disability is an aggravating circumstance in Andorra, Belgium, Canada, Romania, Spain, the United Kingdom, and the United States.

[12] The 11 states include: California, Colorado, Connecticut, Hawaii, Maryland, Minnesota, Montana, New Jersey, New Mexico, Oregon, and Vermont.

[13] Criminal Code of Portugal (Código Penal Português), http://www.unifr.ch/derechopenal/legislacion/pt/CPPortugal.pdf.

[14] European Union Agency for Fundamental Rights, *Thematic Legal Study on Homophobia and Discrimination on Grounds of Sexual Orientation (Portugal)*, February 2008, http://fra.europa.eu/fra/material/pub/comparativestudy/FRA-hdgso-NR_PT.pdf.

[15] These include article 105 (Murder), article 111 (Deliberate infliction of grievous bodily harm), article 112 (Deliberate infliction of moderate bodily harm), article 117 (Torture), article 214 (Vandalism), article 244 (Desecration).

[16] These include article 115 (Deliberate infliction of mild bodily harm), article 116 (Assault), article 119 (Threatening murder or the infliction of serious bodily harm), article 150 (Involving a minor in the commission of a crime), and article 213 (Hooliganism).

[17] "Antiekstremistkie popravki prinyaty v tret'em chtenii: Kratkij komemtarij," the SOVA Center for Information and Analysis, July 6, 2007, http://xeno.sova-center.ru/89CCE27/89CD14E/975C903.

[18] Human Rights First correspondence with Dr. Andreas Stegbauer, Judge at the County Court of Eggenfelden, July 15, 2008.

[19] These states were joined by the eastern state of Mecklenburg-Vorpommern.

[20] Human Rights First correspondence with Dr. Andreas Stegbauer, Judge at the County Court of Eggenfelden, July 15, 2008.

[21] "Hate Crimes, Norway," Submission to ODIHR, 2004-2005, Legislationline, http://www.legislationline.org/?tid=218&jid=38&less=false.

[22] "Lov om endringer i straffeloven 20. mai 2005 nr. 28 mv.," Lovdata, http://www.lovdata.no/cgi-wift/wiftldles?doc=/usr/www/lovdata/ltavd1/filer/nl-20080307-004.html&emne=homofile*&.

[23] Bjorn Lacompte, "Skal knuse hatvold," Nettavisen, February 14, 2008, http://www.nettavisen.no/innenriks/ioslo/article1601485.ece.

[24] "Offenses (Aggravated by Prejudice) (Scotland) Bill," Policy Memorandum, SP Bill 9-PM, Session 3 (2008), http://polfest.org/s3/bills/09-AggPrej/b9s3-introd-pm.pdf.

[25] The 1968 "Federal Hate Crime Statute," 18 USC 245, outlines the six federally protected activities as follows: " (1) A student at or applicant for admission to a public school or public college; (2) A participant in a benefit, service, privilege, program, facility or activity provided or administered by a

state or local government; (3) An applicant for private or state employment; a private or state employee; a member or applicant for membership in a labor organization or hiring hall; or an applicant for employment through an employment agency, labor organization or hiring hall; (4) A juror or prospective juror in state court; (5) A traveler or user of a facility of interstate commerce or common carrier; (6) A patron of a public accommodation or place of exhibition or entertainment, including hotels, motels, restaurants, lunchrooms, bars, gas stations, theaters, concert halls, sports arenas or stadiums."

[26] The data challenge is complicated in part because sentences may take into consideration a wide range of other aggravating and mitigating factors, while monitoring systems have not been established to register whether the "racist" or other bias element was in fact taken into account in sentencing.

[27] Official response of the Government of Canada to a Human Rights First questionnaire, July 2, 2008.

[28] Human Rights First correspondence with Tas Floris, Discrimination focal point in the Dutch National Police, September 14, 2008.

[29] The Minister of State for Communities and Local Government, *All-Party Inquiry into Antisemitism: Government Response One year on Progress Report*, May 12, 2008, http://www.official-documents.gov.uk/document/cm73/7381/7381.pdf.

[30] Crown Prosecution Service, *Guidance on Prosecuting Cases of Homophobic and Transphobic Crime*, November 2007, http://www.cps.gov.uk/publications/doc/htc_guidance.pdf.

[31] Centre for Equal Opportunities and Opposition to Racism, *Discriminatie, Diversiteit, Jaarverslag 2007*, http://www.diversiteit.be/?action=publicatie_detail&id=32&thema=2.

[32] Human Rights First correspondence with the Office of the Ombudsman against Discrimination on Grounds of Sexual Orientation, February 5, 2008.

[33] The Office of the Ombudsman against Discrimination on Grounds of Sexual Orientation, *Homophobic Motives as Aggravating Circumstances*, http://www.homo.se/o.o.i.s/2078.

[34] Galina Kozhevnikova, *Radical Nationalism and Efforts to Counteract it in 2007*, the SOVA Center for Information and Analysis, March 14, 2008, http://xeno.sova-center.ru/6BA2468/6BB4208/AC15D1E.

[35] Tony Grew, "Pride petrol bomber jailed for attempted attack," *Pink News*, February 26, 2008, http://www.pinknews.co.uk/news/articles/2005-6961.html.

[36] Vyacheslav Likhachev, *Ksenofobiya v Ukraine: Materialy Monitoringa 2007-2008*, Kyiv, May 2008, p. 38.

[37] Vyacheslav Likhachev, *Ksenofobiya v Ukraine: Materialy Monitoringa 2007-2008*, Kyiv, May 2008, p. 39.

[38] Mihail Sergushev, "Apellyatsionnyj sud Kieva prigovoril chetveryh kievlyan, zabivshih do smerti 31-letnego Kang Dzhonvonga, k 13 godam lisheniya svobody kazhdogo," *Fakty*, May 16, 2008, http://www.facts.kiev.ua/2008/05/16/08.htm#1.

The Fighting Discrimination Website

Our website—**www.humanrightsfirst.org/discrimination**—offers this and many other reports for free, in both html and pdf formats. The website is updated regularly to demonstrate the latest developments in our advocacy efforts as well as the most recent publications. We invite all interested parties to use our online resources.

human rights *first*
30th ANNIVERSARY

FIGHTING DISCRIMINATION

| PROGRAMS | ABOUT US | CONTRIBUTE | MEDIA ROOM | SEARCH |

FIGHTING DISCRIMINATION

Human Rights First examines bias-driven violence as a serious human rights violation and advocates methods of combating it.

Our Program »
Reports »
Our Activities »

Hate Crime »

Overview »
Recommendations »

Issues

Racism & Xenophobia »
Antisemitism »
Religious Intolerance »
Muslims »
Roma & Sinti »
LGBT Persons »

Country Focus »

Russia »
Ukraine »
USA »
Others »

Int'l Organizations

OSCE »
U.N. »
Council of Europe »

Hate crime is on the rise around the world.

Read our 2008 Hate Crime Survey »

30th **ANNIVERSARY**
HUMAN RIGHTS AWARD DINNER
THURSDAY, OCTOBER 23 »

GIVE TO
HUMAN RIGHTS FIRST »

TAKE ACTION »

SIGN UP
FOR HRF NEWS »

WATCH
HRF VIDEOS »

READ
HRF BLOGS »

Click Here to subscribe to HRF RSS feeds »

LATEST NEWS

HRF Addresses the 2008 OSCE Human Dimension Implementation Meeting in Warsaw

The Conference, hailed by the ODIHR Director Amb. Janez Lenarcic as "the single most important yearly OSCE event focusing on human rights and democracy in Europe, North America, and Central Asia," features delegations from all 56 member states, as well other high-profile speakers from NGO and IGO communities.

OSCE HDIM 2008

Human Rights First is scheduled to make four interventions during the conference. Our 2008 Hate Crime Survey is also distributed at various side-events and meetings.

Read Tad Stahnke's Statement on "Hate Crimes in the OSCE Region."

Read Paul Legendre's statement at the Tolerance and Non-Discrimination Session.

10/06/08

New Report Finds Violent Hate Crime on the Rise

Incidents of violent hate crime targeting a number of minority groups are increasing or occurring at historically high levels in many of the Organization of Security and Cooperation in Europe (OSCE) member-states, as governments fail to combat such crimes, a new report finds.

Read Press Release

Watch Video & Read Report

09/24/08

2008 Hate Crime Survey

9 780979 999756